THIRD EDITION

SUMMIT 1

ENGLISH FOR TODAY'S WORLD

JOAN SASLOW
ALLEN ASCHER

Summit: English for Today's World   Level 1, Third Edition

Pearson, 221 River Street, Hoboken, NJ 07030

Staff credits: The people who made up the *Summit* team representing editorial, production, design, manufacturing, and marketing are Pietro Alongi, Rhea Banker, Peter Benson, Stephanie Bullard, Jennifer Castro, Tracey Munz Cataldo, Rosa Chapinal, Aerin Csigay, Dave Dickey, Gina DiLillo, Christopher Leonowicz, Laurie Neaman, Alison Pei, Sherri Pemberton, Jennifer Raspiller, Mary Rich, Courtney Steers, Katherine Sullivan, and Paula Van Ells.

Cover credit: Tonis Pan/Shutterstock

Text composition: emc design ltd

Library of Congress Cataloging-in-Publication Data

Names: Saslow, Joan M., author. | Ascher, Allen, author.
Title: Summit : English for today's world / Joan Saslow and Allen Ascher.
Description: Third Edition. | White Plains, NY : Pearson Education, [2017]
Identifiers: LCCN 2016017942| ISBN 9780134096070 (book w/ CD) | ISBN 9780134176888 (book w/ CD) | ISBN 013409607X (book w/ CD)
Subjects: LCSH: English language--Textbooks for foreign speakers. | English language--Rhetoric. | English language--Sound recording for foreign speakers.
Classification: LCC PE1128 .S2757 2017 | DDC 428.2/4--dc23
LC record available at https://lccn.loc.gov/2016017942

Photo credits: Original photography by Libby Ballengee/MPS. Page 2 Trevor Clifford/Pearson Education; p. 3 Jenner/Fotolia; p. 4 (top left to right) Ammentorp/Fotolia, Fotos593/Shutterstock, Mark Bowden/Getty Images, Claudia Paulussen/Fotolia, (bottom left to right) Viorel Sima/Shutterstock, Avava/Fotolia, DragonImages/Fotolia, Antonioguillem/Fotolia; p. 5 CP Cheah/Moment Open/Getty Images; p. 6 (tl) Tatyana Gladskih/Fotolia, (tr) Asife/Fotolia, (bl) michael spring/Fotolia, (br) Minerva Studio/Fotolia; p. 10 Kris Yeager/Shutterstock; p. 11 Nik_Merkulov/Fotolia; p. 14 (tr) Blend Images/KidStock/Getty Images, (mr) Kevin Dodge/Blend Images/Getty Images, (br) Brian A Jackson/Shutterstock, (bottom) DJ/AAD/starmaxinc.com/Newscom; p. 16 (tl) Philip Date/Fotolia, (r) Monkey Business Images/Shutterstock, (bl) nyul/Fotolia, p. 17 V&P Photo Studio/Fotolia; p. 18 (girl) Deposit Photos/Glow Images, (background) karandaev/Fotolia; p. 19 Astarot/Fotolia; p. 20 (bl) Alexander Tihonov/Shutterstock; p. 21 (gears) ShpilbergStudios/Fotolia, (l) RSD/APC/ZOJ WENN Photos/Newscom, (c) DESRUS BENEDICTE/SIPA/Newscom, (r) Graham Whitby Boot/Allstar/Sportsphoto Ltd./Allstar/Newscom; p. 22 (tl) EDHAR/Shutterstock, (tc) rasstock/Fotolia, (tr) aastock/Shutterstock, (bl) Mike Goldwater/Alamy Stock Photo, (br) TommL/Vetta/Getty Images; p. 23 Lance Iversen/San Francisco Chronicle/Corbis; p. 27 Fancy Collection/Superstock; p. 29 Vereshchagin Dmitry/Shutterstock; p. 30 (tl) Blvdone/Fotolia, (r) nyul/Fotolia, (b) vadymvdrobot/Fotolia; p. 31 Karen Roach/Fotolia; p. 33 photobuay/Fotolia; p. 34 Doctors Without Borders, Coral Reef Alliance, (l) dpa picture alliance/Alamy Stock Photo, (r) Vlad61/Shutterstock; p. 35 ballabeyla/Fotolia; p. 38 (left to right) Raisa Kanareva/Fotolia, Olga Bogatyrenko/Shutterstock, Maridav/Fotolia, leungchopan/Fotolia, mimagephotography/Shutterstock, Sundikova/Fotolia; p. 41 (left to right) DRB Images, LLC/E+/Getty Images, Vlad Teodor/Shutterstock, Andrey Kiselev/Fotolia, Andrey Kiselev/Fotolia, Jenner/Fotolia, (b) djoronimo/Fotolia; p. 42 (l) Gstockstudio/Fotolia, (c) Matthew Cole/Shutterstock, (r) michaeljung/Fotolia; p. 44 Meffista/Fotolia; p. 45 (l) RUNGROJ YONGRIT/Newscom, (c) Valua Vitaly/Shutterstock, (r) Pearson Education; p. 46 Imagine China/Newscom; p. 47 Zdenka Darula/Fotolia; p. 48 (tl) ardman/Fotolia, (r) Photodisc/Fotolia; p. 51 Stock Rocket/Shutterstock, (inset) maron/Fotolia; p. 55 Deyan Georgiev/Fotolia; p. 56 davidf/E+/Getty Images; p. 58 (inset) INB/Ivan Nikolov/WENN/Newscom, (bottom) Savostyanov/ZUMA Press/Newscom; p. 59 (left to right) Jerry Sharp/Shutterstock, FiCo74/Fotolia, kalpis/Fotolia; p. 60 icsnaps/Fotolia; p. 61 wavebreakmedia/Shutterstock; p. 62 (spider) Eric Isselee/Shutterstock, (bee) paulrommer/Shutterstock, (worm) Valentina Razumova/Shutterstock, (dolphin) FineShine/Shutterstock, (mouse) Tsekhmister/Shutterstock, (dog) Andresr/Shutterstock, (elephant) Richard Peterson/Shutterstock, (horse) Eric Isselee/Shutterstock, (lion) Eric Isselee/123 RF, (baboon) Eric Isselee/Shutterstock, (bunny) Joshua Lewis/Shutterstock, (sheep) Eric Isselee/Shutterstock, (parrot) Denis Tabler/Fotolia, (eagle) Eric Isselee/Shutterstock, (snake) Kruglov_Orda/Shutterstock, (crocodile) nattanan726/Shutterstock, (frog) Eric Isselee/Shutterstock, (salamander) Vitalii Hulai/Shutterstock, (eel) Eric Isselée/Fotolia, (goldfish) Gunnar Pippel/Shutterstock; p. 63 Ghislain & Marie David de Lossy/Cultura/Corbis; p. 64 (t) Joshua Rainey Photography/Shutterstock, (m) Suna/Fotolia, (b) Yanlev/Fotolia; p. 65 yulia-zl18/Fotolia; p. 66 (t) Tono Balaguer/123rf (b) Alena Ozerova/Shutterstock; p. 67 hin255/Shutterstock; (guinea pig) Inkwelldodo/Fotolia; p. 68 (top, left to right) Feng Yu/123rf, dazb75/Fotolia, Soren Egeberg Photography/Shutterstock, Meoita/Fotolia, (bottom, left to right) Valdecasas/Shutterstock, Lubos Chlubny/Fotolia, John Foxx/Getty Images, sbthegreenman/Fotolia; p. 69 (b) ARTENS/Fotolia; p. 70 (t) Jeff Foott. Alamy, (l) PARIS PIERCE/Alamy Stock Photo, (r) Everett Historical/Shutterstock; p. 75 Jupiterimages/Stockbyte/Getty Images; p. 77 Photosindia/Alamy Stock Photo; p. 78 (tl) Nicolas McComber/E+/Getty Images, (tr) DanielBendjy/E+/Getty Images, (bl) Rob Byron/Shutterstock, (br) Glow Images/Getty Images; p. 80 Tetra Images/Shutterstock; p. 86 bst2012/Fotolia; p. 87 Alistair Berg/DigitalVision/Getty Images; p. 88 Christin Lola/Shutterstock; p. 89 Monkey Business/Fotolia; p. 91 Jetta Productions/Blend Images/Getty Images; p. 92 (background) Anton Gvozdikov/Fotolia; (man) Syda Productions/Fotolia; p. 93 pressmaster/Fotolia; p. 94 (l) Robert Kneschke/Fotolia, (r) Monkey Business Images/Shutterstock; p. 95 (tl) Ana Bokan/Shutterstock, (r) Imtmphoto/Fotolia, (bl) Jim Pruitt/Shutterstock; p. 97 glisic albina/Fotolia; p. 98 (hat) cratervalley/fotolia, (canary) glifeisgood/Fotolia, (coin) MAC1/Shutterstock, (bird) kukies/Fotolia (arms) IgorGoloviov/Shutterstock; p. 99 (l) bokan/Fotolia, (r) DragonImages/Fotolia; p. 102 (l) Leksele/Shutterstock, (r) Everett Collection/Newscom; p. 103 (left to right) meunierd/Shutterstock, Pecold/Shutterstock, Jgz/Fotolia; p. 104 (top and bottom) aleciccotelli/Fotolia, (l) Cimmerian/Getty Images, photoBeard/Shutterstock, (r) photoBeard/Shutterstock; p. 105 sss78/Fotolia; p. 106 Jeremy Craine/REX/Newscom; p. 107 michaeljung/Fotolia; p. 109 Monkey Business/Fotolia; p. 110 (fans) Chris Whitehead/Cultura/Getty Images, (skydivers) Joggie Botma/Shutterstock, (hammock) saras66/Shutterstock, (chess) auremar/Shutterstock; p. 113 Stockbroker/MBI / Alamy Stock Photo; p. 114 (t) Hurst Photo/Shutterstock, (m) khwanchai s/Fotolia, (b) Fotokvadrat/Fotolia; p. 115 paultarasenko/Fotolia; p. 116 Focus Pocus LTD/Fotolia; p. 117 ldprod/Fotolia; p. 118 (left to right) 2happy/Fotolia, creative soul/Fotolia, bikeriderlondon/Shutterstock, Maridav/Fotolia, Digital Vision/Getty Images; p. 119 Photocreo Bednarek/Fotolia; p. 138 Axel Bueckert/Fotolia (male), zea_lenanet/Fotolia (female).

Illustration credits: Aptara pp. 9, 40(b), 69, 74; Steve Attoe pp. 52, 90; Mark Collins p. 65, (map, flag, camel, cat) 98; Francois Escalmel p. 83; Dusan Petricic pp. 28, 100(b), 101; Shannon Wheelie pp. 32, 54, 100(t); el Primo Ramon p. 40(t); Liza Donnelley p. 76; Jerome Studer p. 81.

Printed in the United States of America

ISBN-10: 0-13-409607-X
ISBN-13: 978-0-13-409607-0

ISBN-10: 0-13-449893-3 (with MyEnglishLab)
ISBN-13: 978-0-13449893-5 (with MyEnglishLab)

ABOUT THE AUTHORS

Joan Saslow

Joan Saslow has taught in a variety of programs in South America and the United States. She is author or coauthor of a number of widely used courses, some of which are *Ready to Go*, *Workplace Plus*, *Literacy Plus*, and *Top Notch*. She is also author of *English in Context*, a series for reading science and technology. Ms. Saslow was the series director of *True Colors* and *True Voices*. She has participated in the English Language Specialist Program in the U.S. Department of State's Bureau of Educational and Cultural Affairs.

Allen Ascher

Allen Ascher has been a teacher and teacher trainer in China and the United States, as well as academic director of the intensive English program at Hunter College. Mr. Ascher has also been an ELT publisher and was responsible for publication and expansion of numerous well-known courses including *True Colors*, *NorthStar*, the *Longman TOEFL Preparation Series*, and the *Longman Academic Writing Series*. He is coauthor of *Top Notch*, and he wrote the "Teaching Speaking" module of *Teacher Development Interactive*, an online multimedia teacher-training program.

Ms. Saslow and Mr. Ascher are frequent presenters at professional conferences and have been coauthoring courses for teens, adults, and young adults since 2002.

AUTHORS' ACKNOWLEDGMENTS

The authors wish to thank Katherine Klagsbrun for developing the digital Extra Challenge Reading Activities that appear with all reading selections in *Summit 1*.

The authors are indebted to these reviewers, who provided extensive and detailed feedback and suggestions for *Summit*, as well as the hundreds of teachers who completed surveys and participated in focus groups.

Cris Asperti, CEL LEP, São Paulo, Brazil • **Diana Alicia Ávila Martínez**, CUEC, Monterrey, Mexico • **Shannon Brown**, Nagoya University of Foreign Studies, Nagoya, Japan • **Cesar Byrd**, Universidad ETAC Campus Chalco, Mexico City, Mexico • **Maria Claudia Campos de Freitas**, Metalanguage, São Paulo, Brazil • **Alvaro Del Castillo Alba**, CBA, Santa Cruz, Bolivia • **Isidro Castro Galván**, Instituto Teocalli, Monterrey, Mexico • **Melisa Celi**, Idiomas Católica, Lima, Peru • **Carlos Celis**, CEL LEP, São Paulo, Brazil • **Jussara Costa e Silva**, Prize Language School, São Paulo, Brazil • **Inara Couto**, CEL LEP, São Paulo, Brazil • **Gemma Crouch**, ICPNA Chiclayo, Peru • **Ingrid Valverde Diaz del Olmo**, ICPNA Cusco, Peru • **Jacqueline Díaz Esquivel**, PROULEX, Guadalajara, Mexico • **María Eid Ceneviva**, CBA, Cochabamba, Bolivia • **Erika Licia Esteves Silva**, Murphy English, São Paulo, Brazil • **Cristian Garay**, Idiomas Católica, Lima, Peru • **Miguel Angel Guerrero Pozos**, PROULEX, Guadalajara, Mexico • **Anderson Francisco Guimarães Maia**, Centro Cultural Brasil Estados Unidos, Belém, Brazil • **Cesar Guzmán**, CAADI Monterrey, Mexico • **César Iván Hernández Escobedo**, PROULEX, Guadalajara, Mexico • **Robert Hinton**, Nihon University, Tokyo, Japan • **Segundo**

Huanambal Díaz, ICPNA Chiclayo, Peru • **Chandra Víctor Jacobs Sukahai**, Universidad de Valle de México, Monterrey, Mexico • **Yeni Jiménez Torres**, Centro Colombo Americano Bogotá, Colombia • **Simon Lees**, Nagoya University of Foreign Studies, Nagoya, Japan • **Thomas LeViness**, PROULEX, Guadalajara, Mexico • **Amy Lewis**, Waseda University, Tokyo, Japan • **Luz Libia Rey**, Centro Colombo Americano, Bogotá, Colombia • **Diego López**, Idiomas Católica, Lima, Peru • **Junior Lozano**, Idiomas Católica, Lima, Peru • **Tanja McCandie**, Nanzan University, Nagoya, Japan • **Tammy Martínez Nieves**, Universidad Autónoma de Nuevo León, Monterrey, Mexico • **María Teresa Meléndez Mantilla**, ICPNA Chiclayo, Peru • **Mónica Nomberto**, ICPNA Chiclayo, Peru • **Otilia Ojeda**, Monterrey, Mexico • **Juana Palacios**, Idiomas Católica, Lima, Peru • **Giuseppe Paldino Mayorga**, Jellyfish Learning Center, San Cristobal, Ecuador • **Henry Eduardo Pardo Lamprea**, Universidad Militar Nueva Granada, Colombia • **Dario Paredes**, Centro Colombo Americano, Bogotá, Colombia • **Teresa Noemí Parra Alarcón**, Centro Anglo Americano de Cuernavaca, S.C., Cuernavaca, Mexico • **Carlos Eduardo de la Paz Arroyo**, Centro Anglo Americano de Cuernavaca, S.C.,

Cuernavaca, Mexico • **José Luis Pérez Treviño**, Instituto Obispado, Monterrey, Mexico • **Evelize Maria Plácido Florian**, São Paulo, Brazil • **Armida Rivas**, Monterrey, Mexico • **Luis Rodríguez Amau**, ICPNA Chiclayo, Peru • **Fabio Ossaamn Rok Kaku**, Prize Language School, São Paulo, Brazil • **Ana María Román Villareal**, CUEC, Monterrey, Mexico • **Reynaldo Romano C.**, CBA, La Paz, Bolivia • **Francisco Rondón**, Centro Colombo Americano, Bogotá, Colombia • **Peter Russell**, Waseda University, Tokyo, Japan • **Rubena St. Louis**, Universidad Simón Bolivar, Caracas, Venezuela • **Marisol Salazar**, Centro Colombo Americano, Bogotá, Colombia • **Miguel Sierra**, Idiomas Católica, Lima, Peru • **Greg Strong**, Aoyama Gakuin University, Tokyo, Japan • **Gerald Talandis**, Toyama University, Toyama, Japan • **Stephen Thompson**, Nagoya University of Foreign Studies, Nagoya, Japan • **José Luis Urbina Hurtado**, Instituto Tecnológico de León, Mexico • **René F. Valdivia Pereyra**, CBA, Santa Cruz, Bolivia • **Magno Alejandro Vivar Hurtado**, Salesian Polytechnic University, Ecuador • **Belkis Yanes**, Caracas, Venezuela • **Holger Zamora**, ICPNA Cusco, Peru • **Maria Cristina Zanon Costa**, Metalanguage, São Paulo, Brazil • **Kathia Zegarra**, Idiomas Católica, Lima, Peru.

LEARNING OBJECTIVES

UNIT	COMMUNICATION GOALS	VOCABULARY	GRAMMAR
UNIT 1 **Outlook and Behavior** PAGE 2	• Describe your personality • Discuss someone's behavior • Compare perspectives on world problems • Discuss creative ways to achieve a goal	• Adjectives to describe personality traits **Word Study:** • Adjective suffixes -ful and -less	• Gerunds and infinitives: review and expansion • Verbs that require a noun or pronoun before an infinitive **GRAMMAR BOOSTER** • Infinitives: review, expansion, and common errors • Grammar for writing: parallelism with gerunds and infinitives
UNIT 2 **Music and Other Arts** PAGE 14	• Describe how you've been enjoying the arts • Express a negative opinion politely • Describe a creative personality • Discuss the benefits of the arts	• Elements of music • Negative descriptions of music • Describing creative personalities **Word Study:** • Using participial adjectives	• The present perfect continuous • Cleft sentences with What **GRAMMAR BOOSTER** • Finished and unfinished actions: summary • Noun clauses: review and expansion • Grammar for Writing: noun clauses as adjective and noun complements
UNIT 3 **Money, Finance, and You** PAGE 26	• Express buyer's remorse • Talk about financial goals and plans • Discuss good and bad money management • Explain reasons for charitable giving	• Describing spending styles • Expressing buyer's remorse • Good and bad money management **Word Study:** • Parts of speech	• Expressing regrets about the past: wish + past perfect; should have / ought to have + past participle; if only + past perfect. • Completed future actions and plans: The future perfect and perfect infinitives **GRAMMAR BOOSTER** • The past unreal conditional: inverted form • The future continuous • The future perfect continuous
UNIT 4 **Clothing and Appearance** PAGE 38	• Describe clothing details and formality • Talk about changes in clothing customs • Examine questionable cosmetic procedures • Discuss appearance and self-esteem	• Adjectives to describe fashion • Describing clothes **Word Study:** • Compound words with self-	• Quantifiers: review and expansion **GRAMMAR BOOSTER** • A few / few; a little / little • Quantifiers: using of for specific reference • Quantifiers used without referents • Grammar for Writing: subject-verb agreement of quantifiers followed by of
UNIT 5 **Communities** PAGE 50	• Politely ask someone not to do something • Complain about public conduct • Suggest ways to avoid being a victim of urban crime • Discuss the meaning of community	• Types of locations • Community service activities **Word Study:** • Using negative prefixes to form antonyms	• Possessive gerunds • Paired conjunctions **GRAMMAR BOOSTER** • Conjunctions with so, too, neither, or not either • So, too, neither, or not either: short responses

CONVERSATION STRATEGIES	LISTENING / PRONUNCIATION	READING	WRITING
• Use <u>I'd say</u> to soften an assertive opinion • Use <u>I don't see [myself] that way</u> to politely contradict another's statement • Say <u>I see [you] as</u> to explain your own point of view • Use <u>tend to</u> and <u>seem to</u> to make generalizations	• Listen to activate grammar • Listen to classify • Listen for main ideas • Listen for details • Understand meaning from context **PRONUNCIATION BOOSTER** • Content words and function words	**Texts:** • A survey about positive and negative outlooks • Descriptions of other people's behavior • A newspaper article about a creative solution to a problem **Skills / strategies:** • Understand idioms and expressions • Determine the main idea • Understand meaning from context • Summarize	**Task:** • Write about your outlook on a world problem **Skill:** • Paragraph structure: Review
• Use <u>To tell the truth</u>, <u>To be honest</u>, and <u>I hate to say it, but</u> to politely introduce a contrary opinion	• Listen to activate vocabulary • Listen for main ideas • Listen for supporting information • Listen to take notes • Listen for details **PRONUNCIATION BOOSTER** • Intonation patterns	**Texts:** • A survey about musical memories • Commentaries about enjoying the arts • A short biography **Skills / strategies** • Understand idioms and expressions • Infer information • Identify supporting details • Express and support an opinion	**Task:** • Describe your interests and personality **Skill:** • Parallel structure
• Use <u>You know, …</u> to introduce a new topic of conversation • Use <u>I hate to say it, but</u> to introduce negative information • Ask <u>What do you mean?</u> to invite someone to elaborate • Say <u>That's a shame</u> to show empathy • Say <u>I'll think about that</u> when you're non-committal about someone's suggestion	• Listen for details • Listen to activate vocabulary • Listen to confirm content • Listen to summarize • Listen to evaluate **PRONUNCIATION BOOSTER** • Sentence rhythm: thought groups	**Texts:** • A spending habits self-test • Interview responses about financial goals • A guide to charitable giving **Skills / strategies:** • Understand idioms and expressions • Understand meaning from context • Draw conclusions • Express and support an opinion	**Task:** • Write a personal statement about how you manage financial responsibilities **Skill:** • Organizing information by degrees of importance
• Use <u>Can I ask you a question about…?</u> to introduce a subject you are unsure of • Use <u>I mean</u> to elaborate on a prior statement or question • Use <u>Actually,</u> to assert a point of view • Begin a question with <u>So</u> to affirm understanding of someone's earlier statement • Say <u>I think that might be …</u> to gently warn that something is inappropriate	• Listen for main ideas • Listen for details • Listen to summarize **PRONUNCIATION BOOSTER** • Linking sounds	**Texts:** • Descriptions of personal style • An article about the evolution of "business casual" attire • An article about questionable cosmetic procedures • Advertisements for cosmetic procedures **Skills / strategies:** • Understand idioms and expressions • Understand meaning from context • Identify supporting details • Express and support an opinion	**Task:** • Write two paragraphs comparing tastes in fashion **Skill:** • Compare and contrast: Review
• Use <u>Do you mind…?</u> to ask permission to do something • Use <u>Not at all</u> to affirm that you are not bothered or inconvenienced • Use <u>That's very [considerate] of you</u> to thank someone for accommodating you	• Listen to summarize • Listen for details • Listen to confirm content • Listen to infer **PRONUNCIATION BOOSTER** • Unstressed syllables: vowel reduction to /ə/	**Texts:** • A questionnaire about community • Interview responses about pet peeves • A magazine article about urban crime • A website about community projects **Skills / strategies:** • Understand idioms and expressions • Classify • Understand meaning from context • Critical thinking	**Task:** • Write a formal letter of complaint **Skill:** • Formal letters: Review

UNIT	COMMUNICATION GOALS	VOCABULARY	GRAMMAR
UNIT 6 **Animals** PAGE 62	• Exchange opinions about the treatment of animals • Discuss the pros and cons of certain pets • Compare animal and human behavior • Debate the value of animal conservation	• Categories of animals • Describing pets • Animal social groups and physical features	• Passive modals **GRAMMAR BOOSTER** • Modals and modal-like expressions: summary
UNIT 7 **Advertising and Consumers** PAGE 74	• Evaluate ways and places to shop • Discuss your reactions to ads • Discuss problem shopping behavior • Persuade someone to buy a product	• Verbs for shopping activities • Ways to persuade	• Passive forms of gerunds and infinitives **GRAMMAR BOOSTER** • The passive voice: review and expansion
UNIT 8 **Family Trends** PAGE 86	• Describe family trends • Discuss parent-teen issues • Compare generations • Discuss caring for the elderly	• Describing parent and teen behavior **Word Study:** • Transforming verbs and adjectives into nouns	• Repeated comparatives and double comparatives **GRAMMAR BOOSTER** • Making comparisons: review and expansion • Other uses of comparatives, superlatives, and comparisons with as...as
UNIT 9 **Facts, Theories, and Hoaxes** PAGE 98	• Speculate about everyday situations • Present a theory • Discuss how believable a story is • Evaluate the trustworthiness of news sources	• Degrees of certainty **Word Study:** • Adjectives with the suffix -able	• Perfect modals for speculating about the past: active and passive voice **GRAMMAR BOOSTER** • Perfect modals: short responses (active and passive voice)
UNIT 10 **Your Free Time** PAGE 110	• Suggest ways to reduce stress • Describe how you got interested in a hobby • Discuss how mobile devices affect us • Compare attitudes about taking risks	• Ways to describe people • Ways to reduce stress **Word Study:** • Adverbs of manner	• Expressing an expectation with be supposed to • Describing past repeated or habitual actions: would and the past continuous with always **GRAMMAR BOOSTER** • Be supposed to: expansion • Would: review • Grammar for Writing: placement of adverbs of manner

CONVERSATION STRATEGIES	LISTENING / PRONUNCIATION	READING	WRITING
• Use <u>I've heard</u> to introduce a commonly-held belief or opinion • Respond with <u>In what way?</u> to request further explanation • Use <u>For one thing</u> to introduce a first supporting argument • Use <u>And besides</u> to add another supporting argument • Use <u>But what if</u> to suggest a hypothetical situation	• Listen to activate vocabulary • Listen to define terms • Listen for examples • Listen for details **PRONUNCIATION BOOSTER** • Sound reduction	**Texts:** • Social media posts about treatment of animals • An article about animal conservation **Skills / strategies:** • Understand idioms and expressions • Understand meaning from context • Recognize cause and effect	**Task:** • Write a persuasive essay about the treatment of animals **Skill:** • Supporting a point of view
• Say <u>Quick question</u> to indicate one wants some simple information • Introduce an opinion with <u>I find</u> • Say <u>That's good to know</u> to express satisfaction for information • Use <u>Why don't you...</u> to offer advice	• Listen to activate vocabulary • Listen to infer **PRONUNCIATION BOOSTER** • Vowel sounds /i/ and /ɪ/	**Texts:** • Self-tests about shopping mistakes and behavior • Descriptions of techniques used in advertising • Interview responses about compulsive shopping **Skills / strategies:** • Understand idioms and expressions • Understand meaning from context • Identify supporting details	**Task:** • Write a summary of an article **Skill:** • Summarize and paraphrase someone's point of view
• Ask <u>Why's that?</u> to ask someone to elaborate on an opinion • Say <u>I suppose, but ...</u> to signal partial agreement	• Listen to activate grammar • Listen to activate vocabulary • Listen for supporting information • Listen for details • Listen to compare and contrast **PRONUNCIATION BOOSTER** • Stress placement: prefixes and suffixes	**Texts:** • A survey about parents and teens • A brochure about falling birthrates • A report on the increase in global population of older people **Skills / strategies:** • Understand idioms and expressions • Summarize • Understand meaning from context • Critical thinking • Draw conclusions	**Task:** • Write a blog post of three or more paragraphs about advice for parents and teens **Skill:** • Avoiding run-on sentences and comma splices
• Use <u>I wonder</u> to introduce something you're not sure about • Say <u>I'm sure it's nothing</u> to indicate that something is probably not serious • Say <u>I suppose you're right</u> to acknowledge someone's point of view • Say <u>There must be a good explanation</u> to assure someone that things will turn out OK	• Listen to activate vocabulary • Listen for main ideas • Listen to draw conclusions **PRONUNCIATION BOOSTER** • Reduction and linking in perfect modals in the passive voice	**Texts:** • A quiz about tricky facts • An article about Rapa Nui • Facts and theories about mysteries • An article about a UFO conspiracy theory • A survey about the trustworthiness of information sources **Skills / strategies:** • Understand idioms and expressions • Confirm point of view • Infer information	**Task:** • Write a news article about a mysterious event **Skill:** • Avoiding sentence fragments
• Say <u>Uh-oh</u> to indicate that you realize you've made a mistake • Use <u>I just realized</u> to acknowledge a mistake • Use <u>Well, frankly</u> to indicate that you are going to be honest about something • Use <u>It's just that</u> or <u>Let's face it</u> to introduce an honest criticism or assessment • Use <u>You know what?</u> to introduce a piece of advice	• Listen to activate vocabulary • Listen for main ideas • Listen for supporting details • Listen to understand meaning from context **PRONUNCIATION BOOSTER** • Vowel sounds /eɪ/, /ɛ/, /æ/, and /ʌ/	**Texts:** • A survey about free time • Descriptions of how people got interested in their hobbies • An article about the impact of mobile devices • A survey about mobile device usage **Skills / strategies:** • Understand idioms and expressions • Understand meaning from context • Identify supporting details • Infer point of view	**Task:** • Write a critique of an article **Skill:** • Presenting and supporting opinions clearly

TO THE TEACHER

What is *Summit?*

Summit is a two-level high-intermediate to advanced communicative course that develops confident, culturally fluent English speakers able to navigate the social, travel, and professional situations they will encounter as they use English in their lives. *Summit* can follow the intermediate level of any communicative series, including the four-level *Top Notch* course.

Summit delivers immediate, demonstrable results in every class session through its proven pedagogy and systematic and intensive recycling of language. Each goal- and achievement-based lesson is tightly correlated to the Can-Do Statements of the Common European Framework of Reference (CEFR). The course is fully benchmarked to the Global Scale of English (GSE).

Each level of *Summit* contains material for 60 to 90 hours of classroom instruction. Its full array of additional print and digital components can extend instruction to 120 hours if desired. Furthermore, the entire *Summit* course can be tailored to blended learning with its integrated online component, *MyEnglishLab*. *Summit* offers more ready-to-use teacher resources than any other course available today.

NEW This third edition represents a major revision of content and has a greatly increased quantity of exercises, both print and digital. Following are some key new features:

- **Conversation Activator Videos** to build communicative competence
- **Discussion Activator Videos** to increase quality and quantity of expression
- A **Test-Taking Skills Booster** (and **Extra Challenge Reading Activities**) to help students succeed in the reading and listening sections of standardized tests
- An **Understand Idioms and Expressions** section in each unit increases the authenticity of student spoken language

Award-Winning Instructional Design*

Demonstrable confirmation of progress

Every two-page lesson has a clearly stated communication goal and culminates in a guided conversation, free discussion, debate, presentation, role play, or project that achieves the goal. Idea framing and notepadding activities lead students to confident spoken expression.

Cultural fluency

Summit audio familiarizes students with a wide variety of native and non-native accents. Discussion activities reflect the topics people of diverse cultural backgrounds talk about in their social and professional lives.

Explicit vocabulary and grammar

Clear captioned illustrations and dictionary-style presentations, all with audio, take the guesswork out of meaning and ensure comprehensible pronunciation. Grammar is embedded in context and presented explicitly for form, meaning, and use. The unique "Recycle this Language" feature encourages active use of newly learned words and grammar during communication practice.

Active listening syllabus

More than 50 listening tasks at each level of *Summit* develop critical thinking and crucial listening comprehension skills such as listen for details, main ideas, confirmation of content, inference, and understand meaning from context.

Conversation and Discussion Activators

Memorable conversation models with audio provide appealing natural social language and conversation strategies essential for post-secondary learners. Rigorous Conversation Activator and Discussion Activator activities with video systematically stimulate recycling of social language, ensuring it is not forgotten. A unique Pronunciation Booster provides lessons and interactive practice, with audio, so students can improve their spoken expression.

Systematic writing skills development

Summit teaches the conventions of correct English writing so students will be prepared for standardized tests, academic study, and professional communication. Lessons cover key writing and rhetorical skills such as using parallel structure and avoiding sentence fragments, run-on sentences, and comma splices. Intensive work in paragraph and essay development ensures confident and successful writing.

Reading skills and strategies

Each unit of *Summit* builds critical thinking and key reading skills and strategies such as paraphrasing, drawing conclusions, expressing and supporting an opinion, and activating prior knowledge. Learners develop analytical skills and increase fluency while supporting their answers through speaking.

We wish you and your students enjoyment and success with **Summit**. *We wrote it for you.*
Joan Saslow and Allen Ascher

*Summit is the recipient of the Association of Educational Publishers' Distinguished Achievement Award.

ActiveTeach

Maximize the impact of your *Summit* lessons. Digital Student's Book pages with access to all audio and video provide an interactive classroom experience that can be used with or without an interactive whiteboard (IWB). It includes a full array of easy-to-access digital and printable features.

For class presentation . . .

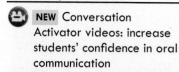 **NEW** Conversation Activator videos: increase students' confidence in oral communication

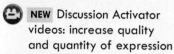 **NEW** Discussion Activator videos: increase quality and quantity of expression

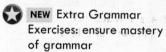 **NEW** Extra Grammar Exercises: ensure mastery of grammar

NEW Extra Challenge Reading Activities: help students succeed at standardized proficiency tests.

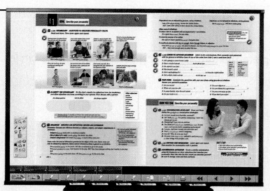

PLUS

• Interactive Whiteboard tools, including zoom, highlight, links, notes, and more.

• ▶ Clickable Audio: instant access to the complete classroom audio program

• *Summit TV* Video Program: fully-revised authentic TV documentaries as well as unscripted on-the-street interviews, featuring a variety of regional and non-native accents

For planning . . .

• A *Methods Handbook* for a communicative classroom

• Detailed timed lesson plans for each two-page lesson

• *Summit TV* teaching notes

• Complete answer keys, audio scripts, and video scripts

For extra support . . .

• Hundreds of extra printable activities, with teaching notes

• *Summit TV* activity worksheets

For assessment . . .

• Ready-made unit and review achievement tests with options to edit, add, or delete items.

MyEnglishLab

An optional online learning tool

• **NEW** Immediate, meaningful feedback on wrong answers
• **NEW** Remedial grammar exercises
• **NEW** Grammar Coach videos for general reference
• Interactive practice of all material presented in the course
• Grade reports that display performance and time on task
• Auto-graded achievement tests

Ready-made Summit Web Projects provide authentic application of lesson language.

Workbook

Lesson-by-lesson written exercises to accompany the Student's Book

Full-Course Placement Tests

Choose printable or online version

Classroom Audio Program

• A set of Audio CDs, as an alternative to the clickable audio in ActiveTeach

• Contains a variety of authentic regional and non-native accents to build comprehension of diverse English speakers

• **NEW** The app *Summit Go* allows access anytime, anywhere and lets students practice at their own pace. The entire audio program is also available for students at www.english.com/summit3e.

Teacher's Edition and Lesson Planner

• Detailed interleaved lesson plans, language and culture notes, answer keys, and more

• Also accessible in digital form in ActiveTeach

For more information: www.pearsonelt.com/summit3e

ix

We hording break

Outlook and Behavior

COMMUNICATION GOALS

1 Describe your personality
2 Discuss someone's behavior
3 Compare perspectives on world problems
4 Discuss creative ways to achieve a goal

PREVIEW

A **FRAME YOUR IDEAS** Complete the quiz by writing your points in the circles. Then calculate your score.

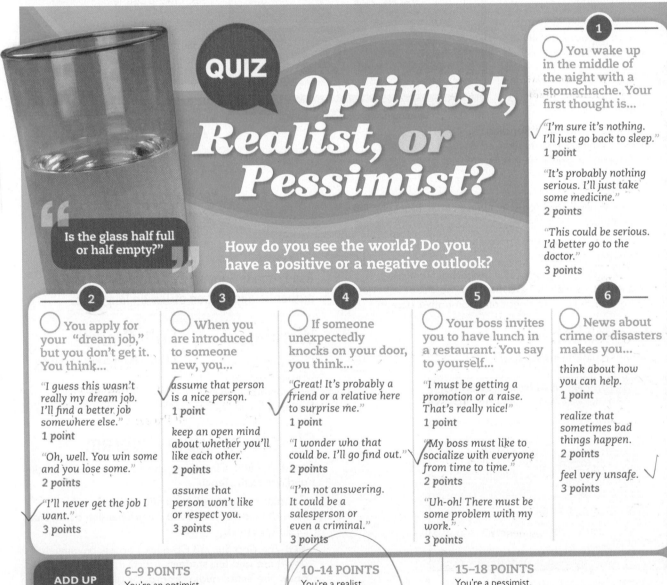

QUIZ

Optimist, Realist, or Pessimist?

"Is the glass half full or half empty?"

How do you see the world? Do you have a positive or a negative outlook?

1
○ You wake up in the middle of the night with a stomachache. Your first thought is...

✓ "I'm sure it's nothing. I'll just go back to sleep."
1 point

"It's probably nothing serious. I'll just take some medicine."
2 points

"This could be serious. I'd better go to the doctor."
3 points

2
○ You apply for your "dream job," but you don't get it. You think...

"I guess this wasn't really my dream job. I'll find a better job somewhere else."
1 point

"Oh, well. You win some and you lose some."
2 points

✓ "I'll never get the job I want."
3 points

3
○ When you are introduced to someone new, you...

✓ assume that person is a nice person.
1 point

keep an open mind about whether you'll like each other.
2 points

assume that person won't like or respect you.
3 points

4
○ If someone unexpectedly knocks on your door, you think...

✓ "Great! It's probably a friend or a relative here to surprise me."
1 point

"I wonder who that could be. I'll go find out."
2 points

"I'm not answering. It could be a salesperson or even a criminal."
3 points

5
○ Your boss invites you to have lunch in a restaurant. You say to yourself...

"I must be getting a promotion or a raise. That's really nice!"
1 point

✓ "My boss must like to socialize with everyone from time to time."
2 points

"Uh-oh! There must be some problem with my work."
3 points

6
○ News about crime or disasters makes you...

think about how you can help.
1 point

realize that sometimes bad things happen.
2 points

feel very unsafe. ✓
3 points

ADD UP YOUR POINTS

6–9 POINTS
You're an optimist. You have a positive outlook and tend to see the glass half full.

10–14 POINTS
You're a realist. You tend to see the world as it really is.

15–18 POINTS
You're a pessimist. You have a negative outlook and tend to see the glass half empty.

B **PAIR WORK** Compare answers with a partner. Are your scores similar, or very different? Which of you has the more optimistic, realistic, or pessimistic outlook on life, according to the quiz?

C **GROUP WORK** Calculate the average score for the members of the class. On average, how optimistic, realistic, or pessimistic is your class?

D ▶ 1:02 **SPOTLIGHT** Read and listen to two friends talking about a new virus they're concerned about. Notice the spotlighted language.

concerned = worries.

Leo: Did you hear about that new virus going around? Chikungunya?

Nora: Chikun-*what*? Oh! You mean the one that comes from mosquitos?

Leo: As a matter of fact, yes. Just like Zika.

Nora: We've never had either of those viruses here before.

Leo: Well, they say it's due to global warming — all those mosquitos from the warmer weather. I suppose **it's just a matter of time** 'til we get all kinds of new diseases.

Nora: You sure are a pessimist. I agree it's scary. But hey, **what are you going to do?**

Leo: I'm just saying this **has started getting to me** and I'm scared. I read that if you come down with Chikungunya, you can be sick for a year … or even more.

Nora: Right. But they say it's still pretty rare around here. These things are just part of life. **You've got to roll with the punches**, if you know what I mean. I'm not going to worry about it.

Leo: Well, *I* am. Anyway, I'm not going to the company dinner at that outdoor restaurant. **You're just a sitting duck** out there, with the mosquitos and everything.

Nora: What about just wearing long sleeves and hoping for the best? I mean, how unlucky could you be?

Leo: Well, I'm going to call in sick and say I can't go. **Better safe than sorry.**

He's getting paranoid about the virus.

E **UNDERSTAND IDIOMS AND EXPRESSIONS** Find the following expressions in Spotlight. Choose the meaning that more closely explains each one.

1 It's just a matter of time.
  a It will take a long time.
  b It will certainly happen in the future.

2 Hey, what are you going to do?
  a There's nothing anyone can do about it.
  b What plans do you have?

3 This has started getting to me.
  a This is beginning to bother me.
  b I'm beginning to get sick.

4 You've got to roll with the punches.
  a You have to deal with life's difficulties and move on.
  b You shouldn't accept the difficulties life brings.

5 You're just a sitting duck out there.
  a There's nothing you can do to protect yourself.
  b You probably won't get sick.

6 Better safe than sorry.
  a It's better to stay safe and have no regrets.
  b I'm sorry, but I'm sick.

F **COMPARE AND CONTRAST** Discuss the questions.

1 How would you describe Leo's and Nora's outlooks? How are they different?

2 Who are you more like, Leo or Nora?

SPEAKING **ROLE PLAY** Take turns responding to the following statements related to the situations in the quiz on page 2. Use idioms from Exercise E in your responses. Then change roles.

❝ I woke up with a stomachache. This could be serious. I'd better go to the doctor. ❞

❝ I'll never get the job I want! ❞

Don't be sad. it is just a matter of time

❝ My boss invited me to lunch in a restaurant. There must be some problem with my work. ❞

❝ Uh-oh. There's someone at the door. I'm not answering. It could be a salesperson or even a criminal. ❞

3

GOAL Describe your personality

(handwritten: He really likes to show off. To show off)

A ▶ 1:03 **VOCABULARY** ADJECTIVES TO DESCRIBE PERSONALITY TRAITS

Read and listen. Then listen again and repeat.

Nothing seems to bother Donna. She just rolls with the punches.

She's pretty **easygoing**.

Jason never wastes time at work and always gets a lot done.

He's quite **hardworking**.

Andrés is always helpful. He's aware of other people's needs.

He's really **considerate**.

Sonia's a tennis champion, but she doesn't think she's better than anyone else.

She's quite **modest**.

Eric is not at all shy. He loves meeting and chatting with new people.

He's so **outgoing**.

You can trust Irene to be reliable. She always does a good job and finishes it on time.

She's very **trustworthy**.

Jared rarely acts silly. He is thoughtful and pays attention to the important things.

He's pretty **serious**.

(handwritten: He really likes to show off his medals)

Isabelle and Anna enjoy chatting with each other.

They're really **talkative**. *(handwritten: Chatterbox)*

B **CLASSIFY THE VOCABULARY** On the chart, classify the adjectives from the Vocabulary, and other adjectives you know, according to your opinion. Then discuss with a partner.

(handwritten left margin: I am a punctual person.)

Are always positive	Can be either	Are always negative
polite	punctual	impolite
Friendly	liberal	Rude
nice	conservative	unfriendly
intelligent	interesting	
interesting	independent	

Other adjectives
polite
impolite
punctual
rude
friendly
unfriendly
nice
liberal
conservative
interesting
intelligent
independent
(handwritten: Able to things by himself.)

❝Hardworking is usually positive. But some people are too hardworking and don't spend enough time with their family. ❞

(handwritten: seeing   to see)

C **GRAMMAR** GERUNDS AND INFINITIVES: REVIEW AND EXPANSION

Remember: Gerunds and infinitives function as subjects, objects, and subject complements in sentences.

Subject: Sharing tasks with co-workers is helpful.
Direct object of a verb: I avoid **calling** the doctor too often.
Subject complement: Our dream is **to make** a trip to Africa next year.

Some verbs can only be followed by gerunds as the object of the verb. Some verbs can only be followed by infinitives. Others can be followed by either a gerund or an infinitive.

We **considered going** to the picnic. NOT We considered ~~to go~~ to the picnic.
They **have decided to invite** their teacher to the play. NOT They have decided ~~inviting~~ their teacher to the play.
BUT
She **prefers going** to the early show. OR She **prefers to go** to the early show.

For lists of verbs followed by gerunds and / or infinitives, see pages 123–124.

For a list of expressions followed by gerunds, see page 123.

For a list of adjectives followed by infinitives, see page 124.

(handwritten: CONSERVATIVE ⟹ OPPOSITE VIEW THINGS.)

Some people can take advantage of you.

Prepositions can be followed by gerunds, not by infinitives.
    I saw a film **about driving** across the United States.
    NOT I saw a film about ~~to drive~~ across the United States.

Other uses of infinitives:
To state a fact or an opinion with an impersonal <u>it</u> + an infinitive.
    It's a good day **to meet** the new boss.

To state the purpose of an action.
    We used an insect repellent **to avoid** mosquito bites.

To modify an adjective with <u>too</u> or <u>enough</u>. Note: Enough follows an adjective.
    They were **too late to make** the plane to Boston, but they were **early enough to catch** the bus.
    NOT ... they were ~~enough early to catch~~ the bus.

Adjectives can be followed by infinitives, not by gerunds.
    We're **ready to go**. NOT We're ready ~~going~~.

> **GRAMMAR BOOSTER** p. 125
> · Infinitives: review, expansion, and common errors
> · Parallelism with gerunds and infinitives

DIGITAL MORE EXERCISES

D ▶ 1:04 **LISTEN TO ACTIVATE GRAMMAR** Listen to the conversations. Then complete each statement with the gerund or infinitive form of one of the verbs from List 1 and a word from List 2.

1 He's going to come home early ....
2 She's worried about ..... *telling* ..... Jack about her ..... *keyboard* .....
3 He says it's too late ..... *waiting never* .....
4 She doesn't mind .... in ....
5 She's apologizing for ..... *to be* ..... *rude* ..... to him the night before.
6 He's a little down about ..... *have to* work late on ..... *Friday* .. .

List 1:	List 2:
paint	~~the bedroom~~
have to	Friday
tell	an office
~~be~~	rude
work	keyboard
watch	~~a movie~~

E **PAIR WORK** Complete the questions with your own ideas, using gerunds or infinitives. Answer your partner's questions.

1 Do you avoid .... ?
2 When are you too old .... ?
3 In your family, who doesn't mind .... ?
4 Do you believe in .... ?
5 Do you object to .... ?
6 Do you think it's a good time .... ?
7 Do you ever stay up late .... ?
8 What don't you mind .... ?

NOW YOU CAN | Describe your personality

A ▶ 1:05 **CONVERSATION SPOTLIGHT** Read and listen. Notice the spotlighted conversation strategies.

A: So how would you describe yourself?
B: Me? Well, **I'd say** I'm pretty easygoing. I don't let things get to me.
A: Easygoing? I see you as serious.
B: You think so? **I don't see** myself **that way**. In any case, can't you be both easygoing and serious?
A: I guess. And how would you describe me?
B: You? **I see you as** pretty outgoing.
A: You do? Why do you say that?
B: Because you **tend to be** talkative and you **seem to** like being with people a lot.

B ▶ 1:06 **RHYTHM AND INTONATION** Listen again and repeat. Then practice the conversation with a partner.

DIGITAL VIDEO
DIGITAL SPEAKING BOOSTER
C **CONVERSATION ACTIVATOR** Create a similar conversation, using the Vocabulary or other adjectives that describe your personality. Start like this: *So how would you describe yourself?* Be sure to change roles and then partners.

DON'T STOP!
• Say more about your personality.
• Ask about other people's personalities.
• Say as much as you can.

RECYCLE THIS LANGUAGE
be an optimist / a pessimist / a realist

GOAL Discuss someone's behavior

A ▶ 1:07 **GRAMMAR SPOTLIGHT** Read how these four people describe other people's behavior. Notice the spotlighted grammar.

My manager, Chris, is a real sweetheart. He **wants all of us to succeed**. And he **encourages us to learn** new skills so we can move up in the company. He's also really kind and understanding. He **permits us to work** at home when we have a sick kid. You'll never find a better boss than Chris!

—— *Sarah Beth Linehan, 30 Melbourne, Australia*

I share an apartment with three roommates, but one of them, Erika, is an annoying pain in the neck! First, she's a total workaholic. Between her studies and her after-school job, she's rarely here, and when she is, she just keeps working. My other two roommates and I do all the chores: shop for groceries, cook, wash the dishes, and so on. When we complain that Erika's not pulling her weight, she just **asks us to do** her chores because she doesn't have time! Time? It's time for her to move out!

Martina Braun, 21 Frankfurt, Germany ——

My colleague Lily at the travel agency where I work is a real people person. Most of us prefer to do everything by e-mail or online, but Lily **invites all her clients** (even the difficult ones!) **to come in** to the office and **tell her** their dream vacation ideas, and she tries to make those a reality for them. And Lily's such a team player. If one of us has too much to do, she offers to help. Everyone loves Lily.

Cindy Yu, 27 Boston, USA ——

I'll never forget my high-school drama teacher, Mr. Mellon. He was such a tyrant! He used to **force us to say** our lines over and over until it drove us crazy. And if anyone forgot even one word, he would **forbid them to go** home until they had learned the line. He would **warn them to learn** every line perfectly by the next class, or they couldn't be in the play. Everyone hated him. He took all the fun out of drama.

Richard Rowan, 43 Saint Louis, USA ——

DIGITAL STRATEGIES

B **RELATE TO PERSONAL EXPERIENCE** Find these words and phrases in the Grammar Spotlight. With a partner, talk about people you know or have known who behave like people described in the Grammar Spotlight. Provide examples.

a pain in the neck	a team player
a people person	a tyrant
a sweetheart	a workaholic

C ▶ 1:08 **LISTEN TO CLASSIFY** Listen to people describe other people's behavior, using noun and pronoun objects before infinitives. Check the description(s) of each person, according to the opinions expressed.

1 Margaret is: ☐ a workaholic ☐ a pain in the neck ☐ a team player

2 Peter is: ☐ a people person ☐ a tyrant ☐ a pain in the neck

3 Tim is: ☐ a tyrant ☐ a pain in the neck ☐ a workaholic

DIGITAL INDUCTIVE ACTIVITY

D **GRAMMAR** **VERBS THAT REQUIRE A NOUN OR PRONOUN BEFORE AN INFINITIVE**
Remember: Some verbs can be followed directly by an infinitive. However, in the active voice, some verbs must have a noun or pronoun object before the infinitive.

Active
He **ordered us to leave** the office.
The sign **warned drivers not to speed**.
We **told them to be** on time.
She **taught them to swim** last year.

Passive
(We were ordered to leave the office.)
(Drivers were warned not to speed.)
(They were told to be on time.)
(They were taught to swim last year.)

Negative infinitives
To make an infinitive negative, place <u>not</u> before the infinitive:

*They advised us **not to come** late to the meeting.*

Remember: To make a gerund negative, also place <u>not</u> before the gerund:

*They complained about **not having** enough time.*

Some verbs, such as <u>would like</u>, <u>want</u>, <u>ask</u>, <u>expect</u>, and <u>need</u>, are used with or without a noun or pronoun object in the active voice, depending on the meaning.

Without an object
We**'d like to eat** healthier food.
She **wants to drive** the new car.
Tom **asked to see** the director.

With an object
We**'d like** <u>our children</u> to eat healthier food, too.
She **wants** <u>me</u> **to drive** the new car.
Tom **asked** <u>Emily</u> to see the director.

These verbs require a noun or pronoun object before an infinitive in the active voice.

advise	convince	force	invite	permit	require
allow	encourage	hire	order	persuade	teach
cause	forbid	instruct	pay	remind	warn

For a list of verbs that can be followed directly by an infinitive in the active voice, see page 124.

DIGITAL MORE EXERCISES

E UNDERSTAND THE GRAMMAR   On a separate sheet of paper, change each sentence to the active voice. Use the <u>by</u> phrase as the subject.

The CEO invited spouses of co-workers to attend the reception.

1 Spouses of co-workers were invited (by the CEO) to attend the reception.
2 Drivers were told (by the hotel security guards) to stop at the entrance to the hotel.
3 Employees were required (by the rules) to return from lunch at 2:00.
4 We were encouraged (by our manager) to tweet our questions to the speaker.
5 They were advised (by the invitation) to be at the restaurant before 8:00 P.M.

F GRAMMAR PRACTICE   Complete the sentences with your own ideas, an object, and an infinitive.

1 The change in the meeting schedule caused ......*us*...... to ...*postpone our flight*... .
2 The bad weather on the day of the game convinced ...*us*... to ...*cancel it.*...
3 Should we remind ...*me*... to ...*study for exam*...?
4 The sign at the entrance to the event warned ...*us*... to ~~not forget to~~ *wear mask*
5 Why don't you pay .... to ....?
6 The article in the newspaper about the accident persuaded ...*me*... to ...*drive slower*... .

G PAIR WORK   With a partner, take turns answering the questions, using the cues provided.

1 **A:** Is Mark bringing the food for the picnic?
   B: No, Mark ......*expects us to bring*...... the food. (expect / us / bring)
2 **A:** Have you spoken to the manager about the broken equipment?
   B: No. I .... to her about it. (ask / Ken / speak)
3 **A:** Who's going to be the first speaker at the event?
   B: Actually, I .... the first one. (would like / you / be)
4 **A:** Do you want to write the summary of what happened at the meeting?
   B: I'd rather not. I .... it. (want / Kathy / write)
5 **B:** Didn't you need to discuss the new e-mail system with Mr. Green?
   A: Actually, I .... with him about it. (want / my assistant / speak)

PRONUNCIATION BOOSTER   p. 141
Content words and function words

NOW YOU CAN   Discuss someone's behavior

A NOTEPADDING   Choose two people you know. Make statements about each person's personality and behavior, using one of the verbs from the list in the chart at the top of this page.

Description	Description	Description
1 My sister is a sweetheart. She encourages everyone to get along.	1	1
	2	2

RECYCLE THIS LANGUAGE

- easygoing
- hardworking
- helpful
- modest
- outgoing
- reliable
- serious
- talkative
- an optimist
- a pessimist
- a realist
- a sweetheart
- a team player

DIGITAL VIDEO

B DISCUSSION ACTIVATOR   Discuss the people you wrote about on your notepads. Say as much as you can about them.

GOAL **Compare perspectives on world problems**

A **LISTENING WARM-UP** How much do you worry about epidemics, terrorism, and crime? Write each one on the graph. Then discuss with a partner.

NOT AT ALL →→→→→ A LOT

B ▶ 1:09 **LISTEN FOR MAIN IDEAS** Listen. Write the problem discussed in each conversation.

Conversation 1 .... Conversation 2 .... Conversation 3 ....

C ▶ 1:10 **LISTEN FOR DETAILS** Listen again. Circle *T* (true), *F* (false), or *ND* (not discussed).

		T	F	ND
1	**a** She says there aren't a lot of newspaper articles about crime.	T	(F)	ND
	b He thinks there's nothing anyone can do about crime.	(T)	F	ND
2	**a** She thinks breathing the air on planes can be dangerous.	T	(F)	ND
	b He thinks international travel will spread the disease all over the world.	T	F	(ND)
3	**a** He worries about terrorism in crowded places.	(T)	F	ND
	b She thinks terrorism is caused by poverty.	(T)	F	ND

D **UNDERSTAND MEANING FROM CONTEXT** Read each quotation. Then listen again and complete each statement.

Conversation 1

1 When the woman says, "Crime is just out of control," she means ....

   a there's a huge amount of crime   **b** we have to control crime

2 When the man says, "What is the world coming to?" he is asking, ...

   a "Where in the world can we go to avoid crime?"   **b** "What is the future of the world?"

3 When he says, "Better safe than sorry," he is saying ....

   a don't tempt criminals by wearing jewelry   **b** just stay home where it's safe

Conversation 2

4 When the man says, "I think I'm getting a little obsessed," he means, ...

   a "I'm thinking about this way too much."   **b** "I'm afraid I'm getting sick."

5 When she says, "Well, I don't think that's crazy," she means ....

   a he's right to be worried   **b** the disease is extremely bad

6 When the woman says, "It's even more contagious," she worries ....

   a it could cause an epidemic   **b** it won't last for long

Conversation 3

7 When the man says, "I don't know about you, but I'm getting a little freaked out about terrorism," he's really saying, ...

   a "Are you as scared as I am about terrorism?"   **b** "I don't know how to stop terrorism. Do you?"

8 When the woman says, "Well, that's no way to live," she means, ...

   a "You are going to die."   **b** "It's impossible to live normally with that outlook."

9 When she says, "It is what it is," she means, ...

   a "What is it?"   **b** "There's nothing anyone can do about it."

10 When the man says, "I guess I'm going a little overboard," he means, ...

   a "I'm making this too important."   **b** "I'm not interested in this issue."

Overboard
To much

(handwritten top) to get away with something.   fraking out.

E GROUP WORK   Answer each question and explain your answers. Listen again if you disagree.

Conversation 1
1 What does the man think we can do about crime?
2 Why does the woman think he is practical?
3 Which speaker's outlook is closer to yours, the man's or the woman's?

Conversation 2
1 What reasons do the speakers give for why so many people will get the Marburg virus sooner or later?
2 Which speaker is more optimistic—the man or the woman?
3 Which speaker's outlook is closer to yours, the man's or the woman's?

Conversation 3
1 What does the woman think we can do about terrorism?
2 Which speaker has a more realistic outlook—the man or the woman?
3 Which speaker's outlook is closer to yours, the man's or the woman's?

(handwritten notes, right)
→ How is everything with you.
That's good to hear that.
Good to relax able.
I am trying to save as much as possible
That's the good thing to do
Good hobby to have.
on to be came

NOW YOU CAN   Compare perspectives on world problems

A NOTEPADDING   Write a list of world problems that you worry about. Or use the ideas in the pictures. Write why you worry about them.

(handwritten) Everyone was giving us a look
She is very optimistic very ol

> Epidemics: I worry that we won't have enough medicines, and lots of people will die.

(handwritten on notepad) I worry about public sanitation. political corruption
Because we are paying a lot of money as a tax.

War

Drug trafficking

Political corruption

Public sanitation

Global warming

DIGITAL SPEAKING BOOSTER

B DISCUSSION   Meet with classmates who listed the same problems on their notepads. Discuss the problem and explain why you worry about it, providing details of experiences you or others you know have had with it. Discuss what, if anything, can be done about the problem.

GOAL Discuss creative ways to achieve a goal

A **READING WARM-UP** In what ways can a person's attitude help in solving a problem or achieving a goal?

DIGITAL STRATEGIES **B** ▶1:11 **READING** Read the newspaper article, which is based on a true story in the news. What was Phil Cooper's mistake?

DAILY NEWS

August 7

FACEBOOK SAVES THE DAY

WESTON—In a painful ending to an otherwise glorious vacation, Phil and Virginia Cooper and their daughters, Miranda and Grace, arrived home without the hundreds of vacation snapshots they had taken.

"We'll always have our memories," said Phil, "but no pictures of our family's activities or the beautiful New England scenery and Cape Cod beaches where we spent the last two weeks of our summer vacation."

"Phil has always been a little absent-minded, but this takes the cake," Virginia said with an affectionate smile. "We were getting settled in the car for the long drive home, and Phil got out to snap one last picture of the sunset. Then he set the camera on the roof of the car while he got his jacket out of the trunk." Needless to say, the camera fell off the car as they drove off. The family discovered the camera was missing when they got home. Then Phil suddenly remembered placing the camera on the top of the car.

"I felt terrible for having been so careless and was sure the situation was

hopeless. Days had passed. The camera would have been lying on the ground through bad weather, or perhaps someone had found it and taken it home," Phil said. The camera case had the Coopers' name and address, but the camera hadn't been in the case.

Last weekend, while training for an Ironman Triathlon event, Adam Secrest, 24, spotted the camera along the side of Callman Road near Barton Beach, Massachusetts. He picked it up, looked for a name, and finding none, stashed it in his car, thinking he would try to locate the owner after his run. Once home, Secrest turned on the camera and scrolled through the photos.

"I felt sort of like a snoop, but my spying was purposeful," he said. "I was looking for clues to the owner's identity, and I was optimistic that I would find something."

Soon he came across a photo of two young girls getting on a yellow school bus with the words WESTON, NJ on the side. In a burst of creative thinking, Secrest thought someone might recognize the girls, so he posted the photo on Facebook and urged his friends to share it, with this message:

Do you know these kids from Weston, New Jersey? I found a camera with this photo in Barton, Massachusetts, and want to locate the owner. Please share.

Facebook friends shared the photo hundreds of times. It was just a matter of time until it appeared on the Weston Community page and someone recognized Miranda and Grace and called Virginia Cooper, who contacted Secrest, first through Facebook, and then by phone. The camera arrived at the Coopers' house by mail yesterday.

"Lots of people say social media is a meaningless waste of time, but here's an example of how powerful and useful it can be," said Secrest.

C **DETERMINE THE MAIN IDEA** Which statement expresses the main idea of the article?

1 There's nothing worse than losing one's vacation memories.

2 Creative thinking can help solve problems in unexpected ways.

3 Being a forgetful person can cause a lot of problems.

D **UNDERSTAND MEANING FROM CONTEXT** Locate these adjectives and expressions in the article and classify them as positive (+) or negative (-). Then, with a partner, try to explain the meaning of each one in your own words.

☐ absent-minded   ☐ hopeless   ☐ meaningless   ☐ useful
☐ affectionate   ☐ purposeful   ☐ powerful

E **SUMMARIZE** Read the article again. Then close your book and, with a partner, summarize the story in your own words.

DIGITAL EXTRA CHALLENGE

F ▶ 1:12 **WORD STUDY** **ADJECTIVE SUFFIXES -FUL AND -LESS** Expand your vocabulary by learning these adjectives from the Reading on page 10 with the suffixes -ful (meaning "with") and -less (meaning "without"). Write one sentence using one of each pair.

-ful	-less	My sentence
careful	careless	
hopeful	hopeless	
meaningful	meaningless	
painful	painless	
powerful	powerless	
purposeful	purposeless	
useful	useless	

G **WORD STUDY PRACTICE** The following pairs of words aren't opposite equivalents. With a partner, discuss the difference in meaning of the words in these pairs.

restful / restless: We had a very restful vacation and didn't do much. / I was so restless last night. I couldn't sleep.

helpful / helpless: Your brother is so helpful. He always offers to do the chores at home. / Babies are so helpless. They can't do anything for themselves.

pitiful / pitiless: It was pitiful to see that poor cat looking for food. / How can people be so pitiless that they'd let a cat starve?

Be careful!
Not all words that end in -ful and -less are opposite equivalents. Restful refers to a calm place or an experience, while restless refers to a person's feeling of physical nervousness. Always check the dictionary to confirm meaning.

NOW YOU CAN Discuss creative ways to achieve a goal

A **NOTEPADDING** Phil Secrest's goal was to find the camera's owner. With a partner, brainstorm and write creative ways to achieve the goals on the notepad.

B **DISCUSSION** Choose one goal and in a small group discuss ways to achieve it, based on your ideas from Exercise A. Present your ideas to the class.

❝ Not everyone will want to donate a lot of money. So it's important to keep a positive attitude. If everyone gives a little, or donates time to help, we can still reach our goal. ❞

OPTIONAL WRITING In a paragraph, present the ideas you developed in Exercise B.

Goals:

To collect money for a good cause

To locate an organ donor for a sick person

To warn people about a danger

To find a lost person

To spread a political message

A **WRITING SKILL** Study the rules.

A paragraph consists of sentences about one topic. The most important sentence in a paragraph is the **topic sentence**. It is often (though not always) the first sentence, and it introduces, states, or summarizes the topic of a paragraph. For example: Workaholics lead unbalanced lives.

In formal or academic writing, all the **supporting sentences** that follow, surround, or precede a topic sentence—details, examples, and other facts—must be related to the topic presented in the topic sentence.

If the last sentence of a paragraph isn't its topic sentence, and especially if the paragraph is a long one, writers sometimes end it with a **concluding sentence** that restates the topic sentence or summarizes the paragraph. Concluding sentences commonly use phrases such as In conclusion or In summary.

> **WRITING MODEL**
>
> **Workaholics lead unbalanced lives.** They spend all their energy on work. They rarely take time to relax and let their minds rest. I know, because my father was a workaholic, and he worked every day of the week. We hardly ever saw him. Even when he was not at work, we knew he was thinking about work. He seemed never to think of anything else. **In summary, not knowing how to escape from work makes it difficult for a workaholic to find balance in his or her life.**

B **PRACTICE** The sentences below form a paragraph, but they are out of order. Write <u>T</u> next to the topic sentence, <u>S</u> next to each of the four supporting sentences, and <u>C</u> next to the concluding sentence. Then, on a separate sheet of paper, put the sentences in order and rewrite the paragraph.

S... **1** She took a night-shift job so she didn't have to do much work.

S..... **2** Since they're very intelligent, some figure out how to do less work.

T... **3** Very intelligent people, or "brains," are sometimes lazy people.

.... **4** I had a friend who was a member of Mensa, an organization for people who are really smart.

.... **5** To sum up, sometimes intelligent people use their intelligence to get out of doing work.

.... **6** She could read novels most of the night and still get a paycheck.

C **PRACTICE** Read the two paragraphs. Find and underline the topic sentence and the concluding sentence in each paragraph.

Terrorist acts take many forms, but all have one thing in common: the senseless targeting of innocent people to achieve maximum pain, fear, and disruption. In one type of act, a terrorist kills or harms a single individual for no apparent reason. In others, terrorists detonate explosives or bombs in crowded markets or at public events. In still others, terrorists attack public transportation, harming or killing many people at once. In conclusion, although I generally have a positive outlook, I think it is just a matter of time until terrorists harm me or people I know and love.

The things that worry many people don't worry me. For example, many people worry about war, epidemics, and natural catastrophes, such as storms and earthquakes. An individual person can't do anything about war, so why worry about it? I believe in hoping for the best. Epidemics can be terrible, but I trust in modern medicine and think scientists are doing everything they can to discover vaccines and treatments for them. And storms and earthquakes are relatively rare and can't be prevented, so it's best just to keep an optimistic outlook. Of course it would be silly not to take precautions that can help. "Better safe than sorry," as they say, but in most cases it's best just to try to roll with the punches.

DIGITAL WRITING PROCESS

D **APPLY THE WRITING SKILL** Choose one (or more) world problems that worry you. Write a paragraph describing your outlook and attitude about the problem. Use the writing models in Exercise C as an example.

> **SELF-CHECK**
>
> ☐ Does my paragraph have a topic sentence?
>
> ☐ Do the supporting sentences in my paragraph all relate to the topic?
>
> ☐ Do I have a concluding sentence?

A ▶ 1:13 **Listen to the people talking about their reactions to events in the news. Decide if each speaker is an optimist, a pessimist, or a realist.**

1 John .... 2 Susan .... 3 Matt ....

B **Now read the statements. Write the name of the person from the listening who is most likely to have said each statement. Listen again if necessary.**

1 "You've got to be practical. There will be some problems in life that you can solve and some that you can't. What's important is realizing when something is beyond your control. I mean, it is what it is." ....

2 "Life is full of hard times. Bad things happen and there's very little you can do about it." ....

3 "It's important to see a problem as both a challenge and an opportunity for success. Difficult experiences can make a person stronger." ....

C **Complete each description in your own words.**

1 An easygoing person is someone who ....

2 An outgoing person is someone who ....

3 A reliable person is someone who ....

4 A helpful person is someone who ....

D **Complete each conversation with one of the words that describe behavior from page 6.**

1 **A:** Looks like I have to work overtime again tonight. My boss just gave me three projects to complete by the end of the day.

   B: You're kidding. He sounds like a real .... !

2 **A:** You know, without Sarah's help, I would never have completed that presentation in time.

   B: Tell me about it. She really helped me out with my sales campaign last month. She's such a ....

3 **A:** Tom is really a .... I ran into him in the park last weekend, and he was sitting on a bench and working on that report.

   B: Yeah, that's Tom all right. He never stops!

4 **A:** I don't think Jill had a very good time at the party—she didn't say a word the whole evening.

   B: Well, Jill doesn't feel comfortable in social situations. She's just not a ....

E **Complete each sentence with one of the adjectives from Word Study on page 11.**

1 Excellent dental anesthesia today makes almost all dental treatment ....

2 Sometimes we feel completely .... ; there's just nothing we can do to make something happen.

3 The Internet can be very .... in helping us communicate with a large number of people at once.

4 I'm .... about the future. I think things will change for the better.

5 Some say the colors of a painting create a more .... impression than the black and white of a pencil drawing.

| TEST-TAKING SKILLS BOOSTER | p. 151 |

Web Project: Personality Types
www.english.com/summit3e

I feel like to dance

PREVIEW

A FRAME YOUR IDEAS Complete the survey. Then tell a partner about the songs and artists you listed. Explain why each one is memorable for you.

WRITE ONE OR MORE EXAMPLES OF YOUR
MUSICAL MEMORIES

1 A song with a really danceable beat that made you want to get up and move to the music

Yes, It was so danceable and I want to get up

2 A song with a catchy, unforgettable melody that you loved—you couldn't get the music out of your head

Yes, It was.

3 A song with an annoying melody that drove you crazy every time you heard it

none

4 A song with really moving lyrics—you got emotional every time you heard the words

Yes It was

5 A song with interesting lyrics that made you really think about the song's meaning

It was really!

6 A group or performer with an innovative sound unlike anything you'd heard before

none

7 A singer that blew you away with his or her extraordinary singing voice

8 A top-notch musician you thought was one of the most talented artists ever

9 A singer, musician, or group that put on an amazing and memorable performance

B ▶1:14 **VOCABULARY ELEMENTS OF MUSIC** Work with a partner to explain the meanings of the words on the right. Use the survey to support your explanation. Then listen and repeat.

a beat	a sound
a melody	a voice
lyrics	a performance

C PAIR WORK Tell your partner about the performers you'd like to see, or not like to see, in the future. Explain your reasons.

❝I'd love to see Bastille. They have a really unique sound.❞

D ▶1:15 **SPOTLIGHT** Read and listen to three colleagues discussing what to do after a meeting. Notice the spotlighted language.

ENGLISH FOR TODAY'S WORLD
Understand a variety of accents.
Amalia = Spanish
Sandy = Chinese
Paul = American English (standard)

Amalia: Hey, guys, we've got a free evening tonight. Why don't we see if there's anything to do?

Sandy: Good idea! Let me see if I can find something online.

Paul: **I'm in** … Check out eTix. They usually have some great deals.

Sandy: Let's see … Hey, *The Phantom of the Opera* is at the Palladium. I saw the movie, but I've never seen it live. What do you think?

Paul: I saw it back home in Chicago at least ten years ago. Hasn't that thing been playing for like twenty years now?

Amalia: At least! I've actually seen it on stage. But I guess I wouldn't mind seeing it again. The music is awesome.

Paul: Yeah, it's got some catchy melodies, but the story**'s nothing to write home about**.

Sandy: Hey, here's something that might be good! It looks like tickets are still available for *Swan Lake*. That's supposed to be an amazing ballet.

Paul: Uh, no offense, but ballet **isn't my thing**.

Amalia: I can see Paul's going to be **hard to please**!

Paul: Sorry, **I don't mean to be a pain**. I guess I'm not really in the mood for a show tonight. Maybe there's a museum that stays open late.

Sandy: Hold on! Here's something that might be **right up your alley**, Paul. There's an exhibit of modern American art at the Grant Gallery. And they're open late on Thursdays.

Paul: **Now you're talking**!

Sandy: And what I really love is the location. The gallery's right around the corner from here.

E **UNDERSTAND IDIOMS AND EXPRESSIONS** Find these expressions in Spotlight. Match each with its correct usage.

...f... **1** I'm in.
...e... **2** It's nothing to write home about.
...g... **3** It isn't my thing.
...d... **4** He's hard to please.
...b... **5** I don't mean to be a pain.
...a... **6** It's right up your alley.
...c... **7** Now you're talking.

a You think someone will definitely be interested in something.
b You want to apologize for making trouble.
c You think someone has made a good suggestion.
d You think someone is difficult to satisfy.
e You think there's nothing special about something.
f You want to indicate your willingness to participate.
g You indicate that something isn't to your personal taste.

F **THINK AND EXPLAIN** Discuss these questions.

1 Who's willing to see *The Phantom of the Opera* and who's not? Explain each person's point of view.

2 Why do you think Sandy thinks the art exhibit might be just right for Paul?

SPEAKING **PAIR WORK** Rate the events on a scale of 1 to 5 (with 5 being most enjoyable). Then tell your partner about the kinds of events you'd like to attend. Explain your reasons in detail.

> 66 Musicals aren't really my thing. They just seem silly to me. But a rock concert's right up my alley. 99

- [ ] an art exhibit
- [4] a rock concert
- [5] a comedy show
- [ ] a modern dance performance
- [ ] a classical music concert
- [ ] a jazz performance
- [ ] a play
- [ ] a musical
- [ ] a ballet

It is so fast for me.

15

GOAL Describe how you've been enjoying the arts

A ▶ 1:16 **GRAMMAR SPOTLIGHT** Read the commentaries. Notice the spotlighted grammar.

Over the past few years, **I've been going** to see a lot of live theater. I've seen some classic but still-popular shows like *Les Misérables* and *The Phantom of the Opera*. Recently, I booked a trip to New York, and **I've been checking** online to see what's playing. I couldn't go to the Big Apple without seeing a few good shows, right?

Amy Chen, 18 San Francisco, USA

I try to get to MASP—that's the São Paulo Museum of Art— whenever I can. Because it's not far from work, **I've been dropping by** about every month or so to see what's new and visit its excellent library. Lately, **I've been exploring** the Antiques Market outside as well. They always have a lot of interesting stuff to look at.

Music plays a pretty big part in my life. Lately **I've been using** music to wake me up in the morning, get me moving at the gym, and help me unwind after work. Speaking of work, **I've been listening** to music more during the day and I've noticed that it actually makes me more productive.

Nicole Clarkson, 34 Chicago, USA

Fabiano Valle, 22 São Paulo, Brazil

B **MAKE PERSONAL COMPARISONS** Which person's tastes, interests, and activities are the most like (or the least like) your own? Explain why.

DIGITAL INDUCTIVE ACTIVITY

C **GRAMMAR** **THE PRESENT PERFECT CONTINUOUS**

Use the present perfect continuous to express a continuing action that began in the past and continues in the present. Depending on the context, the action may continue in the future. Use <u>have</u> / <u>has</u> + <u>been</u> and a present participle.

Statements
She**'s been practicing** ballet for years.
I**'ve been listening** to classical music since I was a kid.

Questions
Have you **been playing** the piano for a long time?
How long **has** your son **been painting** portraits?

These words and phrases are often used with the present perfect continuous (and the present perfect) when describing continuing actions:

for [two months]	lately	these days
for a while	recently	this [year]
since [2013]	all day	How long ... ?

Note: The present perfect continuous, rather than the present perfect, is generally used to describe a recent continuous action, especially when there is visible evidence that the action has just ended.

What's Nora's violin doing on the table? **Has** she **been practicing**?

Remember:
The present perfect can also be used to describe a continuing action that began in the past. There is no significant difference in meaning.

She**'s practiced** ballet for years.
I**'ve listened** to classical music since I was a kid.
Have you **played** the piano for a long time?
How long **has** your son **painted** portraits?

However, use the present perfect, not the present perfect continuous, in sentences with <u>already</u>, <u>yet</u>, <u>before</u>, and <u>ever</u>, because they describe finished actions.

She**'s already practiced** ballet this week.
Have you **ever studied** piano?

GRAMMAR BOOSTER p. 126
Finished and unfinished actions: summary

D **NOTICE THE GRAMMAR** Find an example of the present perfect continuous in Spotlight on page 15. Does it describe an action that has finished or one that may continue in the future?

E **UNDERSTAND THE GRAMMAR** Check the sentences in which the present perfect continuous can also be used. Then, on a separate sheet of paper, rewrite those sentences in the present perfect continuous.

☐ **1** He's played with their band for almost ten years.

☐ **2** Justin Timberlake has already given two concerts in my town.

☐ **3** She's looked online this morning for a good deal on show tickets.

☐ **4** Since he got promoted to stage manager, Mark's arrived early at the theater every day.

☐ **5** We've gone to a lot of concerts lately.

☐ **6** Have you ever visited the Museum of Contemporary Art?

☐ **7** How many times have you seen the musical *Les Misérables*?

☐ **8** Lately, audiences have asked them to play more songs from their new album.

F **GRAMMAR PRACTICE** Complete the questions, using the present perfect continuous when possible. Otherwise, use the present perfect.

1 A: .... music videos on my tablet?
   ‹‹you / watch››

   B: Yes, I have. But I'm done.

2 A: .... the musical *Wicked* yet?
   ‹‹Max / see››

   B: No, he hasn't. But he should. It's unforgettable.

3 A: .... ?
   ‹‹what / you / do››

   B: Just now? I've been checking to see if there are any interesting art exhibits this week.

4 A: .... late again?
   ‹‹Vickie / work››

   B: I'm afraid so. But she'll be heading home in a few minutes.

5 A: .... to a Broadway musical?
   ‹‹Jerry / go››

   B: Never. But he's going to his first one tonight.

6 A: .... in line to get in to the concert?
   ‹‹how long / you / wait››

   B: About twenty minutes. But it looks like we're finally moving now.

> **PRONUNCIATION BOOSTER** p. 142
> Intonation patterns

NOW YOU CAN Describe how you've been enjoying the arts

A **NOTEPADDING** Write about your experiences with the arts recently. Explain why you've been doing some things and not doing others. Use the present perfect continuous.

Music	Art
I've been listening to a lot of jazz these days. It helps me unwind.	I haven't been going to any art exhibits lately. But to tell the truth, it's not really my thing.

Music	Art	Theater

B **DISCUSSION ACTIVATOR** Discuss the role the arts have been playing in your life recently. Use your notes to discuss what you've been doing (or not doing) lately. Ask your partner questions. Say as much as you can.

> ❝ Have you been going to many plays or musicals recently? ❞

GOAL Express a negative opinion politely

DIGITAL STRATEGIES **A** ▶1:17 **VOCABULARY** **NEGATIVE DESCRIPTIONS OF MUSIC**

Read and listen. Then listen again and repeat.

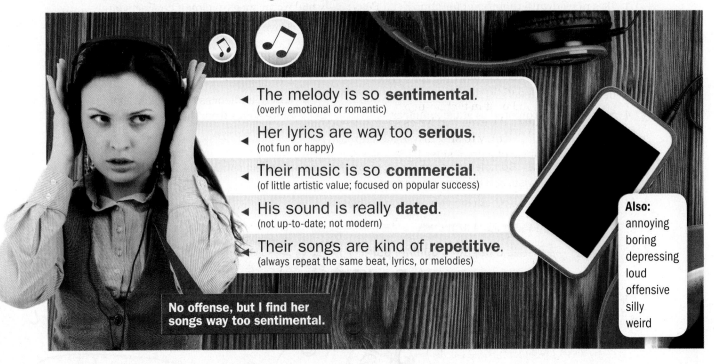

◄ The melody is so **sentimental**.
(overly emotional or romantic)

◄ Her lyrics are way too **serious**.
(not fun or happy)

◄ Their music is so **commercial**.
(of little artistic value; focused on popular success)

◄ His sound is really **dated**.
(not up-to-date; not modern)

◄ Their songs are kind of **repetitive**.
(always repeat the same beat, lyrics, or melodies)

Also:
annoying
boring
depressing
loud
offensive
silly
weird

No offense, but I find her songs way too sentimental.

B ▶1:18 **LISTEN TO ACTIVATE VOCABULARY** Listen to each conversation. Then complete the description.

1 He finds Jackie Evancho's music way too (repetitive / commercial / sentimental / serious).

2 She finds Maná very (repetitive / commercial / dated / serious).

3 He finds Caetano Veloso a little too (repetitive / sentimental / dated / serious).

4 She thinks reggae music is really (repetitive / sentimental / dated / commercial).

5 He thinks Anthony Hopkins's music is too (repetitive / sentimental / dated / serious).

C **APPLY THE VOCABULARY** With a partner, describe singers and bands you don't like, using the Vocabulary.

❝In my opinion, Phil Collins's music is way too commercial. And I hate to say it, but it's pretty dated, too. Do you agree?❞

DIGITAL INDUCTIVE ACTIVITY **D** **GRAMMAR** **CLEFT SENTENCES WITH WHAT**

One way to emphasize the action in a sentence is to use a noun clause with <u>What</u> as the subject of the sentence + the verb <u>be</u>. Make sure the form of the verb <u>be</u> agrees with its complement.

Cleft sentences

(**I really don't like** traditional music.) →	**What I really don't like is** traditional music.
(**He doesn't understand** jazz.) →	**What he doesn't understand is** jazz.
(**They really loved** the lyrics.) →	**What they really loved were** the lyrics.
(The melody **made everyone cry**.) →	**What made everyone cry was** the melody.

GRAMMAR BOOSTER p. 128
· Noun clauses: review and expansion
· Noun clauses as adjective and noun complements

DIGITAL MORE EXERCISES **E** **NOTICE THE GRAMMAR** Find an example of a cleft sentence with <u>What</u> in Spotlight on page 15.

F **GRAMMAR PRACTICE** Rewrite each statement as a cleft sentence with <u>What</u>.

1 I can't stand long classical music concerts. .....*What I can't stand are long classical music concerts.*.....

2 I didn't care for Adele's overly sentimental lyrics. ....

3 Jessica doesn't particularly like Bono's voice. ....

4 I'd really enjoy seeing a live Lady Gaga performance. ....

5 The song "I Gotta Feeling" by the Black Eyed Peas really makes me want to dance. ....
....

G **PAIR WORK** Take turns reading a statement aloud. Your partner restates it as a cleft sentence with <u>What</u>.

1 "Jazz always puts me to sleep."
2 "I can't stand the loud beat in techno-pop."
3 "A good melody can make even bad lyrics seem acceptable."
4 "Listening to my brother try to sing drives me crazy."
5 "Dancing to the music of a great salsa band helps me unwind."
6 "I love downloading songs by unknown new artists."

NOW YOU CAN **Express a negative opinion politely**

A ▶ 1:19 **CONVERSATION SPOTLIGHT**
Read and listen. Notice the spotlighted conversation strategies.

A: Are you as much of a Michael Bublé fan as I am?

B: Michael Bublé? **To tell the truth,** I'm not crazy about him.

A: How can you not like Michael Bublé?

B: **To be honest,** what I don't like is his sound. It's *so* commercial. But you know who I really like?

A: Who?

B: Sting.

A: Sting? **I hate to say it, but** I find his music a little dated.

B ▶ 1:20 **RHYTHM AND INTONATION** Listen again and repeat. Then practice the conversation with a partner.

C **NOTEPADDING** Write about some of your favorite musical artists and groups. Use cleft sentences with <u>What</u>.

Artists or groups	What I like

Artists or groups	What I like
Black Eyed Peas	What I love are their great dance beats.

D **CONVERSATION ACTIVATOR** Create a conversation similar to the one in Exercise A. Start like this: *Are you as much of a __ fan as I am?* Be sure to change roles and then partners.

DON'T STOP!
• Discuss other artists you like or don't like.
• Say as much as you can.

19

GOAL Describe a creative personality

  A ▶1:21 **VOCABULARY** DESCRIBING CREATIVE PERSONALITIES

Read and listen. Then listen again and repeat.

Positive qualities

gifted   having a natural ability to do one or more things extremely well

energetic   very active, physically and mentally

imaginative able to think of new and interesting ideas

passionate showing a strong liking for something and being very dedicated to it

Negative qualities

eccentric   behaving in an unusual way or appearing different from most people

difficult   never satisfied and hard to please

moody   becoming quickly and easily annoyed or unhappy

egotistical believing oneself to be better or more important than other people

B **READING WARM-UP** It is often said that gifted people have eccentric, moody, or difficult personalities. Do you agree? Explain.

  C ▶1:22 **READING** Read the short biography. What effect did Beethoven's personality have on his life?

A Passionate **Genius**

Born in 1770 in Bonn, Germany, Ludwig van Beethoven started playing the piano before he was four years old. Clearly gifted, he had already composed his first piece of music by the time he was twelve. When Beethoven was just sixteen, he went to study in Vienna, Austria, then the center of European cultural life and home to the most brilliant musicians and composers of the period. Beethoven proved to be both a gifted pianist and an imaginative composer. He went on to create his own unique sound and melodies loved by millions.

Beethoven is remembered not only for his great genius, but also for his strong and difficult personality. In one infamous incident, Beethoven became so annoyed with a waiter that he emptied a plate of food over the man's head. He could also be quite egotistical, saying once, "There are and will be thousands of princes. There is only one Beethoven." During concerts, if people talked while he was performing, he would stop and walk out.

Despite this type of behavior, many in musical and aristocratic circles admired Beethoven, and music lovers were always Beethoven's greatest supporters. This fact did not prevent him from losing his temper with one or another of them. However, because of his talent, Beethoven's friends always forgave his insults and moody temperament.

In addition to being difficult, Beethoven was also well-known for his eccentric behavior. He had the odd habit of putting his head in cold water before he composed any music. He often walked through the streets of Vienna muttering to himself and stamping his feet. He completely neglected his personal appearance; he had wild hair, and his clothes would get so dirty that his friends would come during the night and replace his old clothes with new ones. What amazed his friends was that he never noticed the difference.

Beethoven wrote two famous works, *Moonlight Sonata* and *Für Elise*, for two different women he loved. He was almost always passionately in love, often with a woman who was already married or engaged. Although Beethoven asked several women to marry him, they all rejected him.

The most tragic aspect of Beethoven's life was his gradual loss of hearing, beginning in his late twenties until he became completely deaf in his forties. However, even as his hearing grew worse, Beethoven continued to be energetic and productive; his creative activity remained intense, and audiences were deeply touched by his music. In 1826, Beethoven held his last public performance of his famous *Ninth Symphony*. By this time, the composer was completely deaf. When he was turned around so he could see the roaring applause that he could not hear, Beethoven began to cry.

Beethoven died in Vienna at age fifty-seven. One out of ten people who lived in Vienna came to his funeral. And millions of people all over the world have been enjoying his music ever since.

D **INFER INFORMATION** Infer the information from the Reading. Explain your answers.

1 the year Beethoven moved away from Bonn

2 Beethoven's age when he gave his last public performance

3 the reason he cried

4 the year Beethoven died

E **IDENTIFY SUPPORTING DETAILS** On a separate sheet of paper, write examples from the Reading of Beethoven's behavior that illustrate each personality trait. Use your own words. Explain your answers.

1 that he was gifted
2 that he was energetic
3 that he was imaginative

4 that he was passionate
5 that he was eccentric
6 that he was difficult

7 that he was moody
8 that he was egotistical

F **EXPRESS AND SUPPORT AN OPINION** Discuss the questions. Activate the Vocabulary to support your opinion.

1 Why do you think every woman that Beethoven asked to marry him rejected him? Do you think they made the right decision?

2 Why do you think Beethoven was able to write some of his most popular pieces of music when he could no longer hear?

NOW YOU CAN Describe a creative personality

A **FRAME YOUR IDEAS** Do you think you have a creative personality? Rate yourself for the qualities below on a scale from 0 to 3. Compare answers with a partner.

> **"** I'm not particularly creative, but I'm very **passionate**. I think it's really important to love what you do. What about you? **"**

0 = not at all
1 = a little
2 = somewhat
3 = extremely

...... gifted
...... eccentric
...... passionate
...... imaginative

...... difficult
...... energetic
...... moody
...... egotistical

B **DISCUSSION** Provide details to complete the descriptions of these creative personalities, or write complete descriptions of others you find interesting. Be sure to use the Vocabulary and provide examples. Say as much as you can.

Michael Jackson was a gifted singer, songwriter, and dancer from the U.S. But a lot of people found him eccentric. For example, ...

Frida Kahlo was a famous Mexican painter. They say that, at times, she could be quite moody. For example, ...

Christian Bale is a Hollywood actor who is originally from the U.K. He is very talented and is known to be very passionate about acting. But it is said that he can be egotistical and difficult to work with. For example, ...

OPTIONAL WRITING Write a biography of a creative person. Present it to the class.

RECYCLE THIS LANGUAGE

- a pain in the neck
- a people person
- a sweetheart
- a team player
- a tyrant
- a workaholic

21

GOAL Discuss the benefits of the arts

A **LISTENING WARM-UP** **DISCUSSION** In what ways do you think the arts could be used to help children who are under emotional stress or the elderly with memory problems?

DIGITAL STRATEGIES **B** ▶ 1:23 **LISTEN FOR MAIN IDEAS** Listen to the radio program for descriptions of how the arts are used as therapy. Write the type of therapy that is described by each therapist.

Mark Branch 1 ....   Bruce Nelson 2 ....   Carla Burgess 3 ....

C ▶ 1:24 **LISTEN FOR SUPPORTING INFORMATION** Listen to the radio program again and complete each statement. Then explain what the therapist does to achieve each goal.

1 Mark Branch uses the arts to help patients with intellectual disabilities improve ....
  a their schoolwork   **b** their ability to socialize

2 Bruce Nelson uses the arts to help troubled teens ....
  a talk about their problems more easily   **b** socialize with others more easily

3 Carla Burgess uses the arts to help the elderly ....
  a tell others about their problems   **b** socialize with others

D ▶ 1:25 **LISTEN TO TAKE NOTES** Listen to the radio program again. Work with a partner to define these words and phrases.

1 an intellectual disability: ....

2 a troubled teen: ....

3 a senior: ....

E **APPLY IDEAS** Read each situation. Which therapies mentioned in the radio program would *you* recommend for each situation and why? Compare and discuss your answers with a partner.

1 A number of humanitarian organizations have been working with children who were forced to become soldiers and fight in local wars. In many cases these children have participated in violent acts. Their experiences make it hard to sleep or interact normally with others.

2 Greenwood Hospital specializes in helping patients who have been in car accidents and sports- or work-related accidents. Patients struggle with physical pain, limited movement in arms and legs, and depression. They need emotional support.

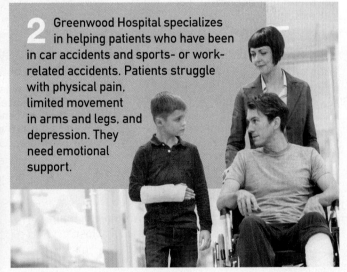

3 The Walker Institute provides support for adults who have suddenly found themselves without a job or a place to live. As a result, these people feel separated from others socially. Understandably, they feel bad about their current circumstances and worry a lot about the future.

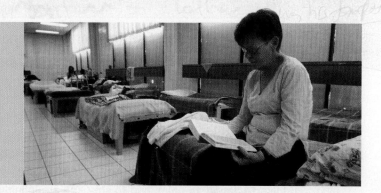

F WORD STUDY   USING PARTICIPIAL ADJECTIVES

The present and past participial forms of many verbs can function as adjectives.

The past participle has a passive meaning. It can usually be restated with a <u>by</u> phrase.

> The patient is **depressed** [by his life].
> I'm **bored** [by this movie].

The present participle does not have a passive meaning. It can usually be restated with an active verb.

> That book is **depressing**. [It depresses everyone.]
> It's so **boring**. [It bores me.]

▶ 1:26 **Participial adjectives**

Verb	Present participle	Past participle
(amaze)	amazing	amazed
(annoy)	annoying	annoyed
(bore)	boring	bored
(depress)	depressing	depressed
(disappoint)	disappointing	disappointed
(entertain)	entertaining	entertained
(excite)	exciting	excited
(interest)	interesting	interested
(please)	pleasing	pleased
(relax)	relaxing	relaxed
(soothe)	soothing	soothed
(stimulate)	stimulating	stimulated
(surprise)	surprising	surprised
(touch)	touching	touched
(trouble)	troubling	troubled

G WORD STUDY PRACTICE   Circle an adjective to complete each sentence.

1 Music can make language students feel (relaxed / relaxing).

2 Drawing pictures about their problems can make patients feel less (depressed / depressing).

3 Some patients find movement therapy to be very (soothed / soothing).

4 For patients in physical pain, the benefits of music therapy can be (surprised / surprising).

5 Researchers are (amazed / amazing) that the results have been so positive.

6 Many doctors report they are (pleased / pleasing) with the progress their patients make.

7 Many teen patients feel that drama therapy is (entertained / entertaining).

H WORD STUDY PRACTICE   With a partner, take turns choosing a present participial adjective from Exercise F and using it in a sentence. Your partner then creates a sentence using the past participial form.

> 66 I think music therapy might be **disappointing**. 99

> 66 I think I might be **disappointed** by music therapy. 99

NOW YOU CAN   Discuss the benefits of the arts

A NOTEPADDING   What are some benefits that music, art, dance, and theater bring to people's everyday lives? With a partner, make a list and discuss. Use participial adjectives.

Benefits	Examples
Music can be soothing.	Playing music at work relaxes people so they're more productive.

Benefits	Examples

B GROUP WORK   Present your ideas to your class or group. Comment on your classmates' ideas and ask questions.

A WRITING SKILL Study the rules.

When listing two or more words in a series, be sure to use parallel structure. All the words, phrases, or clauses should be in the same form. Study the examples.

> I like **dancing, painting**, and **singing**. (All are gerunds.)
> I like **to dance, to paint**, and **to sing**. (All are infinitives.)
> The picture **was painted, framed**, and **sold**. (All are passives.)
> She's a **friendly, helpful**, and **intelligent** human being. (All are adjectives.)

If you are listing two or more infinitives, either use <u>to</u> with all of them or use it only with the first one.

> She wants **to eat, to drink**, and **to go** to sleep. OR She wants **to eat, drink**, and **go** to sleep.

With a pair or series of nouns, either use the article with all of them, or use it only with the first one.

> I'm **a student, a musician**, and **a mother**. OR I'm **a student, musician**, and **mother**.

If another word refers to all of the words in the series, you can use it with all of them or only with the first.

> I don't think I'm **very interesting** or **very smart**. OR I don't think I'm **very interesting** or **smart**.
> I prefer people **who make me laugh** and **who like outdoor activities**.
>   OR I prefer people **who make me laugh** and **like outdoor activities**.

B ERROR CORRECTION Find and correct the errors.

My personality

Some people think I am moody, a pessimistic person, and cautious, because I sometimes worry about the future. However, this is very surprising to me. What I think is that I have always been a passionate, a positive, and optimistic person. The fact that I love traveling, to meet new people, and learning about new places proves that I don't have a pessimistic outlook. Most of my friends find me to be energetic and imaginative.

C PRACTICE On a separate sheet of paper, complete each statement with the words in parentheses, using parallel structure. Then write at least two similar sentences about your own personality and interests.

1 I like (read, listen to music, go to movies).

2 I've been (teacher, stay-at-home mom, office manager).

3 I enjoy (hike, ski, swim in the ocean).

4 (see new places, have new experiences, make new friends) are all reasons I like to travel.

5 Last year I (join the volleyball team, play in ten games, win an award).

6 What energizes and relaxes me is (paint portraits, cook great meals, play my guitar).

DIGITAL WRITING PROCESS

D APPLY THE WRITING SKILL Write a paragraph describing your interests and personality. Try to include at least one sentence using the present perfect continuous and one using a cleft sentence with <u>What</u>. Use the Vocabulary from Units 1 and 2.

SELF-CHECK

☐ Does my paragraph have a topic sentence and supporting sentences?

☐ Do I have a concluding sentence?

☐ Did I use parallel structure?

A ▶ 1:27 **Listen to the conversations about musical preferences. Check the person who doesn't like the music. Then listen again and write what the person doesn't like about it.**

	The man	The woman	What he or she doesn't like
1 One Direction	☐	☐	....
2 Vanessa-Mae	☐	☐	....
3 Josh Groban	☐	☐	....
4 Lady Gaga	☐	☐	....
5 Antonio Carlos Jobim	☐	☐	....

B **Complete the statements with an appropriate adjective from the box.**

eccentric	egotistical	energetic	gifted	moody	passionate

1 Sarah is a very .... musician. She started playing the piano when she was three.

2 My neighbor has thirty cats. You could say he's a bit ....

3 Franco is an extremely .... person. He only thinks of himself.

4 Dalia has been so .... lately. She gets angry at the smallest thing.

5 My brother is really .... He's always doing something productive.

6 My boss is so .... about the products we sell. She really believes in them.

C **Check the sentences in which the present perfect continuous or present perfect are used correctly. Correct and rewrite the incorrect sentences on a separate sheet of paper.**

☐ **1** I've already been writing two reports for my boss this month.

☐ **2** Kate hasn't seen the movie *Interstellar* yet, but all her friends have been telling her how great it is.

☐ **3** They've never been hearing about art therapy before.

☐ **4** Most likely, Lance studied late. His bedroom light is still on.

☐ **5** We haven't been making reservations for our flight yet.

☐ **6** I'll bet you've done the laundry. I can hear the washing machine.

D **Rewrite each statement as a cleft sentence with <u>What</u>.**

1 Life without the arts wouldn't be much fun.

....

2 I don't like a band whose music is really commercial.

....

3 The beat made everyone feel like dancing.

....

4 I like to listen to music that has fun lyrics and a great melody.

....

5 They should go see anything that's playing on Broadway.

....

TEST-TAKING SKILLS BOOSTER p. 152

Web Project: Benefits of the Arts
www.english.com/summit3e

Money, Finance, and You

A **FRAME YOUR IDEAS** Take the test to learn about your personal spending style. Circle the letter that best describes you.

SPENDING HABITS SELF-TEST

1 **You hear about the latest (expensive!) smart phone with the coolest new features. You …**

A run to the store and stand in line to be one of the first people to have it.
B compare prices online so you can get the best deal right away.
C tell yourself that the price always comes down after a while and decide to wait.
D other _____

2 **You are invited to a birthday party and know a gift is expected, but you're short on cash right now. You …**

A spend more on the gift than you can afford anyway.
B try to find a nice gift that's not too expensive.
C say you are busy and don't go, so you don't have to buy a gift.
D other _____

3 **You discover a hole in your pants. You …**

A go out and buy new pants.
B have the pants repaired.
C fix the pants yourself.
D other _____

4 **You would love to have a fancy high-tech entertainment system in your living room, but you just don't have the money right now. You …**

A buy it with your credit card and hope you find the money to pay for it later.
B cut back on other expenses until you've saved enough to buy it.
C decide you have more important spending priorities than buying an entertainment system.
D other _____

5 **You always split the restaurant bill equally with two work colleagues when you eat lunch. This time you weren't hungry and ate very little. You …**

A pay your usual 1/3 of the bill.
B offer to pay for just the small amount you ate.
C ask the others to treat you, since your amount was so small.
D other _____

If you circled three or more A's:	**If you circled three or more B's:**	**If you circled three or more C's:**	**If you wrote your own answers (D) for three or more questions:**
You are definitely a big spender. Your motto is: **Easy come, easy go.**	You've got a good head on your shoulders about money. Your motto is: **Everything in moderation.**	You are thrifty and don't waste money. Your motto is: **Waste not, want not.**	How would you describe your spending style?

B ▶ 2:01 **VOCABULARY** DESCRIBING SPENDING STYLES
Listen and repeat.

a big spender	a person who regularly spends a lot of money
thrifty	careful not to spend too much money
a cheapskate	a person who hates to spend money

C **DISCUSSION** Do you know anyone you would call a big spender, thrifty, or a cheapskate? Give one or more examples of that person's behavior to support your opinion.

D ▶ 2:02 **SPOTLIGHT** Read and listen to a conversation between a father and son about spending. Notice the spotlighted language.

Brad: Dad! Check out the smart bikes! Are they cool, or what? And there's a place for your smart phone on the handlebars so you can get texts. You don't have to look for your phone while you're riding!

Dad: You've got to be kidding. "*Smart* bike"? Sounds more like a dumb bike. Don't tell me you text while you're riding your bike!

Brad: Oops. I shouldn't have said that. What I meant is that I could just stop and take a look.

Dad: Look. Even if this were a great bike, which it isn't, it's **way over our budget**. Look at the price—it's **astronomical**! And what's so special about it except for the ridiculous handlebars?—which should be illegal in my opinion …

Brad: Well, I could **chip in** part of the cost. I've **saved up a little for a rainy day**, like you've always told me to.

Dad: Hey, I'm really proud of you for not spending all your money. But this isn't a rainy day. The bike is a totally unnecessary **impulse item**. They want you to buy it without thinking. And the handlebars are just a **gimmick** to get you to want it.

Brad: But for once, I'd like to be the *first* person to have something cool, you know?

Dad: Well, if you **have your heart set on** this smart bike, then you'll have to save up and pay for it yourself. But I'll need your **word of honor** you won't text while you're riding.

Brad: OK. But Dad, by the time I have enough money to buy a smart bike myself, all my friends will have already gotten theirs!

Dad: That may be true, but Mom and I won't **shell out** that much money for this bike, even if you do chip in. It's a **matter of principle**. You know, money doesn't grow on trees.

E **UNDERSTAND IDIOMS AND EXPRESSIONS** Match the expressions from Spotlight with their meaning.

.... **1** way over our budget

.... **2** astronomical

.... **3** chip in

.... **4** saved up a little for a rainy day

.... **5** impulse item

.... **6** gimmick

.... **7** have your heart set on

.... **8** word of honor

.... **9** shell out

.... **10** matter of principle

a promise

b very, very high

c more than we can spend

d pay

e contribute some of the cost

f kept some money in case of an emergency

g something you buy without thinking much about it

h something that's right

i a valueless feature

j really want

F **THINK AND EXPLAIN** Support your answers to the questions with information from Spotlight.

1 In your opinion, will Brad buy the smart bike for himself?

2 Do you think Brad sees his dad as a big spender, thrifty, or a cheapskate? How does his dad see him?.

SPEAKING **GROUP WORK** Discuss some worthless gimmicks and worthwhile features you've seen promoted for the following products.

1 an electronic product ....

2 a personal-care product ....

3 a shoe for a specific sport ....

4 another product ....

GOAL Express buyer's remorse

A ▶ 2:03 **VOCABULARY** EXPRESSING BUYER'S REMORSE

Read and listen. Then listen again and repeat.

It costs so much to maintain.

It takes up so much room.

It's so hard to operate.

It's so hard to put together.

It just sits around collecting dust.

B ▶ 2:04 **LISTEN FOR DETAILS** Listen to conversations about items people bought. Write the product they're discussing.

1 ....
2 ....
3 ....
4 ....
5 ....

C ▶ 2:05 **ACTIVATE VOCABULARY** Listen again. Pay attention to the people's regrets. From what they say, infer the reason for the regrets, using expressions from the Vocabulary. Use each Vocabulary expression only one time.

1 ....*It takes up too much room.*...............
2 ....
3 ....
4 ....
5 ....

D **GRAMMAR** EXPRESSING REGRETS ABOUT THE PAST

Wish + the past perfect

I **wish** I **had bought** a smart bike. And I **wish** I **hadn't bought** this car!
Do they **wish** they **had joined** a gym instead of buying that treadmill?
Don't you **wish** the store **had had** the uPhone a month ago?
Why does Ann **wish** she **had gotten** the more expensive model?

> **GRAMMAR BOOSTER** p. 129
> The past unreal conditional: inverted form

Should have or ought to have + past participle

I **should have waited** to buy a food processor = I **ought to have waited** to buy a food processor.

Note: American English speakers use <u>should have</u>, not <u>ought to have</u>, in negative statements and in questions.

He shouldn't have bought the shoes in size 40. NOT He ~~ought not to have bought~~ the shoes in size 40.
Should you have sold your house? NOT ~~Ought you to have sold~~ your house?

If only + the past perfect

Express very strong regret with <u>If only</u> + the past perfect. You can also use <u>if only</u> in a past unreal conditional statement and include a result clause.

If only I had bought an underwater camera! (regret: I wish I had.)
If only we hadn't bought that car! (regret: We wish we hadn't.)
If only I had bought an underwater camera, I **would have taken** pictures of the coral reef.

E **NOTICE THE GRAMMAR** Find one regret about the past in Spotlight on page 27.

F **UNDERSTAND THE GRAMMAR** On a separate sheet of paper, rewrite the statements and questions, changing <u>wish</u> or <u>if only</u> + the past perfect to <u>should have</u> or <u>ought to have</u>.

1 She wishes she had bought a new car. (ought to)

> *She ought to have bought a new car.*

2 Do you wish you had read the owner's manual before you tried to use the espresso maker? (should)

3 We wish we had gone to a discount store instead of this fancy department store. (ought to)

4 If only I hadn't been in such a hurry to sell my house! (should)

5 Doesn't he wish he had taken the tutorial for his new computer? (should)

6 I wish I hadn't bought these gimmicky basketball shoes! (should)

G **PAIR WORK** Read each quotation. Then take turns asking each question. Your partner answers with a statement using <u>wish</u> + the past perfect.

1 Steven said, "I should have exchanged those shoes." **What does Steven wish?**

> ❝ He wishes he had exchanged those shoes. ❞

2 Kate said, "I shouldn't have tried to repair this air-conditioner myself." **What does Kate wish?**

3 Michelle's husband said, "You should have bought a convertible." **What does Michelle's husband wish?**

4 Clark said, "My dad should have returned the defective tires as soon as he read about the problem in the news." **What does Clark wish?**

5 The teacher told Suzanne, "The kids ought to have taken the school bus this morning." **What does Suzanne's children's teacher wish?**

NOW YOU CAN Express buyer's remorse

A ▶ 2:06 **CONVERSATION SPOTLIGHT** Read and listen. Notice the spotlighted conversation strategies.

A: You know, I wish I hadn't gotten that exercise machine.

B: What do you mean?

A: Well, **I hate to say it, but** it's pretty hard to operate.

B: **That's a shame.** Can you return it?

A: It's too late. If only I'd thought about that sooner.

B: Well, maybe you can sell it.

A: **I'll think about that.** Thanks.

- Return it.
- Sell it.
- Give it away.
- Give it to someone.
- Donate it.

B ▶ 2:07 **RHYTHM AND INTONATION** Listen again and repeat. Then practice the conversation with a partner.

C **NOTEPADDING** Answer the questions on the notepad about something you regret buying.

D **CONVERSATION ACTIVATOR** Create a conversation expressing regret. Use the Vocabulary and the Grammar. Start like this: *You know, I wish...* Be sure to change roles and partners.

What did you buy?
Do you still have it?
If not, what did you do with it?
Would you ever buy a similar item again?

DON'T STOP!
- Make other suggestions about what to do with the item.
- Accept or decline the suggestion.
- If you decline, explain why.
- Say as much as you can.

GOAL Talk about financial goals and plans

A ▶2:08 **GRAMMAR SPOTLIGHT** Read the interview responses. Notice the spotlighted grammar.

Q: Tell us about your short-term and long-term financial goals and plans.

I've decided to set a long-term goal for myself—to save enough money to buy a new car. By this time next year, **I'll have put away** enough cash for a down payment. I'm optimistic that I'll be able to afford the monthly payments after that. My short-term goal is to make a budget for my monthly expenses and stick to it.

Hana Sung, 28
Incheon, South Korea

I find it helpful to try to picture where I want to be in the next few years. By next year, if I play my cards right, I figure **I'll have gotten** a good job as a financial consultant. That's a short-term plan, I guess. My long-term goals? They're still a little up in the air, but my goal is to be financially independent, able to retire if I want to, before I'm fifty.

Paul Drake, 24
Sydney, Australia

I'm not a big spender, but my college expenses have been astronomical, and now I'm in debt. My salary from my part-time job helps a bit, but I still had to borrow money from my family, and paying back those loans will take some time. Here's my plan: By this time next year, **I'll have graduated.** My immediate goal is to find a job and make enough money to be able to put away 10% every month, which I'll use to begin paying off the loans. After I've advanced in my career, say after four or five years, **I expect to have started** earning enough so that 10% of my salary will amount to more money. **I really hope to have paid back** all my loans by the time I turn thirty.

Sara Williams, 21
Detroit, USA

B **MAKE PERSONAL COMPARISONS** Discuss the questions.

1 How are you similar to or different from any of the people in the Grammar Spotlight?

2 Do you cut back on your spending to buy something you want? Are you financially independent? Give specific examples from your own life.

DIGITAL INDUCTIVE ACTIVITY

C **GRAMMAR** **COMPLETED FUTURE ACTIONS AND PLANS: THE FUTURE PERFECT AND PERFECT INFINITIVES**

Use the future perfect to indicate an action that will be completed by a specified time in the future. It's common to state the particular time somewhere in the sentence. Form the future perfect with <u>will have</u> or <u>won't have</u> + a past participle. You can contract <u>will</u>.

By the time Cleo gets her visa, she **will have waited** for two years.
I'll have finished paying for my car before the end of the year.
They **won't have eaten** lunch before 2:00.
Will she **have finished** work by 9:00? (Yes, she will. / No, she won't.)

Use a perfect infinitive after <u>hope</u>, <u>expect</u>, <u>intend</u>, or <u>plan</u> to indicate that an action will or might take place before a specified time in the future. Form the perfect infinitive with <u>to have</u> + past participle.

By this time next year, I **plan to have saved** enough cash to buy a car.
They **intend to have completed** their studies by June 10th.
Do you **expect to have paid back** your loans in the next year? (Yes, I do. / No, I don't.)

Note: These are some expressions that commonly accompany statements in the future perfect:
before / after [May 15]
on / by [Tuesday]
by the time [she arrives]
in the next [month]

GRAMMAR BOOSTER p. 130
· The future continuous
· The future perfect continuous

D **NOTICE THE GRAMMAR**   Find a statement in Spotlight on page 27 with the future perfect.

E **GRAMMAR PRACTICE**   On a separate sheet of paper, use the cues to write sentences with the future perfect.

1 By the end of this month / I / put half my paycheck in the bank.

2 By next summer / Stan / save enough to make a down payment on an apartment.

3 Do you think you / lower / your credit card debt by December?

4 When / they / start / spending less than they earn?

F **GRAMMAR PRACTICE**   Complete the paragraph, using perfect infinitives.

Ed Compton has been drowning in debt, so he has some emergency short-term goals.

By the end of the month, he .... a realistic budget that he can stick to.

1 intend / create

As a matter of fact, he .... the last payment on his car loan by October 30th.

2 hope / made

In addition, he .... saving 10% of his paycheck even before that. If he can stick to his

3 plan / begin

budget and savings plan, Mr. Compton .... all the money he owes within the year.

4 expect / pay back

G **ERROR CORRECTION**   These sentences all have errors. On a separate sheet of paper, rewrite them correctly.

1 I expect to will earn enough money to buy a car by the end of the year.

2 Before they come back home, they will to have spent all the money they took with them.

3 We hope having completed our driver training by the end of the week.

4 By the time I'm thirty I will to be married for five years.

> **PRONUNCIATION BOOSTER**   p. 143
> Sentence rhythm: thought groups

NOW YOU CAN   Talk about financial goals and plans

A **NOTEPADDING**   Write your short-term and long-term financial goals.

short-term goals	completion dates	long-term goals	completion dates
buy a racing bike	by this time next year	buy a house	by the time I'm thirty

short-term goals	completion dates	long-term goals	completion dates

B **DISCUSSION ACTIVATOR**   Discuss your financial goals with a partner, using information from your notepad. Make statements in the future perfect and statements with hope, expect, plan, and intend with perfect infinitives. Say as much as you can. Be sure to change roles and then partners.

> 66 A year from now I'll have paid back my loans. 99

> 66 By the time I graduate, I hope to have saved enough to buy a new car. 99

Ideas
- be financially independent
- be out of debt
- cut back on spending
- create a realistic budget
- stick to a budget
- start saving money

GOAL Discuss good and bad money management

DIGITAL STRATEGIES
A ▶ 2:09 **LISTENING WARM-UP** **VOCABULARY** **GOOD AND BAD MONEY MANAGEMENT**

Read and listen. Then listen again and repeat.

Good money management

| I live within my means. | I keep track of my expenses. | I save regularly. | I always pay my credit card bills in full. |

Bad money management

| I live beyond my means. | I don't know where the money goes. | I live paycheck to paycheck. | I'm drowning in debt. |

B **VOCABULARY PRACTICE** Complete each statement about money management, using the Vocabulary. Use each expression only once.

1 Some people say Mr. and Mrs. Strong are thrifty. They don't spend too much, and they always have money in the bank for a rainy day.

Mr. and Mrs. Strong …*save regularly.*…………………………………………………………………

2 Andrew earns a small salary, but he's a big spender, so he's always out of cash.

Andrew ……

3 The Wilsons spend everything they earn and have almost no savings in the bank.

The Wilsons ……………………………………………………………………………………………………

4 When Katherine's credit card statement comes each month, she writes a check for the full balance.

Katherine ………………………………………………………………………………………………………

5 Sam acts as if he thinks money grows on trees. He can't remember where he spent this week's allowance.

Sam ……

6 Every month, Melanie pays a lot of interest and a late fee on her credit card bill. She can't sleep at night because of all that debt.

Melanie ……

7 Martha and Bill have everything they need and never spend more than they earn.

Martha and Bill ………………………………………………………………………………………………

8 Sally always knows where her money goes. Every day she writes down everything she has bought.

Sally ……

C ▶ 2:10 **LISTEN TO CONFIRM CONTENT** Listen to three calls to a radio financial adviser. Check one or more suggestions the host gives each caller.

I live within my means

Caller 1
- ☐ **1** Save all your loose change.
- ☐ **2** Take money out of the ATM.
- ☐ **3** Put money in the bank.
- ☐ **4** Stick to a budget.

Caller 2
- ☐ **1** Avoid impulse items.
- ☐ **2** Talk to your parents.
- ☐ **3** Save some money.
- ☐ **4** Don't complain.

Caller 3
- ☐ **1** Use only one or two cards.
- ☐ **2** Pay each month's bill in full.
- ☐ **3** Stop using credit cards.
- ☐ **4** Stick to a budget.

D ▶ 2:11 **LISTEN TO SUMMARIZE** Listen again. On a separate sheet of paper, write a summary in two sentences of the reason each caller called the radio program.

E ▶ 2:12 **LISTEN TO EVALUATE** Choose one of the callers. Explain to a partner why you think Mack's advice is good or not. If so, add another suggestion. If not, offer your own advice.

NOW YOU CAN Discuss good and bad money management

A **FRAME YOUR IDEAS** Analyze your own money management style. Choose the statements on the survey that best apply to you.

paycheck to paycheck

- ○ I live within my means.
- ○ I live beyond my means.
- ○ I keep track of my expenses.
- ○ I don't know where the money goes.
- ○ I save regularly. *Diane*
- ○ I live from paycheck to paycheck and spend it all. *Diane*
- ○ I always pay my credit card bills in full.
- ○ I'm drowning in debt.

B **PAIR WORK** Compare your answers on the survey. Do you have the same money management style? Explain the reasons for your choices and give real-life examples. Use the Vocabulary.

RECYCLE THIS LANGUAGE
- a big spender
- a cheapskate
- an impulse item
- stick to a budget
- save for a rainy day
- chip in
- way over my budget

GOAL Explain reasons for charitable giving

A READING WARM-UP What are some reasons people donate money to or volunteer for charities?

B ▶ 2:13 READING Read about some charities. How would you describe what a charity is?

HOME NEWS CHARITIES CONTACT US

CHARITIES OF THE WEEK

The following non-governmental, non-profit organizations have been among the most popular charities supported by both philanthropists and other generous people over the past year. Both of them have excellent reputations and both have been shown to use a high percentage of their funds for their work rather than for administrative expenses. They both seek contributions, and you can donate to each one through its website. If you are interested in volunteering your time, information about that can be found on the websites as well.

DOCTORS WITHOUT BORDERS

This well-known charitable organization dates from 1971, when 300 doctors, nurses,  and other staff, including journalists, officially formed it. Originally named (in French) Médecins Sans Frontières (MSF), it became known internationally in English as Doctors Without Borders. MSF's founding belief is that medical care should be available to everyone, regardless of location. Every year MSF provides emergency care to millions of people caught in crises in some 70 countries around the world. It offers assistance when catastrophic events such as armed conflicts, epidemics, malnutrition, or natural disasters overwhelm health resources. MSF also assists people who are neglected by their local health systems or who are otherwise excluded from medical care.

MSF medical personnel wear protective gear to avoid getting Ebola

CORAL REEF ALLIANCE

Pollution, overfishing, and rapid development are threatening coral reefs around the world. The guiding belief of the Coral Reef Alliance is that since these problems are caused by humans, they can be solved by humans. Corals are resilient to change, but if subjected to current levels of stress, they are in danger of extinction within a few decades. Coral Reef Alliance volunteers work in partnership with the people and groups who depend on reefs for their survival. They employ a three-pronged approach: reducing threats such as overfishing and poor water quality; helping communities benefit socially, culturally, and economically from conservation; and working directly with the tourism industry to decrease its environmental footprint. If the Coral Reef Alliance is successful, we will be able to enjoy beautiful coral reefs for a long time to come.

CORAL REEF ALLIANCE

A healthy coral reef teeming with fish

C WORD STUDY PARTS OF SPEECH Write the noun, adjective, or verb form of each of these words used in the Reading. Use a dictionary if necessary.

noun: charity   adjective: ....   verb: assist   noun: ....
noun: contribution   verb: ....   noun: pollution   verb: ....
verb: volunteer   noun: ....   noun: threat   verb: ....
verb: donate   noun: ....   noun: extinction   adjective: ....

D UNDERSTAND MEANING FROM CONTEXT Complete the statements about information in the Reading with a word from Exercise C.

1 Poor water quality is a .... to healthy coral reefs.

2 .... from the Coral Reef Alliance help communities conserve the health of their coral reefs.

3 If we don't improve the environment, coral reefs may face .... within a few years.

4 MSF provides emergency medical .... when there aren't enough local resources.

5 Tourism has contributed to the .... of the water around coral reefs.

6 The .... of philanthropists and others are welcomed by MSF and the Coral Reef Alliance.

E DRAW CONCLUSIONS Complete each statement with the most likely conclusion, based on the Reading.

1 The purpose of the Charities of the Week column is ....
   a to tell readers which charities they should volunteer for
   b to educate the public each week about some good charities

2 The medical personnel of MSF usually ....
   a travel to places where they are needed
   b assist the people mostly in the countries where the medical personnel live

3 The people helped by the Coral Reef alliance are probably ....
   a people who fish for a living near coral reefs
   b tourists who visit areas with coral reefs

F EXPRESS AND SUPPORT AN OPINION Which of the two charities does more important work? Explain your opinion.

NOW YOU CAN | Explain reasons for charitable giving

A FRAME YOUR IDEAS Write a checkmark next to people or organizations you would contribute to. Write an X next to the ones you wouldn't. Then tell your partner your reasons.

a homeless person	a school in a poor neighborhood
an organization that helps the homeless	a museum
a disaster relief agency	a religious institution
an animal protection agency	other

❝ I'd contribute to an animal protection agency. I think it's our responsibility to protect animals. ❞

B PAIR WORK First rate the reasons you think people donate money to charities from 1 to 8, with 1 being the best reason. Compare and discuss your ratings with a partner.

..... to change society
..... so people will admire them
..... to be a good example
..... so people will thank them
..... for religious reasons
..... to feel good
..... to help others
..... other

C DISCUSSION Put together the information from Exercises A and B. Discuss your general and specific reasons for contributing to the charities you checked, saying as much as you can. Use words from Word Study when possible.

❝ My motivation for contributing to charity is mostly to help other people. That's the reason I give money to homeless people and organizations that help the homeless. ❞

OPTIONAL WRITING Choose a charity. Write a paragraph explaining why people should donate or volunteer for this cause. Present your ideas to your class or group.

A **WRITING SKILL** Study the rules.

When writing a paragraph, organize your ideas and sentences logically. Use words and phrases to indicate to the reader the relative importance of the ideas. Write the ideas in order of importance, starting with the most important. Notice the commas.

First, in order of importance,
Most importantly,
To begin with,

Secondly, / Thirdly, etc.
Following that,
After that,

Finally,
Last but not least,
Least importantly,
As a final point,

WRITING MODEL

I am proud to say that I am financially independent. My friends occasionally ask me how I did it and ask me to give them advice. I like to say, "You have to be financially intelligent." How? **First and most importantly**, spend less than you earn. One way to do that is to create a budget and stick to it. **Secondly**, don't charge things on credit cards that you can't pay for at the end of the month. **Last but not least,** put a little money into savings whenever you can.

B **PRACTICE** Complete the paragraph with words and phrases indicating order of importance.

I try to be generous to those in need and always contribute a portion of my income to charities that I think are worthwhile. Since I don't have a lot of money, I have to consider where my money can do the most good. There are several issues I need to think about before sending money. .... , I want to know if the charity is financially sound; that is, does most of the money it receives actually go to the people in need? Or does it spend too much money on salaries for employees of the organization? I get this information from Charity Navigator on the Internet. .... , although nearly as important to me, is does the charity address a crisis of some sort, such as an epidemic? There are so many worthy charities, but to me, the ones that provide immediate help that can prevent death are the most important. .... , I always ask if the charity provides help to all people, regardless of who they are. I don't care if the people I help are in my country or some other country, and I don't care about their religion, race, or nationality.

C **APPLY THE WRITING SKILL** Write a one-paragraph personal statement for a job or university application. Describe three ways you manage your financial responsibilities. Use vocabulary from this unit and organize your ideas in order of importance. Provide examples to support your claims.

DIGITAL
WRITING
PROCESS

SELF-CHECK

☐ Did I present my ideas in order of importance?

☐ Did I use the words and phrases to indicate their relative importance?

☐ Did I use correct punctuation?

A ▶ 2:14 Listen to the conversations. Then write the letter of the statement that best summarizes each conversation. Listen again if necessary.

a He should be more thrifty.

b He's not really a big spender. He's just feeling generous today.

c If he'd known it would be so hard to put together, he never would have bought it.

Conversation 1 ...... **Conversation 2** ...... **Conversation 3** ......

B Complete the statements about bad money management, using four different phrases from the Vocabulary in Lesson 3.

1 Marian Bates receives her salary on the last Friday of every month. By the end of the next month, she has no money left. She ....

2 Paul and Clare Oliver never pay their credit cards in full, and every month the balance on their card is bigger. They're ....

3 Cheryl spends more than she earns. She ....

4 Eleanor's mother gives her money every week for transportation to and from school, but by Thursday the money's gone. Eleanor ....

C Complete each statement with true information, using the future perfect or a perfect infinitive.

1 By this weekend, ...

2 At the end of this school year, I intend ....

3 By the time I retire ....

4 By the year 2020, I hope ....

5 Before I leave this English program, I expect ....

D On a separate sheet of paper, answer each question using <u>wish</u> and the past perfect or <u>should have</u> and a past participle to express a true regret from the past.

1 What do you wish you had done differently in your life? ....
....

2 What decision should you have made that you didn't? ....
....

E Explain in your own words the meaning of the following words and phrases.

1 financially independent: ....

2 a budget: ....

3 a short-term goal ....

4 a long-term goal ....

5 astronomical ....

6 a loan ....

TEST-TAKING SKILLS BOOSTER p. 153

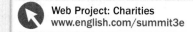
Web Project: Charities
www.english.com/summit3e

Clothing and Appearance

COMMUNICATION GOALS

1 Describe clothing details and formality
2 Talk about changes in clothing customs
3 Examine questionable cosmetic procedures
4 Discuss appearance and self-esteem

A **FRAME YOUR IDEAS** Match each quotation with the person or people you think most likely said it.

WHAT'S YOUR PERSONAL STYLE?

Write the number of a quote for each person.

1 I don't go for a trendy look. I prefer to wear things that will still be in style next year. And I like clothes that are elegant and well made.

2 I prefer being comfortable in my clothes. What I wear may not be the most fashionable or stylish, but I like it that way.

3 Clothing should express your individuality. I don't want to dress the same as everyone else. I prefer to stand out in a crowd, even if it's not the most attractive look.

4 I like to be fashionable, so I usually like the clothes of the best fashion designers. But I don't like loud colors. I just don't like to attract attention to myself. I'm a lot more comfortable in subdued colors and classic designs that will never go out of style.

5 I think I look best in clothes that are funky— a little weird to other people perhaps, but very stylish and in good taste to me.

6 The way you dress affects how people perceive you, so it's important to dress well. Also, I like my clothes to have a designer's logo so people know they're not cheap.

B ▶ 2:15 **VOCABULARY** **ADJECTIVES TO DESCRIBE FASHION** Listen and repeat.

fashionable / stylish	representing a style being worn by many people who dress well
funky	modern and attractive, but in an unconventional way
trendy	a temporarily popular style that probably won't last
classic	an unchanging style that is always fashionable
elegant	beautiful and of high quality
subdued	(of colors) not too bright or too colorful
loud	(of colors) very bright and too attention-getting

Don't forget
wild
conservative
modest
appropriate
inappropriate
casual
formal
informal

C **DISCUSSION** Describe the outfit of each person in the photos above, using one or more of the adjectives from the Vocabulary. Explain, using examples.

<D> ▶ 2:16 **SPOTLIGHT**   Read a conversation between two travelers in an airport duty-free shop. Notice the spotlighted language.

ENGLISH FOR TODAY'S WORLD
Understand a variety of accents.
Karen = American English (standard)
Roya = Arabic

Karen: Roya, could I get your opinion on something?

Roya: Sure. What's up?

Karen: What do you think of these pants? For a teenager, I mean. Not for me.

Roya: The ones with the sequins on the bottom? A bit flashy, don't you think? I think they'd **attract too much attention**, know what I'm saying?

Karen: Funny. To me they're kind of cute, maybe a little funky—but not **over the top**. At least not where I come from.

Roya: Well, it may just be a cultural thing, but in my country, no girl from a nice family **would be caught dead** wearing something as immodest as that. In fact, her parents would never even let her buy them.

Karen: Interesting . . . But you must be right. This has got to be cultural. In the U.S., no one would even **give them a second thought**. If they had a bunch of holes in them, I'd agree that they were in bad taste.

Roya: But they draw attention to a part of the body you don't want people staring at, right?

Karen: Well, come to think of it, **you have a point**. But personally, I think the jeans are pretty cute. I guess customs are different everywhere.

Roya: It's not that I think girls and women should always wear frumpy,* baggy clothes. But people can be modern and fashionable and still show some self-respect.

*frumpy = old-fashioned, loose (only used for women's clothes)

E **UNDERSTAND IDIOMS AND EXPRESSIONS**   Paraphrase these quotations from Spotlight.

1 "I think they'd attract too much attention."

2 "… but not over the top."

> **"** I think they might make too many people look at the person wearing them. **"**

3 "No girl … would be caught dead wearing something as immodest as that."

4 "… no one would even give them a second thought."

5 "… you have a point."

F **THINK AND EXPLAIN**   Discuss these questions.

1 In what way do Karen and Roya's perspectives on good and bad taste differ?

2 Whose opinion represents the opinion of a majority of people in your country?

SPEAKING

A **PAIR WORK**   Read the quotations and sayings about the significance of clothes. Then work with a partner to paraphrase them. Think of sayings in your own language that express similar ideas.

" **FASHIONS** FADE; STYLE IS **ETERNAL.** **"**
Yves Saint-Laurent
French fashion designer

" SO SOON AS A **FASHION** IS **UNIVERSAL,** IT IS OUT OF DATE. **"**
Marie Von Ebner-Eschenbach
Austrian writer

" **FASHION DESIGNERS** ARE DICTATORS OF **TASTE.** **"**
Karl Lagerfeld
German fashion designer

" DON'T BE INTO **TRENDS.** DON'T MAKE **FASHION** OWN YOU, BUT YOU DECIDE WHAT YOU ARE—WHAT **YOU** WANT TO **EXPRESS** BY THE WAY **YOU** DRESS AND THE WAY **YOU** LIVE. **"**
Gianni Versace
Italian fashion designer

" WHOEVER SAID THAT MONEY CAN'T BUY **HAPPINESS** SIMPLY DIDN'T KNOW WHERE TO GO **SHOPPING.** **"**
Bo Derek
American actor and model

B **DISCUSSION**   What, in your opinion, do our clothes tell others about us?

GOAL Describe clothing details and formality

DIGITAL STRATEGIES **A** ▶ 2:17 **VOCABULARY** DESCRIBING CLOTHES
Read and listen.

▶ 2:18 **Adjectives**
long-sleeved
low-cut
print
striped
plaid
short-sleeved
solid

▶ 2:19 **Formal clothes**
a cocktail dress
a dress shirt
an evening gown
a tuxedo

Don't forget
Informal clothes
V-neck
crewneck
turtleneck
sweater
polo shirt
jeans
T-shirt
blazer
cardigan

I've got on a **long-sleeved cocktail dress.** A bit **low-cut**, but appropriate… . What color? Actually, it's a black-and-white **print**.

High heels

You should see my costume for the play! I'm wearing a nice **dress shirt**— like for the office. But I'm also wearing **striped** shorts and carrying a **plaid** jacket! Ridiculous and in terrible taste, but great!

Hi, Mom … Dan and I are on our way to the charity ball. It's formal, so I've got on a **short-sleeved evening gown** in a great **solid** dark purple **color**. Dan's got on a **tuxedo**. I'll send you a selfie!

B ▶ 2:20 **LISTEN FOR DETAILS** Listen to the conversations.
Circle the letter of the illustration that answers each question.

1 Which man are they talking about?

a  b  c

2 Which girl are they discussing?

a  b   c

3 Which dress are they describing?

a   b  c

4 Which shirt will he buy?

a   b   c

shirt + t-shirt

C **PAIR WORK** Take turns describing the clothes in Exercise B. Your partner says which clothes you are describing. Use the Vocabulary.

PRONUNCIATION BOOSTER p. 143

Linking sounds

As for Now *Crown-neck*

D **APPLY THE VOCABULARY** With a partner, discuss your opinions about these fashions. Use the Vocabulary and other adjectives you know to describe the clothing details.

> ❝ I love the long-sleeved solid black dress. I think it's classic and elegant and would look great anywhere. ❞

isnt easy forme

NOW YOU CAN Describe clothing details and formality

A ▶ 2:21 **CONVERSATION SPOTLIGHT** Read and listen. Notice the spotlighted conversation strategies.

A: **Can I ask you a question about** the reception this weekend?
B: Sure. What would you like to know?
A: How formal will it be? **I mean,** what kind of clothes are we expected to wear?
B: **Actually,** it'll be pretty formal, I think.
A: **So** would a nice long-sleeved blouse and a pair of black dress pants be OK?
B: **I think that might be** a little underdressed. Most women will probably wear cocktail dresses.
A: Great! I've got a beautiful cocktail dress I can wear.

Formality
underdressed
overdressed

B ▶ 2:22 **RHYTHM AND INTONATION** Listen again and repeat. Then practice the conversation with a partner.

C **CONVERSATION ACTIVATOR** Create a similar conversation about formality at a different kind of event. Ask about specific clothes, using clothing and adjectives from the Vocabulary. Start like this: *Can I ask you a question about...?* Be sure to change roles and then partners.

DIGITAL VIDEO
DIGITAL SPEAKING BOOSTER

DON'T STOP!

• Ask more questions about the event.
• Provide details about the clothes.
• Make a decision about what to wear.
• Say as much as you can.

RECYCLE THIS LANGUAGE	
· trendy	· subdued
· funky	· loud
· frumpy	· flashy
· classic	· in good taste
· elegant	· in bad taste

OPTIONAL WRITING Write about a real or invented event when someone was underdressed (or overdressed). Use the Vocabulary.

GOAL Talk about changes in clothing customs

A ▶ 2:23 **GRAMMAR SPOTLIGHT** Read the article. Notice the spotlighted grammar.

Dressing up and Dressing down

Walk around any urban business district in the U.S., and you'll see **a majority of** office workers in "business casual" attire. Only **a few** will be wearing the more formal suits, skirts, and dresses seen in more conservative locations around the world. Business casual style developed in several steps, **most** people say, in the U.S. state of Hawaii. Here's **a little** history:

In 1966, the Hawaiian clothing industry was trying to sell **more** Hawaiian, or "aloha," shirts. The industry encouraged Hawaiian businesses to let their employees wear these colorful print shirts to the office one day a week, on Fridays. But the style became so popular that by 1970 it had become standard dress **all** days of the week there.

The trend spread to the state of California, which has always had **less** office formality than the rest of the country. There, people called the trend "casual Friday." Later, in the 1990s, the concept got more of a boost, again by the clothing industry. It was during that time that **a number of** companies began promoting casual khaki pants. **Lots of** ads showed both men and women wearing them with dress shirts and blazers or sweaters. This look quickly became the new office standard.

Some wish the pendulum would swing back towards a more traditional, elegant look, but **plenty of** other people say this is unlikely. In fact, **more and more** companies, particularly in the creative and technology sectors, now permit jeans and even T-shirts in the office. **Many** younger people are used to this look and would resist going back to more conservative office dress.

B **EXAMINE CULTURAL EXPECTATIONS** Discuss the questions.

1 Can clothing affect people's work quality and productivity in offices? How?

2 What should the limits of formality be in office dress? Be specific.

DIGITAL INDUCTIVE ACTIVITY

C **GRAMMAR** **QUANTIFIERS: REVIEW AND EXPANSION**

Some quantifiers can only be used with singular count nouns.

one shoe	**each** man	**every** friend

Some quantifiers can only be used with plural count nouns.

a few sports	**both** stores	**a pair of** shoes
many workers	**several** men	**a number of** trends
a couple of skirts	**at least** three	**a majority of** tuxedos

Some quantifiers can only be used with non-count nouns.

a little formality	**much** choice	**a great deal** of conflict
less fun	**not as much** formality	**a great amount of** interest

Note: The quantifier a majority of can also be used with singular count nouns that include more than one person. Use a third-person singular verb.

A majority of **the class thinks** shorts are inappropriate for school.

A majority of **the population prefers** casual clothes in the office.

Some quantifiers can be used with *both* count and non-count nouns.

Count nouns	Non-count nouns
no people	**no** choice
some / **any** cocktail dresses	**some** / **any** fashion
a lot of / **lots of** windbreakers	**a lot of** / **lots of** style
a third of the offices	**a third of** the money
plenty of young men	**plenty of** interest
most clothes	**most** criticism
all young people	**all** fashion
more evening gowns	**more** music
more and more women	**more and more** clothing

> **GRAMMAR BOOSTER** p. 131
> · Quantifiers: <u>a few</u> and <u>few</u>; <u>a little</u> and <u>little</u>
> · Quantifiers: using <u>of</u>
> · Quantifiers used without referents
> · Subject-verb agreement of quantifiers followed by <u>of</u>

D **UNDERSTAND THE GRAMMAR**   Circle the correct quantifier. Explain your answer.

> 66 **Much** can't be used with count nouns. 99

1 (Most / Much) men and women today like having a wide choice of clothes to wear.

2 (A number of / A great deal of) stores in this mall sell trendy clothes.

3 (All / Every) guest at the dinner wore formal clothing.

4 A more liberal dress code has resulted in (less / fewer) choices in formal clothing.

5 Seventy-five years ago, there were (a little / a few) stores that sold women's pants.

E **GRAMMAR PRACTICE**   Circle the letters of *all* the quantifiers that can complete each sentence correctly. Explain your answer, based on the grammar chart.

> 66 **A great deal of** can only be used with non-count nouns. 99

1 If people go to ...... formal events, they need appropriate clothes.
  a a lot of   **b** several   **c** a number of   **d** a great deal of

2 ...... children don't think much about what clothes to wear.
  a most   **b** a great deal of   **c** every   **d** a majority of

3 Since the invitation doesn't specify the level of formality, it's clear that ...... person needs to decide on his or her own what to wear.
  a some   **b** each   **c** every   **d** most

4 There are ...... tailors who can make anything you buy look great on you.
  a a number of   **b** a few   **c** plenty of   **d** a little

5 I was surprised to read that ...... women didn't wear pants 50 years ago.
  a a lot of   **b** some   **c** every   **d** less

NOW YOU CAN   Talk about changes in clothing customs

A **NOTEPADDING**   Contrast what you imagine young people wore 100 years ago with what they wear today.

Event	100 years ago	Today
a walk in the park		
a formal reception or wedding		
dinner at a nice restaurant		
dinner at a friend's home		
a party at school or in the office		

B **SUMMARIZE**   In a group, compare your classmates' ideas. Use quantifiers to summarize your classmates' ideas.

> 66 **A majority** of the class said they thought ... 99

> 66 **A few** students said ... 99

C **DISCUSSION ACTIVATOR**   How much would you say clothing trends have changed in your country? Describe how they have changed. Use the information from your notepad. Say as much as you can.

> 66 In the old days, everyone wore pretty formal clothes to a dinner in a nice restaurant, but today fewer people do. 99

43

A   READING WARM-UP   Are there any cosmetic procedures you think should be illegal? Explain.

DIGITAL STRATEGIES   **B**   ▶ 2:24   **READING**   Read about fish pedicures. In what ways is this treatment risky?

Questionable
COSMETIC TREATMENTS

In this wide world, there's always someone ready to shell out money for a treatment that promises results.

Is it safe to let *Garra rufa* fish, or "doctor fish," exfoliate your feet in a fish spa pedicure, eating away quantities of dead skin and leaving your feet looking sandal-ready? Although fish pedicures are popular in many parts of the world, the governments of a number of U.S. states and at least two Canadian provinces have banned the practice, making it illegal to provide this service. Although some experts say there is not much of a serious risk to health, and although no actual illnesses have been caused by this procedure, most bans are based on one or more of the following reasons:

Since the fish remain in the pedicure tubs, it's impossible to clean them between clients. Bacteria and other pathogens can build up in the water, and if a client has a cut or break in the skin, these organisms can enter and cause infection. In fact, New York dermatologist Dr. Riya Prasad says, "Today there are so many antibiotic-resistant bacteria that I advise my patients to walk the other way when they see a salon or spa offering these pedicures. Better safe than sorry!"

The fish themselves cannot be disinfected or sanitized to prevent them from spreading bacteria. Due to the cost of the fish, salon owners are likely to use the same fish multiple times with different clients, which increases the risk of spreading infection.

Chinchin, a species often mislabeled as *Garra rufa* and used in pedicures, grows teeth and can break the skin, further increasing the risk. *Garra rufa*, on the other hand, are toothless.

According to the U.S. Fish and Wildlife Service, *Garra rufa* could pose a threat to native plant and animal life if released into the wild in places where it isn't native. Non-native species can reproduce without limit because there may be few natural predators to kill them and control their numbers.

And in addition to the harm these pedicures can do to the environment and human health, the fish at a salon or spa must be contained in an aquarium with no natural food source and depend on human skin to survive. In order to get the fish to eat the skin on a client's feet, they must be starved, and this could be considered animal cruelty, which is illegal in many places.

The preponderance of evidence leads one to believe that fish pedicures are doubtful at best and dangerous at worst. And public opinion seems to be building against them, with city after city making them illegal.

> **Fish pedicures? Yuck and double yuck! Just get a nice clean pedicure from a licensed cosmetician. If the hygiene argument doesn't convince you, just think how terrible the experience is for the poor little fishies!**
> –Minnie Edwards, biology teacher

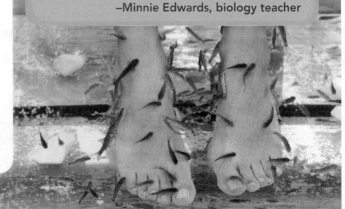

C   UNDERSTAND MEANING FROM CONTEXT   Complete the statements with words from the box.

1 When someone uses something to .... your feet, he or she removes dead skin.

2 Another way to say that a government doesn't permit something is to say it .... it.

3 .... are pathogenic organisms that can grow in water.

4 When you .... something, you clean it to remove harmful organisms.

5 When you .... something, it means that you give it the wrong name.

6 A .... is an animal that kills and eats other animals.

bacteria
bans
disinfect
exfoliate
mislabel
predator

D **IDENTIFY SUPPORTING DETAILS** Choose the correct answer and support it with information from the article.

1 Where can you get a fish pedicure?
a In many countries around the world. **b** In all the U.S. states and Canadian provinces.

2 What is one reason that fish pedicures aren't permitted in some places?
a They have caused serious illnesses. **b** They can cause infection.

3 Where can bacteria enter a client's skin?
a In the fish's mouth. **b** In a cut in the client's skin.

4 What makes chinchin more dangerous than garrra rufa?
a They can reproduce in the wild.
b They have teeth that can break the client's skin, which can cause infection.

5 What would salon owners have to do to keep the water free of pathogens?
a They would have to wash the tank and change the fish after each pedicure.
b They would have to clean each client's feet.

6 Why do some people consider the treatment of pedicure fish cruel?
a Because in order to get them to eat skin, they have to be starved.
b Because keeping them in aquariums is unsanitary and can cause infection.

E **EXPRESS AND SUPPORT AN OPINION** Discuss with a partner. Would you consider getting a fish pedicure? Explain your reasons.

DIGITAL
EXTRA
CHALLENGE

NOW YOU CAN Examine questionable cosmetic procedures

A **FRAME YOUR IDEAS** Read the ads and rate them.
Discuss your ratings and reasons with a partner.

Ratings.
✓ = Looks good to me.
? = I'd have to know more.
✗ = I wouldn't try it even if you paid me!

Face-Slapping Massage ... Based on science!

Rejuvenate your aging face with the ancient practice of face-slapping. Based on scientifically proven physical tapping known as "tapotement" and used extensively in Swedish massage, both gentle and more aggressive slaps with a flat or cupped palm improve circulation and reduce the appearance of wrinkles, resulting in a more youthful appearance.

My rating

The Swiss Chocolate Mud Wrap is a "sweet experience."

Swiss Chocolate Mud Wrap

Soak in the luxury of the finest Swiss chocolate mixed with sticky Mississippi River mud—the ultimate full-body mask to hydrate your skin, slim your silhouette, and stimulate your circulation all at once. Effects are achieved by the natural essential oils in the chocolate that are released as the mud dries and contracts. Emerge from a series of three treatments a newer, smoother, slimmer you.

My rating

Tapeworm Express Diet*

Don't knock it if you haven't tried it! Under a doctor's supervision, you simply swallow a small pill. Within days, one or more tapeworms will absorb all the food you eat, resulting in extra-fast weight loss. Once you have reached your ideal weight, the doctor will administer an anti-parasite pill, killing the tapeworm, which will pass out of your body harmlessly.

"I tried this diet and reached my ideal weight fast!"

* Only for healthy individuals. The tapeworm express diet can cause abdominal complications, meningitis, and dementia.

My rating

B **DISCUSSION** What specific dangerous or harmful procedures have you seen or heard about? What can or should be done about them?

RECYCLE THIS LANGUAGE
· It's just a matter of time until …
· I mean, what are you going to do?
· It is what it is.
· Better safe than sorry.
· Can I ask you a question?

A ▶ 2:25 **LISTENING WARM-UP   WORD STUDY: COMPOUND WORDS WITH SELF-**   Study the words. Then use a dictionary to find two more nouns and two more adjectives with the prefix <u>self-</u>.

NOUNS

self-confidence the belief that one has the ability to do things well
Parents can build their children's self-confidence by helping them develop their talents and abilities.

self-esteem the attitude of acceptance and approval of oneself
High self-esteem can help a person succeed, and low self-esteem can be damaging.

self-image the opinion one has about one's own abilities, appearance, and character
A person's self-image is often formed very early in life.

self-pity the feeling of being sorry for oneself
When you feel that life is unfair and that others have treated you poorly, it's not unusual to feel self-pity.

ADJECTIVES

self-centered interested only in oneself
Children are naturally self-centered, but they usually learn to be more interested in others as they grow up.

self-confident believing that one has the ability to do things well; not shy or nervous in social situations
Janet is a very self-confident young woman. She'll do well at the university.

self-conscious worried about what one looks like or what other people think of one's appearance
Everyone at the meeting was dressed casually, so I felt self-conscious in my suit.

self-critical tending to find fault with oneself
Paul is too self-critical. He always focuses on his mistakes rather than his accomplishments.

B **WORD STUDY PRACTICE**   Complete each statement, using one of the compound words with <u>self-</u>.

1 Eleanor Ricci entered the auditorium with her usual .... and began her presentation.

2 Even though my brother Martin always wears great clothes, he feels .... and usually asks me to tell him if he looks OK.

3 They say that children's .... is built by receiving parental praise for their accomplishments.

4 A positive .... can help people through the difficulties of life without feeling like failures when things go wrong.

5 People who spend a lot of time talking about themselves are ....

6 I don't know why Paul is so .... He's great at everything and more successful than almost everyone else.

7 We tried to encourage Sylvie to look on the bright side, but after she lost her job, she just couldn't stop wallowing in ....

8 .... people don't just sit around worrying about not being able to do things. They try their best and assume their best is good enough.

C ▶ 2:26 **LISTEN FOR MAIN IDEAS**   Listen to a university lecture. Then read the statements and choose the one that expresses the main idea of the lecture.

☐ **1** Female self-image is heavily influenced by messages in the media.

☐ **2** Many fashion models today are super-thin.

☐ **3** Eighty per cent of ten-year-olds are on diets.

☐ **4** Anorexia is a common eating disorder.

Super-thin models are demanded by fashion designers, magazine editors, and advertisers.

D ▶ 2:27 **LISTEN FOR DETAILS** Read the following questions. Answer them, listening again if necessary.

1 What kind of body is currently in style?

2 What change has taken place in the look of fashion models over the last fifty years?

3 What is one serious consequence of feeling like you're fat all the time?

4 How can women help themselves overcome the negative messages in the media?

5 How can people help their daughters avoid a negative self-image?

E ▶ 2:28 **LISTEN TO SUMMARIZE** With a partner, write a summary statement about the lecture.

Photos are often altered to make models and actresses appear thinner than they are.

NOW YOU CAN Discuss appearance and self-esteem

A **FRAME YOUR IDEAS** Take the survey. Then compare ratings with a partner.

HOW MUCH DO YOU AGREE WITH EACH STATEMENT ABOUT MEN AND WOMEN IN YOUR COUNTRY?

	STRONGLY DISAGREE			STRONGLY AGREE	
1 Most women are self-conscious about their bodies.	1	2	3	4	5
2 Most men are self-conscious about their bodies.	1	2	3	4	5
3 Most women are self-conscious about their faces.	1	2	3	4	5
4 Most men are self-conscious about their faces.	1	2	3	4	5
5 Most women want to look more like women in the media.	1	2	3	4	5
6 Most men want to look more like men in the media.	1	2	3	4	5
7 Most women think women need to be beautiful.	1	2	3	4	5
8 Most men think women need to be beautiful.	1	2	3	4	5
9 Most women think men need to be handsome.	1	2	3	4	5
10 Most men think men need to be handsome.	1	2	3	4	5

B **NOTEPADDING** Make a list of positive and negative factors that affect self-esteem.

Build self-esteem	Harm self-esteem
Parental love	"Messages" in the media

Build self-esteem	Harm self-esteem

C **DISCUSSION**

1 How can the positive factors you listed on your notepad be promoted?

2 Which of the negative factors on your notepad can be changed or corrected?

3 Do you think life is easier for people who are attractive? Explain your opinion.

4 In an ideal world, what should one's self-esteem be based on? Explain your opinion.

A **WRITING SKILL** Study the rules.

Compare Connecting words that show similarities	Contrast Connecting words that show differences
like **Like** Sylvia, I wear jeans all the time. OR I wear jeans all the time, **like** Sylvia.	**unlike** **Unlike** her sister, Wendy wears great clothes. OR Wendy wears great clothes, **unlike** her sister.

similarly
 	
I grew up paying little attention to fashion.
    Similarly, my brother was not very
    interested in clothes. OR
I grew up paying little attention to fashion;
    similarly, my brother was not very interested
    in clothes.
	in contrast
	
	I've always liked to wear black to evening events.
	    In contrast, my sister prefers white. OR
	I've always liked to wear black to evening events;
	    in contrast, my sister prefers white.

likewise
 	
My mother always liked elegant clothes.
    Likewise, her two sisters did, too. OR
My mother always liked elegant clothes;
    likewise, her two sisters did, too.
	however
	
	Lily had to wear a uniform when she was in
	    school. **However,** I was allowed to wear
	    anything I wanted. OR
	Lily had to wear a uniform when she was in
	    school; **however,** I was allowed to wear
	    anything I wanted.

as well / not either
 	
Many people spend too much money on clothes.
    Some spend too much on shoes **as well.**
Our parents' generation didn't worry so much
    about fashion. Their own parents **didn't
    either.**
	while / whereas
	
	Sam spends a lot of money on clothes **while**
	    (or **whereas**) Jeff rarely does. OR
	While (or **whereas**) Sam spends a lot of money
	    on clothes, Jeff rarely does.

B **PRACTICE** Read the paragraph, inserting logical connecting words for comparing and contrasting.

My husband, Jack, generally appreciates fashion, but we don't always agree on clothes and what to wear. I like to shop in small boutiques; .... , my husband also appreciates the attention a shopper gets in a small store. .... , I always buy funky, trendy clothes. .... , Jack is more conservative. And it won't be surprising for anyone to learn that .... my husband, I tend to like loud colors and bold prints, ... he prefers a more subdued look. .... I feel self-confident that whatever I wear will be OK .... Jack can be a little self-conscious and always tries to wear non-controversial clothes. But, as they say, "opposites attract," and we both like the way the other person dresses, even if our tastes for ourselves aren't the same.

C **APPLY THE WRITING SKILL**

Choose a topic below. Write two paragraphs comparing and contrasting ideas. In your first paragraph, write about the differences. In your second paragraph, write about the similarities. Use connecting words and include a topic sentence for each paragraph.

Topics
- Compare and contrast your fashion style and tastes with those of someone you know.
- Compare and contrast fashion today with fashion five, ten, or twenty years ago.

SELF-CHECK

☐ Did I use connecting words for comparing?
☐ Did I use connecting words for contrasting?
☐ Does each paragraph have a topic sentence?

A ▶ 2:29 **Listen to the conversations about fashion and style. Choose the adjective that best summarizes each speaker's point of view.**

1 They think the purses in the magazine are ....
  a frumpy   **b** trendy   **c** flashy

2 He thinks the jacket Carl is wearing is ....
  a funky   **b** subdued   **c** loud

3 They think the girl's hair is ....
  a elegant   **b** in bad taste   **c** classic

4 The salesperson is suggesting that the dress is ....
  a elegant   **b** funky   **c** trendy

5 She thinks the blouse her friend is holding isn't ....
  a in bad taste   **b** stylish   **c** frumpy

B **Complete each statement with an appropriate word or phrase.**

1 A piece of clothing that's all one color is ....

2 A shirt with different color lines making square patterns is ....

3 A piece of clothing with vertical or horizontal lines in different colors is ....

4 A very formal suit a man might wear to a wedding or a reception is ....

5 A short, elegant dress for a party in the evening is ....

6 A long, very formal dress for a wedding or a reception is ....

7 When a person is wearing something much too informal for an occasion, he or she is ....

8 If a man comes to the office in a tuxedo, people will say that he's ....

9 Many people think that a dress or blouse that's .... is too revealing and in bad taste.

10 When it's cold outside, it's better to wear a .... shirt.

C **Cross out the one quantifier that cannot be used in each sentence.**

1 (Every / A few / Most) older people find flashy clothes in bad taste.

2 The company where I work says that it will permit us to come to the office in jeans (one / a couple of / a few) days a month.

3 (Most / Many / Every) young girls aren't worried about the way they look.

4 (Much / A majority of / A number of) parents are concerned about the effect the media has on young boys as well.

5 When my great-grandparents were young, (many / most / much) women wore only dresses.

6 I'd say your friends could use (some / a little / a few) fashion advice.

7 There are (several / most / many) reasons so many young women have eating disorders.

8 A new study says that (most / many / every) children who watch TV for more than six hours a day may have problems with self-esteem as teenagers.

D **On a separate sheet of paper, write five sentences, each one using one of the quantifiers from the box.**

several	a majority	few	little	more and more

TEST-TAKING SKILLS BOOSTER p. 154

Web Project: Trend Spotters
www.english.com/summit3e

COMMUNICATION GOALS

1 Politely ask someone not to do something
2 Complain about public conduct
3 Suggest ways to avoid being a victim of urban crime
4 Discuss the meaning of community

PREVIEW

A **FRAME YOUR IDEAS** Complete the questionnaire about your ideal community. How closely do your answers describe where you live now? In what ways are they different?

| Home | About | Questionnaires | Top stories | | Search | 🔍 |

Whether you're planning to move soon or just dreaming about your future, this questionnaire will help you focus on what's most important to you.

1. What kind of environment would you prefer to live in?

○ a densely-populated urban area with skyscrapers

○ a medium-sized urban area

○ a suburb, just outside a city, with convenient transportation

○ a small town in a rural area with a slower pace of life

a rural town

2. Which of the following describe your ideal neighborhood?

○ is near my school or job

○ is peaceful and quiet

○ is lively and bustling with activity

○ is friendly, with people who say hello to each other

○ has a mix of apartment buildings and private homes

○ has mainly private homes

○ has mainly modern high-rise apartment buildings

○ has lots of well-maintained historical buildings

○ is safe, with very little crime

○ is very secure, with security cameras and guards

other: ⬚

an urban area

3. Which neighborhood amenities would you want easy access to?

○ reliable public transportation

○ a large modern mall

○ a variety of small businesses, such as hair salons, dry cleaners, florists, etc.

○ a large supermarket

○ a market where you can buy fresh farm produce

○ theaters and stadiums

○ a hospital and clinics

○ parks and fitness centers

○ other: ⬚

B ▶ 3:01 **VOCABULARY** **TYPES OF LOCATIONS** Listen and repeat. Then, with a partner, write a definition for each of these location types.

an urban area
a rural area
the suburbs

C **PAIR WORK** Compare your answers in the questionnaire to determine if you have the same preferences. Discuss and explain the reasons for your choices.

D ▶ 3:02 **SPOTLIGHT**   Read and listen to a conversation between two former colleagues. Notice the spotlighted language.

Bill: Hi, Luiz!

Luiz: Bill? What a surprise!

Bill: I just wanted to see how you're doing. How's your new place? You and Lourdes must be all settled in by now.

Luiz: Pretty much. But city life sure **takes some getting used to**.

Bill: In what way?

Luiz: Well, for one thing, not only do we have to deal with bumper-to-bumper traffic every day, but it's almost impossible to find on-the-street parking.

Bill: Yeah, that *is* a pain. Hey, what about your building? How's that worked out?

Luiz: Pretty well. It's safe and well-maintained. But, to be honest, it's been **a mixed blessing**.

Bill: What's the problem?

Luiz: Well, it's the neighbors on our floor. Whenever they hear someone get off the elevator, they look out their door to check who it is. I don't mean to sound unfriendly, but I wish they'd **mind their own business**.

Bill: Well, I'm sure they **mean well**. You should **look on the bright side**. It's good to be in a building where people **look out for each other**.

Luiz: That's true. We're very lucky. And I have to say, I've fallen in love with the neighborhood.

Bill: That's great!

Luiz: It's really **got a lot to offer**; we're never bored. Sometimes we go out for coffee and just people watch.

Bill: Well, all in all, it sounds like things are going well.

Luiz: They are. Hey, give my regards to Judy. And let me know if you're ever in town.

Bill: Will do!

E **UNDERSTAND IDIOMS AND EXPRESSIONS**   Write an expression from Spotlight for each definition.

1 choose to have an optimistic viewpoint ....

2 take care of other people ....

3 something that has both a good and bad side ....

4 not intrude in other people's lives ....

5 requires time to get comfortable with something ....

6 have good intentions ....

7 has many advantages ....

F **THINK AND EXPLAIN**   Answer the questions, supporting your answers with information from Spotlight.

1 What does Luiz like about the neighborhood he lives in, and what doesn't he like?

2 What does Luiz like about his building, and what doesn't he like?

SPEAKING **PAIR WORK**   On a separate sheet of paper, list the pros and cons of living in a small town, a big city, and a suburb. Then compare opinions with a partner. Use expressions from Spotlight.

❝ What I don't like about living in the city is the bumper-to-bumper traffic. ❞

❝ Life in a small town is a mixed blessing. It's clean and quiet. But there's not much to do! ❞

GOAL Politely ask someone not to do something

A ▶ 3:03 **WORD STUDY** USING NEGATIVE PREFIXES TO FORM ANTONYMS

Listen and repeat.

		Negative prefixes
		dis- ir-
		im- un-
		in-

1 acceptable → **un**acceptable
2 considerate → **in**considerate
3 polite → **im**polite
4 proper → **im**proper
5 respectful → **dis**respectful
6 responsible → **ir**responsible

B **WORD STUDY PRACTICE** Use a dictionary to find antonyms for these words. Then make a list of other adjectives with negative prefixes.

1 appropriate ....
2 courteous ....
3 excusable ....
4 imaginable ....
5 honest ....
6 pleasant ....
7 rational ....
8 mature ....

C **ACTIVATE WORD STUDY** Write sentences that describe inappropriate public behavior. Use adjectives from Exercises A and B.

Example: *It's inconsiderate to play loud music in the library.*

1 ....
2 ....
3 ....
4 ....
5 ....

D **PAIR WORK** Compare the examples you wrote in exercise C. Explain why you consider the behavior inappropriate.

E **GRAMMAR** USING POSSESSIVE GERUNDS

You can use a possessive gerund when you want to indicate the performer of the action.

I object to **their playing** loud music late at night.
Jack's talking during the movie was annoying.
Does **my daughter's playing** video games bother you?
What bothers me is **his not apologizing** for texting during class.

In informal spoken English, it is acceptable to use a name, a noun, or an object pronoun instead of a possessive, but only if the gerund phrase is the direct object in the sentence.

I object to **them playing** loud music late at night.

BUT Never use a name, noun, or object pronoun if the gerund is the subject of the sentence. Use a possessive.

Their playing music late at night is a problem. NOT ~~Them playing~~ music late at night is a problem.

F **UNDERSTAND THE GRAMMAR** Write a check mark next to the sentences that are incorrect in speaking or writing. Correct them.

☐ 1 "Do you mind me eating lunch at my desk?"

☐ 2 "Your brother not saying hello to her was disrespectful."

☐ 3 "Kevin not agreeing to remove his shoes in my house was kind of impolite."

☐ 4 "Isn't Paula honking her car horn early in the morning inexcusable?"

☐ 5 "I don't like you answering your phone while we're eating dinner."

G **GRAMMAR PRACTICE** Combine the two statements, using a possessive gerund.

1 They allow smoking. I'm not in favor of it.
   I'm not in favor of their allowing smoking.

2 He texted his friends during the concert. I didn't appreciate that.
   ....

3 They eat fast food in the car. Does your mother object to it?
   ....

4 She's talking on her cell phone. We don't mind it.
   ....

> **PRONUNCIATION BOOSTER** p. 144
> Unstressed syllables: vowel reduction to /ə/

5 My brother didn't apologize. I'm really annoyed by it.
   ....

NOW YOU CAN Politely ask someone not to do something

A ▶ 3:04 **CONVERSATION SPOTLIGHT** Read and listen. Notice the spotlighted conversation strategies.

A: **Do you mind** my smoking here?
B: **Actually,** smoking kind of bothers me. I hope that's not a problem.
A: **Not at all.** I can step outside.
B: **That's very** considerate **of you.** Thanks for asking.

B ▶ 3:05 **RHYTHM AND INTONATION** Listen again and repeat. Then practice the conversation with a partner.

C **NOTEPADDING** Make a list of situations in which you would probably ask for permission to do something.

> ▶ 3:06 **Ways to soften an objection**
> I hope that's not a problem.
> I hope you don't mind.
> I hope it's OK / all right.
> I don't mean to inconvenience you.

Your list
turning on the TV in a doctor's waiting room
making a phone call while having dinner with someone

Your list

D **CONVERSATION ACTIVATOR** Create a conversation similar to the one in Exercise A, using a situation from your notepad. Start like this: *Do you mind my … ?* Be sure to change roles and then partners.

DON'T STOP!
• Explain why the behavior bothers you.
• Express understanding of your partner's point of view.
• Say as much as you can.

GOAL Complain about public conduct

A ▶3:07 **GRAMMAR SPOTLIGHT** Read the interview responses. Notice the spotlighted grammar.

What are some of your pet peeves?

"Well, it really bugs me when people cut in line at the theater! They should **either** arrive early enough for a good seat **or** wait in line patiently like everyone else does. Who do they think they are?"

cutting in line

Jean Seyedi
San Francisco, USA

"I'll tell you what really gets to me. I can **neither** tolerate **nor** understand people's littering in public places. Do they really expect others to clean up after them? That's just so inconsiderate. **Either** they should throw their garbage in a trash can **or** they should hold on to it till they find one."

littering on the street

Ken Becker
Philadelphia, USA

"It really gets on my nerves when people spit on the street. **Not only** do I find it disgusting, **but** it's also unhygienic. It's important to think about public health and other people's feelings."

spitting on the sidewalk

Nancy Shen
Shanghai, China

"Here's a pet peeve of mine: I hate it when people forget to turn off their phones during a lecture or workshop. **Not only** is it distracting to the speaker, **but** it's also annoying to the audience. They should **either** have the courtesy to turn their phones off **or** simply leave them at home. It really ticks me off."

forgetting to turn off one's phone

Paulo Acosta
Salvador, Brazil

B **EXPRESS YOUR IDEAS** Which of the examples of public behavior described in the interviews bug you the most? With a partner, compare your opinions and explain your reasons.

DIGITAL
INDUCTIVE
ACTIVITY

C **GRAMMAR** **PAIRED CONJUNCTIONS**

You can connect related ideas with paired conjunctions.

either ... or
    Either people should smoke outside **or** they shouldn't smoke at all.
    Phones should **either** be turned off **or** left at home.

neither ... nor
    I would allow **neither** spitting **nor** littering.
    Neither eating **nor** drinking is allowed in the lab.

not only ... but
Invert the subject and verb after Not only. Use a comma after the first clause.
    Not only is it dangerous to text while driving, **but** it may be illegal.
    Not only did they forget to turn off their phones, **but** they also talked during the concert.

Be careful!
When joining two subjects with either or neither, make sure the verb agrees with the subject nearer to the verb.
    Either the mayor or local businesspeople **need** to decide.
    Either local businesspeople or the mayor **needs** to decide.

| GRAMMAR BOOSTER | p. 133 |

· Conjunctions with so, too, neither, or not either
· So, too, neither, or not either: short responses

DIGITAL
MORE
EXERCISES

D **NOTICE THE GRAMMAR** Find an example of paired conjunctions in Spotlight on page 51.

1 People should speak up about what bothers them. They should just learn to live with other people's habits. (either)

2 It's rude when people talk on their phones in theaters. It's also rude when they talk on them on buses. (not only)

3 I hate the smell of cigarette smoke. I worry about the danger to my health. (not only)

4 My uncle isn't willing to give up smoking. My grandparents aren't willing to give up smoking. (neither)

NOW YOU CAN Complain about public conduct

A **NOTEPADDING** Make a list of some of your pet peeves in public places. Then write sentences with paired conjunctions to express your opinion. Use some of the adjectives with negative prefixes.

> In restaurants: *reading e-mail and texting during the meal*
> *Not only is it annoying, but it's also very impolite.*

In restaurants:

In stores:

On buses and trains:

On the street:

In offices:

In movie theaters:

Other:

Ideas
- cutting in line
- talking in theaters
- playing loud music
- honking a car horn
- not saying "Excuse me"

Adjectives with negative prefixes
disrespectful
immature
impolite
inconsiderate
inexcusable
irresponsible
unacceptable
unpleasant

B **APPLY THE GRAMMAR** In a group, role play on-the-street interviews, with one student as the interviewer. Use your notepads and the Grammar Spotlight on page 54 as a guide.

❝ What really ticks me off is … ❞

❝ Here's what really gets on my nerves … ❞

❝ I'll tell you what really gets to me … ❞

❝ Do you want to know what bugs me? ❞

C **DISCUSSION ACTIVATOR** Discuss the questions. Say as much as you can.

1 In your opinion, how should people behave in public places? Do you think it's important to speak up when people behave inconsiderately in public?

2 Do *you* ever do things that annoy other people? Explain.

RECYCLE THIS LANGUAGE
· It takes getting used to.
· It's a mixed blessing.
· [They] should mind [their] own business.
· [They] mean well.
· Look on the bright side.

GOAL Suggest ways to avoid being a victim of urban crime

A **READING WARM-UP** Why do you think tourists might make ideal victims for criminals?

DIGITAL STRATEGIES **B** ▶ 3:08 **READING** Read the interview. Do you agree with Miller's advice?

DON'T LET URBAN CRIME SPOIL YOUR VISIT

Since the beginning of the century, there has been a steady increase in the number of foreign visitors to the great cities of the world. In this interview, travel writer Hanna Miller suggests ways for visitors to avoid becoming victims of urban crime.

You claim that tourists are particularly vulnerable to criminal activities. Why is that?

Miller: Well, for one thing, tourists are more likely than local people to be carrying large sums of money or valuables such as jewelry and electronics. They are also out of their comfort zone, being unfamiliar with local customs or places that should be avoided. Because they're enjoying themselves, tourists are more likely than locals to let their guard down, thinking they are safe when in fact they are not. And let's face it: tourists stand out. They look different and dress differently from the residents of the place they're visiting.

What kinds of crime do tourists need to be concerned about?

Miller: All kinds, including violent crime, unfortunately. Tourists, however, are primarily targeted for theft of the valuables they have on them and the information gained from passports, credit cards, and other forms of identification. Because out-of-town visitors tend to congregate at tourist attractions, it's easier for criminals to do their work. Not only does this provide the opportunity for a pickpocket to take someone's wallet unnoticed, but it also makes it easier for a purse-snatcher to quickly grab something and run. A mugger can follow a victim until he or she is alone at an ATM machine, for example, where the criminal can demand the victim's money and property.

So what precautions do you recommend?

Miller: Before you leave home, use the Internet to learn about your destination so you can avoid high-crime neighborhoods. The more you know, the better you can protect yourself. Photocopy your passport and make sure you have a list of all your credit card numbers. When you're packing, choose clothes that don't make you stand out as a tourist. By the way, the inside pocket of a jacket may seem like a good place for a wallet or passport, but it's a favorite target for pickpockets. You should either bring pants and jackets with zippered or buttoned pockets or consider buying a money belt. And leave unnecessary valuables at home!

And what extra precautions should tourists take in urban areas?

Miller: It goes without saying: Avoid streets that are not well-lit at night. And avoid going out alone, if you can. While there's usually safety in numbers, remember that tourist attractions also attract thieves. Stay aware of what's happening around you—as if you had eyes in the back of your head. On the street, avoid using a smart phone or tablet—or fumbling with a map or guidebook— if you don't need to. Be wary if a stranger asks for directions or starts up a conversation. He or she may be sizing you up as a potential victim. Be particularly careful in crowds at festivals or on buses or trains. Be suspicious of any sudden disruption. Thieves are known to intentionally create a distraction so you won't realize what they're actually doing. And a warning to women: Be careful if you wear a cross-body purse. It may be harder for a criminal to grab, but you could be injured if the purse snatcher is on a motorcycle.

Do people need to worry about leaving valuables in their hotel room?

Miller: Good point! Don't leave valuables unprotected in your room, where a burglar might break in and take them. Ask the front desk to keep them for you. Better safe than sorry! Finally, I should mention that, all in all, crime rates are going down worldwide, and the chances you will become a crime victim are low. So don't let worrying about crime interfere with your having a great time!

C **CLASSIFY** Look for the words pickpocket, purse snatcher, mugger, and burglar in the reading. Then choose the kind of criminal who committed each crime below.

1 "I was looking for souvenirs at the market when this kid grabs my bag!"

☐ a pickpocket ☐ a purse snatcher ☐ a mugger ☐ a burglar

2 "I left my laptop in a dresser drawer under my dirty clothes, but when I got back to the hotel it was gone!"

☐ a pickpocket ☐ a purse snatcher ☐ a mugger ☐ a burglar

3 "I was watching the parade when all of a sudden I realized someone had taken my passport!"

☐ a pickpocket ☐ a purse snatcher ☐ a mugger ☐ a burglar

4 "We were walking on the beach, and three big guys surrounded us and demanded our wallets!"

☐ pickpockets ☐ purse snatchers ☐ muggers ☐ burglars

D **UNDERSTAND MEANING FROM CONTEXT** Read each statement from the interview. Match each underlined expression with its meaning.

.... **1** They are also out of their comfort zone.

.... **2** Tourists are more likely than locals to let their guard down.

.... **3** Tourists stand out.

.... **4** … there's usually safety in numbers.

.... **5** He or she may be sizing you up.

a not be careful

b be more noticeable than others

c checking to see if you might be a good victim

d less risk by doing things with others

e doing what they're not accustomed to doing

E **CRITICAL THINKING** Discuss the questions. Support your ideas with examples.

1 What are some ways that tourists might let their guard down when traveling?

2 What should a visitor to your country do to not "look like a tourist?" What would *you* do to not look like one when you travel?

DIGITAL
EXTRA
CHALLENGE

NOW YOU CAN Suggest ways to avoid becoming a victim of urban crime

A **NOTEPADDING** With a partner, discuss ways to avoid becoming a crime victim in your own town or city for each situation on the notepad. Summarize your ideas.

B **ROLE PLAY** Imagine that you are a tourist visiting a new city, and your partner is a local. Tell your partner about what you've been doing during your visit. Your partner makes suggestions for how to avoid crime. Summarize your ideas on the notepad.

OPTIONAL WRITING Write a short guide for visitors to your city. Suggest how to stay safe and avoid becoming a crime victim.

while riding in a car

while using public transportation

while walking on the street

while staying in a hotel

while getting cash at an ATM machine

other

GOAL Discuss the meaning of community

 A ▶ 3:09 **LISTENING WARM-UP** VOCABULARY: COMMUNITY SERVICE ACTIVITIES

Read and listen. Then listen again and repeat.

GET INVOLVED WITH YOUR COMMUNITY!

| Home | About | News | Community projects | Search 🔍 |

BEAUTIFY YOUR TOWN

Plant flowers or trees where there aren't any.

CLEAN UP LITTER
Pick up trash from parks, playgrounds, or the street.

RAISE MONEY

Mail letters, make phone calls, knock on doors, or set up a table to raise money for a charity or cause.

VOLUNTEER YOUR TIME

Work without pay in the fire department, a hospital, or a school.

DONATE BLOOD
Give the gift of life to someone who's very sick or has been in a serious accident.

B **VOCABULARY PRACTICE** Would you ever consider doing any community service activities? With a partner, explain what you would, or would never, do.

> ❝ I would never consider **volunteering my time** to **clean up litter**. I think they should pay people to do that. ❞

 C ▶ 3:10 **LISTEN TO SUMMARIZE** Listen to the report about the Ice Bucket Challenge. What was it? Describe the idea in your own words.

Pete Frates is credited with starting the Ice Bucket Challenge.

D ▶ 3:11 **LISTEN FOR DETAILS** Read the questions. Then listen again and answer them.

1 How much money did the Ice Bucket Challenge suggest donating if someone didn't take the challenge?

2 How much money was donated in just one month?

3 What percentage of the videos posted on Facebook actually led to donations?

E ▶ 3:12 **LISTEN TO CONFIRM CONTENT**   The report mentions that some people criticized the Ice Bucket Challenge. Read the list of criticisms. Then listen again and check the ones that are actually mentioned in the report.

- ☐ **1** It made people feel bad if they chose not to participate in the challenge.
- ☐ **2** There are more serious problems for which people could have donated money.
- ☐ **3** People should have paid more attention to the cause rather than on having fun.
- ☐ **4** The challenge didn't raise a lot of money for research.
- ☐ **5** Dumping ice water on your head could be dangerous.
- ☐ **6** Some celebrities took the challenge just to call attention to themselves.

F **EXPRESS AND SUPPORT AN OPINION**   Discuss the questions, using information from the report and your own ideas.

1 Do you think the Ice Bucket Challenge was a good idea? Do you agree with the critics or the supporters? Why?

2 Why do you think people on social media responded so strongly to the Ice Bucket Challenge?

NOW YOU CAN   Discuss the meaning of community

A **FRAME YOUR IDEAS**   With a partner, consider each situation and discuss what you might do. Based on your answers, how would you define the meaning of "community"?

1

There has been a terrible storm, and many homes have been destroyed. You're asked to let a family live with you until their home is fixed.

What would you say if they were …

- **a.** your relatives?
- **b.** your neighbors?
- **c.** your colleague's family?
- **d.** complete strangers?

2

There has been a natural disaster with casualties, and someone needs a blood transfusion to survive. You have the same blood type and can donate your blood to save that person's life.

What would you do if the person were …

- **a.** a family member?
- **b.** your neighbor?
- **c.** your classmate?
- **d.** a complete stranger?

❝ My first responsibility is to my family. I can't imagine doing this for a total stranger. ❞

❝ Of course I'd help a stranger! It's the right thing to do. ❞

3

Developers plan to destroy a historic tourist attraction so they can build a new office building. You're asked to donate your time to write letters and talk to your friends and colleagues to help save it.

What would you say if the tourist attraction were …

- **a.** in your neighborhood?
- **b.** in another part of the city?
- **c.** in another city in your country?
- **d.** in another country?

DIGITAL SPEAKING BOOSTER

B **PAIR WORK**   Make a list of ideas for community projects in which you and your classmates could possibly participate. Share your list with the class and explain why you think your ideas would be worthwhile.

A WRITING SKILL Study the rules.

When writing to a friend or relative, it is acceptable to use an informal tone, casual language, and abbreviations. However, when writing to the head of a company, a boss, or someone you don't know, standard formal language should be used, and regular spelling and punctuation rules apply. Formal letters are usually typed, not handwritten. The following salutations and closings are appropriate for formal letters:

Formal salutations		Formal closings
If you know the name:	Dear Ms. Krum: Dear Mr. Paz: Dear Professor Lee: Dear Dr. Smith:	Sincerely, Respectfully, Best regards, Cordially,
If you don't know the name:	Dear Sir or Madam: To whom it may concern:	

Letters of Complaint

When writing a formal letter of complaint, first state the reason you are writing and describe the problem. Then inform whomever you are writing what you would like him or her to do about it, or what *you* plan to do. The language and tone in your message should be formal and polite.

WRITING MODEL

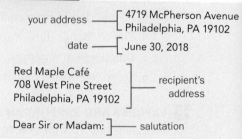

your address ⎡ 4719 McPherson Avenue
          ⎣ Philadelphia, PA 19102

date ⎡ June 30, 2018

Red Maple Café
708 West Pine Street   recipient's
Philadelphia, PA 19102   address

Dear Sir or Madam: ⎯ salutation

   I live a few blocks from your restaurant. For the past several months, I have noticed that in the evenings there is a lot of trash on the side of your building. Cats in the neighborhood turn over the garbage cans, and the trash goes everywhere. This is not only unpleasant to look at, but it is also a health hazard.

   Could you please make sure that when the trash is put out, the garbage cans are closed? Your helping keep our neighborhood clean and beautiful would be greatly appreciated.

Respectfully, ⎯ closing

Olivia Krum ⎯ signature
Olivia Krum

B PRACTICE Write a salutation appropriate for a formal letter to each of these people.

1 a teacher at a university whose family name is Smith ....

2 a company manager whose name you don't know ....

3 a female company manager whose family name is Costa ....

4 a male bank manager whose family name is Takata ....

5 a physician who manages a clinic and whose family name is Grimond ....

C APPLY THE WRITING SKILL On a separate sheet of paper, write a letter of complaint about a problem in your city or town. State what you would like to see done to fix the problem. Remember to be polite and appropriately formal.

OPTIONAL WRITING Exchange letters with a partner. Write an appropriate response to your partner's letter, as if you were the person to whom it was addressed.

SELF-CHECK

☐ Did I use the proper salutation and closing?

☐ Are the tone and language in my letter appropriate for the intended reader?

☐ Did I use regular spelling and punctuation and avoid abbreviations?

A ▶ 3:13 Listen carefully to each story. Infer the type of criminal being described and complete the statements with the details of the crime.

1 A .... took his .... while he was riding on a ....

2 A .... stole .... from her while she was walking with a ....

3 He saw a .... running down the street with a girl's ....

4 A .... broke into her .... and took her husband's ....

B Respond to each statement or question in your own way.

1 "Your texting during the movie kind of bothers me."

    You: ....

2 "Would you mind not smoking in here?"

    You: ....

3 "What bugs you about living in your town?"

    You: ....

4 "Who does things that really get to you?"

    You: ....

C Make each sentence logical by attaching a negative prefix to the adjective. Use a dictionary if necessary.

1 Smoking on public buses and trains is really ~~excusable~~. *inexcusable*

2 I believe littering and spitting on the street are both ~~responsible~~.

3 People who play loud music without consideration for the people around them are exhibiting really ~~proper~~ behavior.

4 I think it's ~~appropriate~~ for people to text their friends during movies.

5 When a salesperson is rude, I find it not only ~~respectful~~ but also annoying.

6 I should warn you that the air pollution downtown is really ~~pleasant~~.

7 I think it's ~~honest~~ to sell souvenirs to tourists at higher prices than people usually pay.

8 It doesn't help when people are ~~courteous~~ to each other.

D Combine the sentences, using paired conjunctions.

1 Restaurants shouldn't allow smoking. Theaters shouldn't allow smoking. (neither … nor)

    ....

2 Smoking should be banned. It should be restricted. (either … or)

    ....

3 Littering doesn't offend me. Spitting doesn't offend me. (neither … nor)

    ....

4 I think loud music is rude. I think loud people are rude. (Not only … but)

    ....

TEST-TAKING SKILLS BOOSTER p. 155

Web Project: Urban Communities
www.english.com/summit3e

COMMUNICATION GOALS

1 Exchange opinions about the treatment of animals
2 Discuss the pros and cons of certain pets
3 Compare animal and human behavior
4 Debate the value of animal conservation

PREVIEW

A **FRAME YOUR IDEAS** Complete the activity. With a partner, explain your choices.
Which categories of animals invite the most negative or positive responses?

YOUR ATTITUDES TOWARD / ANIMALS Write one or more of the adjectives below.

a bee

INVERTEBRATES

a spider

a worm

FISH

a goldfish

an eel

AMPHIBIANS

a salamander

a frog

BIRDS

a parrot

an eagle

a lion

an elephant

MAMMALS

a horse

REPTILES

a crocodile

a snake

a lizard

a rabbit

a monkey

a sheep

a dog

a mouse

a dolphin

ADJECTIVES
attractive cute dangerous disgusting energetic fascinating
frightening funny hardworking independent intelligent
lazy noisy patient quiet relaxed tasty ugly useful

B ▶ 3:14 **VOCABULARY** **CATEGORIES OF ANIMALS** Look at the categories and photos in Exercise A.
Listen and repeat.

C **DISCUSSION** Discuss the questions.

1 Would your responses have been different if any of the animals had been babies instead of adults? How?

2 Did any other physical factors affect your choices, such as color or size? In what ways?

3 Did any experiences you've had with any of these animals affect your choices? How?

D ▶ 3:15 **SPOTLIGHT** Read and listen to a conversation over lunch at an international meeting. Notice the spotlighted language.

Pam: Nice picture. Hey, are those your cats?

Karina: Yeah, they're my babies. We've had the gray one a long time. She's almost seventeen now.

Pam: No way! She still looks so healthy. What about the white one?

Karina: We think he's pretty young. Actually, he was hanging around outside our house all summer, and it didn't seem like anyone was taking care of him. We **felt sorry for** him, so we took him in.

Pam: Lucky cat! He looks like a member of the family now. But I'll bet the older one wasn't too crazy about having a new cat around.

Karina: Well, he thinks he's still a kitten; he just wants to play all the time. But I'd say she **puts up with** him pretty well. She's really patient.

Pam: From the picture, it looks like she's the one **in charge**.

Karina: Definitely. She doesn't fool around. If he gets too rough, she knows how to **put him in his place**. Hey, do you have any pets?

Pam: No, we don't. When we feel like being around animals, we go to the zoo.

Karina: Actually, I'm not too crazy about zoos. I just don't think animals should be **cooped up** in small cages.

Pam: Normally I'd agree with you. But our local zoo isn't like that at all. The larger mammals have plenty of outdoor space. It's pretty humane, I think.

Karina: Well, that's good. I guess we shouldn't just assume that animals in captivity aren't treated well.

E **UNDERSTAND IDIOMS AND EXPRESSIONS** Find each expression in Spotlight. Then complete the statements.

1 When Karina says they "felt sorry for" the younger cat, she means they ….. him.
  a apologized to   **b** were concerned about   **c** were annoyed with

2 When she says the older cat "puts up with" the younger one, she means the older cat ….. .
  a is annoyed with him   **b** accepts his behavior   **c** is concerned about him

3 When she says the gray cat is the one "in charge," she means the gray cat ….. .
  a obeys the white one   **b** is obeyed by the white one   **c** is older than the white one

4 When she says the gray cat put the white one "in his place," she means the gray one ….. .
  a is the boss   **b** isn't the boss   **c** is his friend

5 When she refers to animals being "cooped up in" cages, she means they ….. .
  a are made comfortable   **b** don't get to go outside   **c** often go outdoors

F **PAIR WORK** Choose one or more of these topics. Tell your partner about:
 • a time when you or someone you know felt sorry for an animal and took it in.
 • a time when someone's pet had to put up with another animal.
 • a home where the pet was the one in charge.

SPEAKING **GROUP WORK** Discuss the questions.

1 Do you care if an animal is cooped up in a cage? Why or why not? Are there times when an animal should be?

2 Which animals on page 62 do you think need lots of outdoor space? Why?

GOAL Exchange opinions about the treatment of animals

A ▶3:16 **GRAMMAR SPOTLIGHT** Read the social media posts. Notice the spotlighted grammar.

David Suchet   June 30 / Seattle, USA

I really feel sorry for animals that are mistreated. Does anyone else get as fed up as I do about their inhumane treatment? In my opinion, animals **should** never **be killed** just for sport or entertainment. Hunting, bullfighting, and any other "sport" that involves the killing of defenseless animals **should be** completely **banned**. And the idea that monkeys or dogs **have to be used** in medical research seems ridiculous to me. What do you all think? Is inhumane treatment of animals ever justified?

Reiko Yamamoto   July 1 / Atami, Japan

Maybe you're right about killing animals for sport, but don't you think the needs of people **should** sometimes **be considered**? For example, it seems clear to me that small mammals like mice or rabbits **have to be used** for medical research to make sure new medications are safe. It just **can't be avoided**. Otherwise, new medical treatments **might not be discovered**. We can't fool around when it comes to medicine.

Marie Colbert   July 1 / Lyon, France

I agree with Reiko—people first. But that doesn't mean animals **should be treated** inhumanely. I'm sure research methods **could be improved**. And recently I was reading about factory farms that raise chickens or beef cattle, and I was shocked at how crowded and filthy the conditions were. I know animals **have to be slaughtered** for food, but I'm sure they **could be raised** more humanely.

B **EVALUATE IDEAS**   Do you agree with any of the opinions expressed in the posts? Why or why not?

> **GRAMMAR BOOSTER** p. 134
> · Modals and modal-like expressions: summary

DIGITAL INDUCTIVE ACTIVITY

C **GRAMMAR** **PASSIVE MODALS**

Remember: We use the passive voice to focus on the receiver of an action rather than the person or thing that performs the action. Form passive modals with a modal + <u>be</u> and a past participle.

Conditions for cattle on factory farms	**could**	**be improved.**
Alternatives to using mice for research	**might**	**be found.**
The hunting of bears	**should**	**be prohibited.**
Traditions like bullfighting	**have to***	**be preserved.**

*Note: <u>Have to</u> is a modal-like expression, not a true modal. It has two present forms: <u>have</u> and <u>has</u>. It uses <u>Do</u> or <u>Does</u> in questions and <u>don't</u> and <u>doesn't</u> in negative statements.

<u>Yes</u> / <u>no</u> **questions**

Should chickens **be cooped up** in cages?
Can't factory chicken farms **be shut down**?
BUT **Do** large mammals **have to be kept** in zoos?

Information questions

Why **shouldn't** reptiles or amphibians **be used** for research?
Why **must** all animals' lives **be respected**?
How **might** people's attitudes **be changed**?

> **Remember:**
> **have to** = obligatory
> **don't have to** = not obligatory
> **must** OR **must not** = obligatory

D **NOTICE THE GRAMMAR**   Find one passive modal in Spotlight on page 63.

E **UNDERSTAND THE GRAMMAR**   With a partner, decide who the performer of the action
is. Then choose the active or passive voice to complete each statement.

1 People (should treat / should be treated) animals humanely.

2 Large mammals like lions (shouldn't keep / shouldn't be kept) in zoos.

3 In order to help people with disabilities, dogs (have to train / have to be trained) when they are young.

4 They say people (can teach / can be taught) bears to do tricks like dancing or standing up on command.

5 Horses (shouldn't force / shouldn't be forced) to run in races.

6 Sometimes, in order to protect people, aggressive dogs that live on the street (have to kill / have to be killed).

> ❝ In item 1, <u>people</u> is the performer of the action. ❞

F **GRAMMAR PRACTICE**   Write sentences, using passive modals.

1 People / shouldn't / allow to hunt elephants. ....

2 New medicines / might / discover through animal research. ....
....

3 Monkeys / shouldn't / keep as pets. ....

4 A lot / could / do to improve conditions for cattle on factory farms. ....
....

5 The treatment of research animals / must / improve. ....
....

6 Can't / zoos / use for performing scientific research to protect animals? ....
....

7 Why / chickens / have to / raise in such crowded conditions? ....
....

NOW YOU CAN | **Exchange opinions about the treatment of animals**

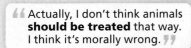

A **DISCUSSION ACTIVATOR**   Use the ideas to exchange
opinions with a partner about the ways animals
are used or treated. Ask and answer questions, using
passive modals. Say as much as you can.

> ❝ Do you think animals **have to be used**
> for medical research? I do. We can't
> experiment on humans, can we? ❞

> ❝ Actually, I don't think animals
> **should be treated** that way.
> I think it's morally wrong. ❞

B **SUMMARIZE THE DISCUSSION**
Compare your classmates' opinions
about the treatment of animals.
Does the majority of the class
share the same opinions?

Ideas

- using animals in medical research
- slaughtering animals for food
- keeping animals in zoos
- raising animals for sports, such as racing or fighting
- killing animals for their hides and fur

a fur coat

RECYCLE THIS LANGUAGE

Express an opinion
- I think [it's morally wrong].
- I believe [it's OK under some circumstances].
- I feel [it's wrong no matter what].
- I'm in favor of ____ .
- I'm opposed to ____ .

Disagree
- I see what you mean, but ____ .
- That's one way to look at it, but ____ .
- On the one hand ____ , but on the other hand ____ .
- I completely disagree.

Agree
- I couldn't agree with you more.
- I completely agree.
- You're so right.

GOAL Discuss the pros and cons of certain pets

DIGITAL STRATEGIES **A** ▶ 3:17 **VOCABULARY** **DESCRIBING PETS** Read and listen. Then listen again and repeat.

Positive traits	
playful	active and fun-loving
affectionate	friendly and loving
gentle / good-natured	easygoing; good with kids and other pets
low-maintenance	easy to care for and inexpensive to keep
loyal / devoted	attentive to its owner; reliable
protective	good at protecting its owner from danger

Negative traits	
high-strung / excitable	nervous; easily frightened
costly	expensive to buy and to take care of
destructive	harmful to furniture and other things
filthy	unclean; makes a mess
high-maintenance	time-consuming to take care of
aggressive	hard to control; possibly dangerous

Puppies are great for kids because they're affectionate and playful. However, they're also high-maintenance.

B ▶ 3:18 **LISTEN TO ACTIVATE VOCABULARY** Listen to each conversation and complete the chart with the pet and its pros and cons. Use the Vocabulary. Listen again if necessary.

	Pet	Possible pros	Possible cons
1			
2			
3			
4			

C **EXPRESS AND SUPPORT AN OPINION** Discuss the questions.

1 In what ways can an animal be a good companion to a child? An adult? An older person?

2 Do you know anyone who is too attached to his or her pet? Why do you think some people get emotionally close to their animals?

D **GROUP WORK** Use the vocabulary to tell your classmates about your past or present pets or about those of people you know.

PRONUNCIATION BOOSTER p. 145

Sound reduction

A ▶ 3:19 **CONVERSATION SPOTLIGHT** Read and listen. Notice the spotlighted conversation strategies.

A: Do you think a poodle would make a good pet?
B: Actually, I'm not so sure. **I've heard** they're really high-maintenance.
A: **In what way?**
B: Well, **for one thing**, they need a lot of attention. I'd consider getting a guinea pig instead.
A: Why a guinea pig?
B: Well, they're very low-maintenance. **And besides,** they're really gentle.
A: **But what if** you were looking for something a bit more affectionate than a guinea pig?
B: Then I'd get a cat. They're affectionate *and* they're low-maintenance.

a poodle

a guinea pig

B ▶ 3:20 **RHYTHM AND INTONATION** Listen again and repeat. Then practice the conversation with a partner.

C **NOTEPADDING** With a partner, complete the chart with animals that make good and bad pets. Explain why, using the Vocabulary. Choose animals from page 62 or others you know.

Animals that make exceptionally good pets	Reasons

Animals that make really bad pets	Reasons

D **CONVERSATION ACTIVATOR**
Create a conversation similar to the one in Exercise A, using the information on your notepad. Start like this: *Do you think a __ would make a good pet?* Be sure to change roles and then partners.

DON'T STOP!
• Make more suggestions.
• Describe the pros and cons of other pets.
• Say as much as you can.

RECYCLE THIS LANGUAGE
· attractive   · funny
· cute   · intelligent
· dangerous   · noisy
· disgusting   · patient
· energetic   · quiet
· fascinating   · ugly
· frightening

GOAL Compare animal and human behavior

A ▶ 3:21 **LISTENING WARM-UP** VOCABULARY: ANIMAL SOCIAL GROUPS AND PROTECTIVE PHYSICAL FEATURES
Read and listen. Then listen again and repeat.

ANIMAL SOCIAL GROUPS

a flock of birds

a herd of cattle

a school of fish

a pack of wolves

PHYSICAL FEATURES

claws

hooves (singular: a hoof)

a beak

horns

B **APPLY NEW VOCABULARY** Complete the chart with a partner.

Animals with claws	Animals with hooves	Animals with horns
Birds with powerful beaks	**Animals that travel in packs**	**Animals that gather in herds**

C ▶ 3:22 **LISTEN TO DEFINE TERMS** Listen to Part 1 of the lecture to answer this question:
What is the difference between an animal that is a predator and one that is prey?

D ▶ 3:23 **LISTEN FOR EXAMPLES** Listen to Part 1 of the lecture again. With a partner, find
an example from the listening to explain each of the following:

1 a benefit of a social group for animals of prey ....

2 a benefit of a social group for predators ....

3 the role of a dominant animal in a social group ....

4 the meaning of "fight or flight" ....

E ▶ 3:24 **LISTEN FOR DETAILS** Now listen to Part 2 of the lecture and answer the questions.

1 What is the difference between learned behavior and instinct?

2 What are two examples of learned behavior from the lecture?

F **THINK AND EXPLAIN** Which of these situations do you think illustrate learned behavior as opposed to instinct? Explain your reasons, based on information from the lecture.

A
Hungry baby birds open their beaks wide so that an adult will put a worm inside.

B
Baby rabbits quickly follow their mother away from a potential predator.

C
Young cats respond to perceived danger by getting ready to run away or to fight.

G **APPLY IDEAS** Discuss the questions.

1 Look at the animals in Preview on page 62. Which are predators and which are prey? Which are both?

2 What are some ways in which you think humans behave: a) like herd animals or flocks or b) like animals who socialize in packs? Provide examples.

NOW YOU CAN Compare animal and human behavior

A **NOTEPADDING** In what ways do you think humans are the same as other animals? In what ways do you think we're completely different? Write some ideas.

How we're the same or similar	How we're very different
Groups provide safety and social interaction.	Humans are more able to respond to danger using their intelligence.

How we're the same or similar	How we're very different

B **DISCUSSION** Share your ideas with your classmates. Do you think we have more similarities to or differences from other animals? Use the examples from your notepad.

RECYCLE THIS LANGUAGE

· aggressive
· dangerous
· devoted
· in charge
· intelligent
· patient
· protective
· useful

A **READING WARM-UP** What are some endangered animals you can think of? What are some threats to their survival?

DIGITAL STRATEGIES **B** ▶ 3:25 **READING** Read the stories. What do you think ensured the survival of the buffalo in the U.S.?

an American bison

The Will to **Make a Difference**

We live on a planet that is rich in biodiversity—there are millions of different species of animals and plants across the globe. Yet many species are disappearing at an alarming rate as the habitats in which plants and animals live together are reduced year after year. Currently, 11,000 species of plants and animals—including over 180 mammals—are at risk of becoming extinct because of this loss of habitat. Once gone, their disappearance is irreversible—they cannot be brought back. In its fast development as a nation over the last three hundred years, the United States has experienced some dramatic shifts in animal populations. Here is the story of a dismal failure and a remarkable success story.

The **Passenger Pigeon** FAILURE

Early European visitors to North America told amazing stories about huge flocks of passenger pigeons that darkened the sky for hours as they flew south for winter. They were easy targets for hunters, delicious to eat, and useful for making feather beds. Estimates put their total population at about five billion—the same number as the population of all birds combined in the U.S. today.

By the mid-1800s, the hunting of passenger pigeons had become a large-scale commercial enterprise, supplying east coast cities with a steady supply of birds. Around 300,000 a year were sent to New York City alone. At the same time, their habitat and food sources were shrinking as forests were cut down for farming and construction. In addition, approximately 250,000 birds were killed simply for sport each year. Making matters worse, a female passenger pigeon laid only one egg each year. By the turn of the twentieth century, any attempts to save the passenger pigeon were too late. The last surviving pigeon died in the Cincinnati Zoo in 1914—a species lost forever.

The **American Bison** (or **Buffalo**) SUCCESS

Before European settlers came to North America, there were more than 50 million buffalo roaming in huge herds across the continent's central flatlands, which are today known as the Great Plains. These strange-looking, magnificent creatures—with their furry heads and shoulders and distinctive horns—were an important resource for food, clothing, and shelter for Native Americans living on the plains. And they played an enormous part in the plains ecosystem, sustaining other animals and plants. Weaker buffalo provided food for predators like bears and wolves. Herds attracted birds that picked at buffalo fur for insects. Thousands of hooves walking over the landscape prevented aggressive plants from taking over.

Buffalo hides were important in Native American life, including for shelter.

In the 1800s, as new settlers moved from the East to settle the West, whole herds were slaughtered, often just for sport. Buffalo were considered an obstacle to the settlers' desire to grow crops and raise cattle. The resource that sustained Native Americans for centuries began to disappear. By the end of the 1800s, there were as few as 750 buffalo remaining.

Many people were shocked that the buffalo, long considered a symbol of the West, had been allowed to come so close to extinction. Fortunately, efforts to save them were begun in 1905. The remaining herds were gathered together and protected. Their number steadily increased to today's population of about 350,000.

What conclusion can we draw from these stories?

In the case of the passenger pigeon, extinction was occurring so fast that, even with efforts to save them, it was too late to act. However, we can see that with the American buffalo, conservation efforts can make a difference if they are begun early enough.

C UNDERSTAND MEANING FROM CONTEXT Choose the correct meaning for each word.

1 biodiversity
  a the place where animals live
  b the variety of living things
  c the disappearance of a species

2 a habitat
  a the food animals eat
  b the place animals live
  c the number of species

3 extinction
  a the protection of a species
  b the hunting of a species
  c the disappearance of a species

4 conservation
  a the protection of animals from extinction
  b a danger to animals
  c a source of food

5 an ecosystem
  a a danger to animals
  b the protection of a species
  c a community of living things

D RECOGNIZE CAUSE AND EFFECT Discuss these questions with a partner.

DIGITAL
EXTRA
CHALLENGE

1 What are four reasons the passenger pigeon became extinct? Why did conservation efforts fail?

2 Why did settlers hunt the buffalo? How did the buffalo come so close to extinction?

NOW YOU CAN Debate the value of animal conservation

A FRAME YOUR IDEAS With a partner, read and discuss the arguments for and against animal conservation. Which arguments are the strongest for each side of the animal conservation debate? Which are the weakest?

For	Against
• Human beings have a responsibility to protect all living things.	• Extinctions are simply part of the natural process—it's the principle of "survival of the fittest."
• Species should be preserved for future generations.	• Environmental protection costs a lot of money. It's "a luxury" for countries that have more serious problems.
• Natural parks that protect wildlife are big tourist attractions that generate jobs and income for local economies.	• Millions of species have already become extinct with no significant impact on the environment—it's no big deal.
• Species extinction is happening at such a fast rate we'd be foolish not to act quickly.	• Conservation limits land available to farmers, who really need it for their livelihood.
• For every species lost to extinction, humans miss the chance to make new discoveries—for example, new medicines.	• Do we really need 2,000 species of mice?
• Your own ideas: ……………………………………	• Your own ideas: ……………………………………

DIGITAL
SPEAKING
BOOSTER

B DEBATE Form two groups—one for and one against this statement: *It's important to protect all species of animals from extinction.* Take turns presenting and supporting your views with reasons and examples.

❝I don't see why we should worry about conserving one type of endangered frog or salamander. There are many other kinds that are not endangered.❞

❝But the extinction of one type of frog could affect mammals and reptiles that may depend on that species for food.❞

OPTIONAL WRITING Write at least two paragraphs about the reasons some animals become endangered. Describe the threats to their survival and what can be done to save them.

❝Come to think of it, you have a point!❞

RECYCLE THIS LANGUAGE
· amphibians
· birds
· fish
· invertebrates
· mammals
· reptiles

A WRITING SKILL Study the rules.

To persuade readers to agree with your point of view in an essay:

· State your point of view in the introduction to your essay.
· Then provide examples, facts, or experts' opinions that support your point of view.
· Another effective technique is to demonstrate the weakness of opposing arguments.
· Summarize your main point in a concluding sentence.

Use expressions like these to support your point of view.
Pay attention to correct punctuation when needed.

Support your point of view	Offer experts' opinions
For one thing, For example, For instance, Furthermore,	[Smith] states that … According to [Rivera], … Studies suggest that …

Refute opposing arguments	Conclude your argument
It can be argued that … [Some people] think … } However, It [may be] true that …	In conclusion, In summary, To sum up,

WRITING MODEL

Many people question whether it's humane to keep animals in zoos. However, **today's zoos can play an important role in animal conservation.** They can do this in a number of ways.

For one thing, studies suggest that animal conservation research and observation may be conducted more easily in zoos. In that way, new methods for ensuring the survival of endangered species might be discovered. **Furthermore,** in her report on conservation efforts at the Parkland Zoo, **biologist Ann Fisher states that** zoos can protect the young of endangered species until they are old enough to be released into the wild. **It can be argued that** all animals should be free and that it is unethical to keep any animals in zoos. **However,** the survival of these species in the wild may actually depend on the results of the scientific studies many zoos provide.

In conclusion, I believe endangered animals should be kept in zoos in order to support conservation efforts. It's one way that we can help ensure their survival.

B PRACTICE Complete the arguments to support the point of view.

Zoos can play an increasingly important role in animal conservation.
1 (For one thing, / However,) a zoo is a good environment for scientists to observe the behavior of endangered animals. Information from this research can be used to ensure their survival. **2** (Many people think / For example,) animals are simply cooped up in cages at zoos. **3** (Furthermore, / However,) today's modern zoos try to imitate their natural habitats by providing healthy food and lots of space for exercise and play. Without this intervention, many species would not survive in the wild. **4** (According to / To sum up) Dutch scientist Frans de Wall, zoos also serve an important educational purpose.
5 (Furthermore, / For example,) by visiting zoos with their families or school classes, children learn about endangered animals and grow up appreciating the importance of protecting them. **6** (To sum up, / It may be true that) there are good reasons for keeping endangered animals in zoos.

C APPLY THE WRITING SKILL Write a short essay in which you express your opinion on the treatment of animals on farms or in research. Use persuasion to get the reader to agree with your point of view. State your point of view in the introduction. Support it with examples, facts, or experts' opinions. Refute opposing arguments. Conclude by restating your main point.

OPTIONAL WRITING Exchange paragraphs with a partner. Do you agree or disagree with your partner's point of view? Write a short response, explaining why. Start like this: *I [agree / disagree] with your argument because …*

SELF-CHECK

☐ Did I state my point of view clearly in the introduction?

☐ Did I provide examples, facts, or experts' opinions to support my point of view?

☐ Did I discuss opposing arguments?

☐ Did I include a concluding sentence?

A ▶ 3:26 **Listen to Part 1 of a radio program. Choose the phrase that best completes each statement, according to the program.**

1 Capuchin monkeys can be ....
   a used for medical research   **b** loyal friends to humans   **c** trained to help people with disabilities

2 These monkeys are useful to humans because they ....
   a can do simple jobs   **b** can push a wheelchair   **c** can wash dishes

B ▶ 3:27 **Now listen to Part 2 and choose the phrase that best completes each statement.**

1 Dolphin-assisted therapy had a positive effect on children's ....
   a moral or ethical development   **b** speech development   **c** physical development

2 Children respond to dolphins because dolphins are ....
   a good swimmers   **b** intelligent   **c** playful

3 Many of these children respond better to people after ....
   a a year of treatment   **b** a few treatments   **c** a few weeks of treatment

C **Change the adjective in each statement so it makes sense.**

1 A relaxed pet that is good with kids is ~~destructive~~. ....

2 A cat that often scratches people with its claws is ~~affectionate~~. ....

3 A pet that is loving and friendly is ~~aggressive~~. ....

4 A dog that damages furniture is ~~playful~~. ....

5 An animal that is easy to care for is ~~filthy~~. ....

6 A dog that is easily frightened is ~~protective~~. ....

7 A pet that is expensive to buy and take care of is ~~good-natured~~. ....

8 A parrot that has fun holding a ball in its beak is ~~loyal~~. ....

D **Complete each statement with vocabulary from the unit.**

1 Passenger pigeons used to fly together in very large ....

2 A cat is a mammal, and a frog is an ....

3 Dogs that do not have owners sometimes hang out together in ....

4 Lions use their teeth and .... to kill their prey.

5 Buffalo have a pair of .... on their furry heads.

6 An eel is a kind of fish, and a crocodile is a kind of ....

7 Dominant male sheep fight with their horns to choose who will be the one in charge of the ....

8 Humans have feet, and horses have ....

9 A bird may use its .... to protect itself from a predator.

E **Choose four of the topics. Use passive modals to state your own opinion about each topic.**

Topics
medical research   dog fighting   pets
hunting   extinction   zoos

Example: *Hunting should be banned because it is inhumane.*..............................

1 ....

2 ....

3 ....

4 ....

TEST-TAKING SKILLS BOOSTER p. 156

Web Project: Treatment of Animals
www.english.com/summit3e

Advertising and Consumers

A FRAME YOUR IDEAS   Read four examples of shopping behavior and rate them.

READ ABOUT FOUR SHOPPING MISTAKES.

Number the mistakes in order of seriousness, from 1 to 4, with 4 being the most serious.

When I'm feeling blue, it cheers me up to go shopping and splurge on a few luxury items.

I may have gone a little overboard this time. But I just can't pass up a good sale, even if I don't need anything at the moment.

Everyone's buying it, so it must be terrific. I guess I'll buy it, too.

When I see a famous person I respect endorsing a product, then I know it's good.

B DISCUSSION   In your opinion, what causes people to behave in the ways the people in the pictures do? In what way is their behavior similar? Do you know anyone like these people? Explain.

C ▶ 4:01 **SPOTLIGHT** Read and listen to a conversation between two colleagues. Notice the spotlighted language.

Aldo: Oh, no! **I could kick myself!**

Sofia: About what?

Aldo: You know how much I've been wanting to learn Spanish, right? Look at this great system I could have gotten for half price. Well, until yesterday, that is.

Sofia: Oh, come on. **Don't fall for that.** You can't learn a language while you sleep.

Aldo: I don't know. They say it's based on brain science. And it's risk-free. You get your money back if you don't learn. So it must be true.

Sofia: Oh, Aldo. **That's just wishful thinking.** Think about how long it took you to learn English.

Aldo: But **you're comparing apples and oranges.** Learning Spanish is a whole lot easier than learning English for Italian speakers like me.

Sofia: **That's debatable.** Not everyone would agree with that. But whatever. Any new language takes plenty of study and practice.

Aldo: I know. But I hate being forced to learn grammar. In this method I don't think you have to.

Sofia: Sorry. **There are no two ways about it.** Learning a language takes work … . **Tell you what.** I'll teach you Spanish myself! Between now and the end of the year, we'll have dinner together a couple of evenings a week. We'll converse in Spanish. You'll learn fast.

Aldo: You really mean it? I'd be willing to pay you for the lessons.

Sofia: No way. Just make me a nice Italian dinner on those nights, and **we'll call it even.** It'll be fun!

Aldo: Dinner? No problem! I'd be making that anyway… . Sofia, this is really generous of you.

Sofia: Well, you've done me a bunch of favors at work. I figure **I owe you one!**

RISK FREE! *Miracle Method*

Be fluent in Spanish in 6 weeks. Just listen while you sleep.

HURRY! Half-price offer ends November 15th.

Your money back if you can't speak Spanish by December 31st.

D **UNDERSTAND IDIOMS AND EXPRESSIONS** Write an expression from Spotlight with a similar meaning to each sentence below.

1 I'm going to suggest something to you.
....

2 You won't owe me anything. ....
....

3 These two things are completely different.
....

4 There is more than one opinion about that.
....

5 I regret something I did. ....

6 There's only one correct opinion about that.
....

7 Don't believe what they say. ....

8 You are hoping that it's true, but it isn't.
....

9 It's my turn to do something nice for you.
....

E **THINK AND EXPLAIN** With a partner, answer each question. Support your answers with specific information from Spotlight.

1 What is it about the ad that makes Aldo want to kick himself?

2 What does Sofia think of the Miracle Method?

3 What do you think Aldo hates about traditional language courses? Explain why.

SPEAKING **PAIR WORK** Discuss whether you think any of the people in the pictures on page 74 have anything in common with Aldo. Explain your reasons.

GOAL Evaluate ways and places to shop

A ▶ 4:02 **VOCABULARY** **VERBS FOR SHOPPING ACTIVITIES** Read and listen to what the people are saying. Then listen and repeat.

browse take one's time looking at things without necessarily wanting to buy anything

bargain hunt look around for things one can buy cheaply for less than their usual price

comparison shop look at the prices of the same or similar items in order to decide which to buy

window shop look at things in store windows without going inside or intending to buy them

B ▶ 4:03 **LISTEN TO ACTIVATE VOCABULARY** Listen to the conversations about shopping. Infer what the people are doing. Complete each statement with the correct verb phrase.

1 The shoppers are (browsing / bargain hunting).

2 The people are (comparison shopping / window shopping).

3 The men are (window shopping / comparison shopping).

4 The woman is (window shopping / browsing).

PAIR WORK First, complete the chart. Then compare information with a partner.

Activity	When and why you do this activity
browsing	
bargain hunting	
window shopping	
comparison shopping	

> **"** I go window shopping when I have time on my hands and don't feel like spending money. **"**

NOW YOU CAN Evaluate ways and places to shop

A ▶ 4:04 **CONVERSATION SPOTLIGHT** Read and listen. Notice the spotlighted conversation strategies.

A: Quick question. Where would you go if you needed some new furniture?

B: Well, **I find** Morton's a good place to go bargain hunting.

A: Morton's? They can be a little pricey, can't they?

B: But when their things go on sale their prices are rock bottom.

A: That's good to know.

B: Why don't you check out Morton's online? Maybe you'll get lucky.

B ▶ 4:05 **RHYTHM AND INTONATION** Listen again and repeat. Then practice the conversation with a partner.

C **NOTEPADDING** Make a list of four places to shop, the best items to buy in each place, and the best shopping activities there.

place	items to buy there	ways to shop there
the public market	handicrafts and gifts	bargain hunt

	place	items to buy there	ways to shop there
1			
2			
3			
4			

D **CONVERSATION ACTIVATOR**
Create a conversation similar to the one in Ex. A, using information from your notepad. Start like this: *Quick question. Where ...* Be sure to change roles and then partners.

DON'T STOP!
- Discuss other places for bargains.
- Ask for recommendations for places to buy other things.
- Suggest shopping together.
- Say as much as you can.

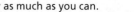

RECYCLE THIS LANGUAGE	
· expensive	· a bargain
· cheap	· save money
· affordable	· cost an arm and a leg
· pricey	· rock bottom

GOAL Discuss your reactions to ads

A ▶4:06 **GRAMMAR SPOTLIGHT** Read the interviews. Notice the spotlighted grammar.

What's the most annoying commercial or ad you've ever seen?

That would be the toothpaste ad they keep playing on my favorite music station. It's loud and obnoxious, and it totally gets on my nerves. I hate **to be forced** to listen to a dumb ad over and over. It just drives me crazy.

Nadia Basri, English teacher Amman, Jordan

What's the funniest ad you've ever seen?

There's this one really funny TV commercial for a language school. This cat sticks its claw into a goldfish bowl. Suddenly, the goldfish starts barking like an angry dog and the terrified cat runs away. The words "It never hurts to know another language" appear on the screen. It just cracks me up every time I see it. I enjoy **being entertained** like that.

Alex Winston, architect Pusan, South Korea

What's the most interesting ad you've ever seen?

An ad I saw yesterday really blew me away. There's this company that produces sports drinks. Their ad presents actual statistics of how the drink enhances athletic performance. It was so convincing I totally forgot it was an ad! Like most people, I resent simply **being sold to** and really appreciate **being informed** about a product's benefits. Ads like that can really build goodwill for a product.

Theresa Selden, advertising executive Minneapolis, USA

What's the most touching ad you've ever seen?

Actually, there's a billboard for a tablet that I see on my way to work. It shows this elderly woman having a video chat with her daughter and brand-new granddaughter. The tablet and the video chat are obviously something really new for the grandma. I'm not an emotional guy, but this ad just hits me in the heart and chokes me up. I know it's just an ad, but once in a while it doesn't hurt **to be reminded** about the important things in life.

Marcos Teixeira, medical student Fortaleza, Brazil

B **UNDERSTAND MEANING FROM CONTEXT** Match the expressions with their meaning.

.... **1** It blows me away.

.... **2** It gets on my nerves.

.... **3** It cracks me up.

.... **4** It chokes me up.

a It makes me feel like crying.

b It annoys me.

c It amazes me.

d It makes me want to laugh.

> **Remember:**
> • Some verbs are followed by gerunds, some by infinitives, and some by either.
> • Certain adjectives are often followed by infinitives.
> • Certain expressions are followed by gerunds.
> See pages 123–124 for a complete list.

C **GRAMMAR** PASSIVE FORMS OF GERUNDS AND INFINITIVES

DIGITAL INDUCTIVE ACTIVITY

Use the passive form of a gerund (being + a past participle) or an infinitive (to be + a past participle) to focus on an action instead of on who performed the action.

Gerunds: affirmative and negative
I don't like **being forced** to watch commercials.
Susan hates **not being told** the truth.

Infinitives: affirmative and negative
We would like **to be called** when it goes on sale.
They were angry **not to be told** about the meeting.

Questions
Do you enjoy **being entertained** by commercials on TV?
Don't you resent **being required** to watch ads in movie theaters?
Doesn't your sister want **to be called** by her first name?
Who likes **being shown** commercials every few minutes?
Where do you like **being seated** in a restaurant?

> **GRAMMAR BOOSTER** p. 136
> The passive voice: review and expansion

D **GRAMMAR PRACTICE**   Complete the conversations with passive gerunds or infinitives.

1 A: I think people enjoy (informed) .... about new products.

   B: True, but I don't want (treat) .... as if I don't know anything. Advertisers sometimes make me feel that way.

2 A: I don't like (show) .... pictures of suffering animals in ads for animal charities. They're just too upsetting.

   B: I agree. I'm happy (ask) .... to contribute just based on the facts. I don't need (show) .... pictures.

3 A: This midnight sale is going to be great. Don't you love (give) .... a chance to get everything at half-price?

   B: Actually, I'm annoyed at (force) .... to wait in line all day and evening just to get in.

4 A: When I read an ad in a magazine, I would like (tell) .... the whole truth, not half-truths.

   B: I know how you feel. I expect (treat) .... with respect.

5 A: Companies want their products (advertise) .... on TV during prime time—when the most people are watching.

   B: Maybe that's why advertisers complain about (charge) .... so much for every minute they buy. They say that's why the products are so expensive.

PRONUNCIATION
BOOSTER   p. 146

Vowel sounds /i/ and /ɪ/

E **GRAMMAR PRACTICE**   Rewrite each sentence, using a passive gerund or infinitive to replace the underlined words. Don't use a by phrase.

Example: I don't mind when advertisers inform me about new products.

1 I can't stand advertisers' forcing me to watch ads over and over again.

2 I resent one company's telling me that I shouldn't buy another company's product.

3 We can't tolerate telemarketers' calling us while we're eating dinner.

I don't mind being informed about new products.

Types of ads
• TV commercials
• pop-up ads on websites
• radio ads
• magazine or newspaper ads
• billboards on highways and buildings
• other online ads

NOW YOU CAN   Discuss your reactions to ads

A **FRAME YOUR IDEAS**   Complete the chart with ads you are familiar with.

	Name or type of product	Type of ad
An ad that's interesting		
An ad that cracks me up		
An ad that gets on my nerves		
An ad that blows me away		
An ad that chokes me up		
An ad that drives me crazy		

B **DISCUSSION ACTIVATOR**   Describe and compare the ads on your chart. Use passive forms of gerunds and infinitives. Say as much as you can.

“There's a TV commercial for shampoo that really gets on my nerves. I'm sick of being forced to watch it over and over!”

Describing how you feel
• I like ...
• I appreciate ...
• I love ...
• I enjoy ...
• I hate ...
• I prefer ...
• I need ...

• I don't like ...
• I don't appreciate ...
• I can't stand ...
• I dislike ...
• I resent ...
• I miss ...
• I want ...

GOAL Discuss problem shopping behavior

A READING WARM-UP Are you a careful shopper? Or do you lack self-control when you shop?

DIGITAL STRATEGIES **B ▶ 4:07 READING** Read the article. In what ways is compulsive shopping a problem?

COMPULSIVE SHOPPING: An addiction or just something to get under control?

For some people, shopping is a favorite pastime and harmless, as long as they have the money to pay for their purchases. For others, unfortunately, shopping can spiral out of control and become as serious as other destructive addictions like alcoholism, drug abuse, and compulsive gambling.

Research has shown that compulsive shopping, like other addictions, causes the physical effect of a "high," when brain chemicals such as endorphins and dopamine are released. This causes the addict to feel pleasurable sensations. These sensations make shopping hard to resist, and thus the habit hard to kick. What are the warning signs of a shopping addiction, or as it is sometimes called, "shopaholism"?

First, just as alcoholics tend to hide their bottles, shopaholics commonly hide their purchases. Shopaholics often lie to people in their families about how much money they've spent.

Second, the problem is long-lived, or "chronic," meaning that the behavior doesn't occur just once or twice a year. Rather, it's a continuous problem that repeats itself over and over.

Third, shopaholics, like many people, purchase items on impulse. But unlike normal people who sometimes splurge and pick up an impulse item like a sweater they don't need, shopaholics might buy ten.

Fourth, as with any addiction, a problem exists when the behavior has obvious consequences: going into debt, going shopping instead of taking care of family or work responsibilities, or uncontrollable spending that may deprive others in the family of money needed for other things.

What can true shopaholics do to get help? For some, self-help and group programs can be effective. For others, whose addiction results from underlying depression, seeing a psychotherapist or a physician can help, reducing the need to shop compulsively.

Thankfully, many people are able to splurge or buy things on impulse from time to time without being addicts. However, if you are concerned you may be a compulsive shopper, here are some tips that can help.

- Shop with a list. It keeps you focused on the things you really need and want. And it ensures that you don't get distracted by impulse items and go overboard, buying a lot of unneeded things.

- Avoid sales, coupons, and special offers. Spending any money on something you don't need is overspending, even if it's a bargain. Remember: Special offers are a way for store owners to get you into the store.

- Follow the "thinking time" rule: Don't buy anything new on the spot. Make yourself wait a day, a week, or some other amount of time before making a purchase. Or do some comparison-shopping. You may find you don't want the item after all, or you may find it at a much better price.

- Always try to be aware of your motivations when you shop. Don't go shopping when you're angry or upset. In the long run, the problem that upset you in the first place will still be there.

C UNDERSTAND MEANING FROM CONTEXT Find each of these words and phrases in the article. With a partner, discuss what they mean and write a sentence using each one.

1 an addiction
2 get something under control
3 a high
4 hard to kick
5 a shopaholic
6 chronic
7 splurge
8 go overboard
9 on the spot

D **IDENTIFY SUPPORTING DETAILS** Answer the questions, providing details from the article to support your answer.

1 In what ways is compulsive shopping like other addictions? Be specific.

2 Why are addictions so hard to overcome?

3 What are some consequences of shopaholism?

4 What is one possible cause for compulsive shopping in some people?

5 In what way is going overboard occasionally different from a true shopping addiction?

NOW YOU CAN Discuss problem shopping behavior

A **FRAME YOUR IDEAS** Check the statements that are true for you.

What kind of SHOPPER are you?

Everyone goes a little overboard shopping from time to time. Take the survey to determine if your shopping is out of control.

◯ I could sometimes kick myself for how I spend my money.

◯ When I go shopping, I can't resist the temptation to buy something—I just can't come home empty-handed.

◯ I feel uncomfortable if I haven't bought anything in a week.

◯ I go shopping for an item I need, but I lose control and come home with a lot of things I don't need.

◯ I spend more than I should in order to get more expensive designer names and labels.

◯ I can't pass up a good sale. Even if I don't need anything, I just have to indulge myself and buy something.

◯ I sometimes lie to people about how much my purchases cost.

◯ I get more pleasure out of spending money than saving money.

◯ I don't have the patience to wait a day before buying something. If I want it, I buy it on the spot.

TOTAL THE NUMBER OF BOXES YOU CHECKED. IF YOUR TOTAL IS:

0–3 Great!
Keep up the good habits!

4–5 Not too bad!
Congratulations for admitting you're not perfect!

6–7 Uh-oh!
Sounds like trouble may be around the corner!

8–9 Red alert!
It's time to take the bull by the horns and change some of the ways you shop and spend money.

B **DISCUSSION** Choose one of the topics and meet in small groups with other classmates who have chosen the same topic. Share your conclusions with the class.

1 Do you think most people tend to go a little overboard with their shopping? Explain.

2 Do you think people should spend money only on things they need and never on things they don't need? Is it OK to buy on impulse sometimes?

RECYCLE THIS LANGUAGE
- That's debatable.
- You're comparing apples and oranges.
- There are no two ways about it.
- That's just wishful thinking.
- You really mean it?
- Whatever.

OPTIONAL WRITING Write a brochure offering help or advice for people with problem shopping behavior. Include a list of tips.

81

GOAL Persuade someone to buy a product

A **LISTENING WARM-UP** **PAIR WORK** Read about eight advertising techniques used to persuade people to buy products. With a partner, discuss the techniques and write the letter of the example that illustrates each technique.

8 Eight techniques used by SUCCESSFUL ADVERTISERS

1 PROVIDE FACTS AND FIGURES
Prove the superiority of a product with statistics and objective, factual information. ☐

2 CONVINCE PEOPLE TO "JUMP ON THE BANDWAGON"
Imply that *everyone* is using a product, and that others should too, in order to be part of the group. ☐

3 PLAY ON PEOPLE'S HIDDEN FEARS
Imply that a product will protect the user from some danger or an uncomfortable situation. ☐

4 PLAY ON PEOPLE'S PATRIOTISM
Imply that buying a product shows love of one's country. ☐

5 PROVIDE "SNOB APPEAL"
Imply that use of a product makes the customer part of an elite group. ☐

6 ASSOCIATE POSITIVE QUALITIES WITH A PRODUCT
Promote a product with words and ideas having positive meanings and associations. ☐

7 PROVIDE TESTIMONIALS
Use a famous person or an "average consumer" to endorse a product so the consumer wants it too. ☐

8 MANIPULATE PEOPLE'S EMOTIONS
Use images to appeal to customers' feelings, such as love, anger, or sympathy. ☐

Examples

a A professional soccer player recommends a particular brand of shirts.

b A hotel chain shows a businesswoman in her room, calling home to talk to her children.

c A soft drink manufacturer shows young people having a great time drinking its product at the beach.

d A car manufacturer states how quickly its car can go from 0 to 100 kilometers per hour.

e A coffee manufacturer shows people dressed in formal attire drinking its brand of coffee at an art exhibition.

f A credit card company claims that its card is used by more people than any other card.

g A clothing manufacturer promotes its clothes by saying they are made by and for people in this country.

h An educational toy company suggests that other children will do better in school than yours will if you don't buy its toy today.

B ▶ 4:08 **VOCABULARY** **WAYS TO PERSUADE** Listen and repeat. Then, based on the way they are used in Exercise A, write the correct word for each definition.

endorse
promote
imply
prove

1 personally recommend a product in exchange for payment: ....

2 show that something is definitely true, especially by providing facts, information, etc.: ....

3 suggest that something is true, without saying or showing it directly: ....

4 make sure people know about a new product in order to persuade them to buy it: ....

C ▶ 4:09 **LISTEN TO INFER** Listen to each ad. Write two techniques from Exercise A that the advertiser uses in the ad. Then listen again and take notes of what the ad says to support your choice of techniques.

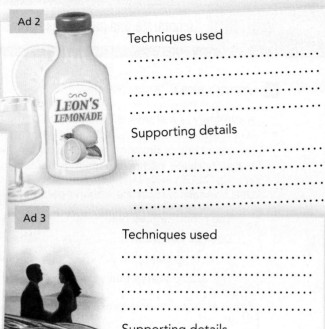

Ad 2

Techniques used

....
....
....

Supporting details

....
....
....

Ad 1

Techniques used

....
....
....

Supporting details

....
....
....

Ad 3

Techniques used

....
....

Supporting details

....
....
....
....

D **APPLY IDEAS** With a partner, discuss some ads you know and decide which techniques they use.

NOW YOU CAN Persuade someone to buy a product

A **NOTEPADDING** In a group, choose a product and create a magazine, newspaper, Internet pop-up, or radio advertisement for it. Use one or more advertising techniques to persuade your classmates to buy the product. Make notes.

Ideas
- a car
- an airline
- a drink
- a smart phone
- a language school
- a brand of toothpaste
- your own idea: _____

Plan your ad

Type of product:

Name of product:

Type of ad:

Technique(s):

B **PRESENTATION** Present your ad to your class. Show it, read it, or act it out. Analyze your classmates' ads and discuss which techniques were used. As a class, assign awards for these categories:

- the funniest ad
- the most annoying ad
- the most persuasive ad
- the most interesting ad
- the most touching ad

A **WRITING SKILL** Study the rules.

A summary is a shortened explanation of the main ideas of an article. When writing a summary, include only the author's main points, not your own reactions or opinions. In your summary, be sure to paraphrase what the author said, putting the main idea into your own words.

Use a variety of reporting verbs to paraphrase the writer's ideas:

The report **argues** that …   The writer **points out** that …

Doctors **believe** that …   The journalist **reports** that …

Experts **explain** that …   The author **concludes** that …

The article **states** that …

Some other common expressions for reporting another person's ideas:

According to [Smith], …   **As** [the article explains], …

In [the writer's] **opinion**, …   **From** [García's] **point of view**, …

MODEL

The original text: "For some people, shopping is a favorite pastime and harmless, as long as they have the money to pay for their purchases. For others, unfortunately, shopping can spiral out of control and become as serious as other destructive addictions like alcoholism, drug abuse, and compulsive gambling."

Your summary and paraphrase:
The author points out that shopping can be harmless for some but a serious addiction for others.

B **PRACTICE** Paraphrase these sentences from the article on page 80.

1 "Research has shown that compulsive shopping, like other addictions, causes the physical effects of a "high," when brain chemicals, such as endorphins and dopamine, are released."

....

2 "For others, unfortunately, shopping can spiral out of control and become as serious as other destructive addictions like alcoholism, drug abuse, and compulsive gambling."

....

C **PRACTICE** Reread the paragraphs that begin with *First*, *Second*, *Third*, and *Fourth* in the article on page 80. Then, in your own words, state the main idea of each paragraph, using reporting verbs and expressions suggested in Exercise A Writing Skill.

First	
Second	
Third	
Fourth	

D **APPLY THE WRITING SKILL** Write a summary of the article on page 80 by combining the main ideas from your notepad. Be sure to paraphrase what the author says, using your own words. Your summary should be no more than four to six sentences long.

OPTIONAL WRITING Write a short article in which you suggest how to avoid compulsive shopping.

SELF-CHECK

☐ Does the summary include only the author's main ideas?

☐ Did I paraphrase the author's ideas?

☐ Was I careful not to include my opinion in the summary?

A ▶ 4:10 Listen to each statement or question. Choose an appropriate response.

1 a There are no two ways about it.
b They're comparing apples and oranges.

2 a Thanks! I owe you one.
b That's just wishful thinking.

3 a Don't worry. We'll call it even.
b That's debatable.

4 a Don't fall for that.
b There are just no two ways about it.

5 a I know. I could kick myself!
b Tell you what.

B On a separate sheet of paper, answer the questions.

1 What always cracks you up about your favorite TV comedy or movie?

2 Whose music blows you away?

3 What songs choke you up?

4 What gets on your nerves about public transportation?

C Complete the statements with passive forms of gerunds or infinitives.

1 I don't recall .... any information.
                                    send

2 They want .... more time for the project.
                           give

3 She arranged .... to the airport.
                               take

4 I was disappointed .... the news.
                                      tell

5 He risked .... from his job.
                        fire

6 We were delighted .... to the wedding.
                                   invite

D On a separate sheet of paper, answer the questions in your own way.

1 What kinds of things do you like to splurge on?

2 Have you ever gone a little overboard when you were shopping? Explain.

3 What can't you resist the temptation to do? Why?

E Complete each statement with the correct form of one of the verbs.

promote	endorse	prove	imply

1 I'm sure Shiny Teeth toothpaste is the best. After all, it's being .... by that British actor with the gorgeous teeth. What's his name again?

2 This month Banana computers is .... a new laptop. It's smaller than a tablet and bigger than a smart phone, but it has full computer functionality.

3 Well, they don't have the statistics to .... that their shampoo grows hair, but all the pictures and testimonials .... that it probably will.

TEST-TAKING SKILLS BOOSTER p. 157

Web Project: Advertising Techniques
www.english.com/summit3e

Family Trends

COMMUNICATION GOALS

1 Describe family trends
2 Discuss parent-teen issues
3 Compare generations
4 Discuss caring for the elderly

A FRAME YOUR IDEAS Fill out the opinion survey of your attitudes about parent-teen relationships.

Check the opinion in each pair that YOU agree with more.

1 Teens should have to help around the house. It helps them develop a sense of responsibility.

Teens shouldn't have to help around the house. They already have enough to do with their schoolwork.

2 Parents should buy things that teens demand in order to "keep the peace."

Teens shouldn't always get everything they ask for. It would be a bad lesson for life.

3 Parents should set curfews. Teens who stay out late are likely to get in trouble.

Teenagers shouldn't have curfews. They should be able to decide what time to come home.

4 Parents should make rules for teen behavior so teens learn right from wrong.

Teens need to learn by making their own mistakes.

5 Parents should always ground teens if they misbehave. If they can't go out with their friends, they'll stop misbehaving and won't become troublemakers.

Teens who don't obey the rules should be given a second chance before being grounded.

6 Parents should control what their teenage children do on the Internet. It's their job to protect their children from danger.

Teenagers have a right to privacy, and their parents ought to respect it. What teens do on the Internet should be off-limits to parents.

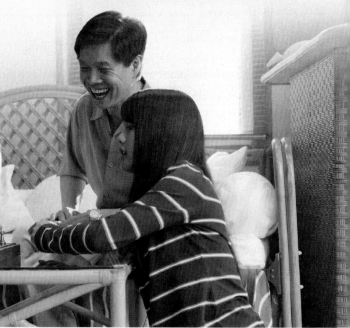

B PAIR WORK Compare your opinions on the survey with a partner. Support your opinions with reasons.

❝Parents don't have the right to know everything their kids do on the Internet. It isn't possible, anyway, because kids can delete their online history if they don't want their parents to see what they're doing.❞

❝I think that depends on the age of the kid.❞

C ▶ 4:11 **SPOTLIGHT**   Read and listen to a conversation about relationships. Notice the spotlighted language.

Grace: Did you hear the good news? Emma and Max **patched things up**!

Margot: They got back together? I didn't even know they**'d split up**! Shows you how out of touch I am. What happened?

Grace: Well, from what I understand, first they **had a falling out** about money, and then one thing led to another, and the marriage started **going downhill**.

Margot: What a shame. It's incredible how little things can snowball…. You know what, though? There's usually some bigger underlying issue when a marriage gets into trouble.

Grace: Actually, I think you**'ve hit the nail on the head**. Emma's been making more money than Max for the last couple of years, and then about six months ago he lost his job. So they figured it would be economical for him be a stay-at-home dad. I mean, why pay a babysitter?

Margot: Makes sense.

Grace: But that's just about the time things began to **fall apart**, and they started arguing about who should make financial decisions. And then the more they fought, the worse things got. Apparently, the constant conflict affected the kids' behavior. They just stopped obeying family rules and started texting friends and playing on their phones during dinner—you know what kids do these days…

Margot: You know, I'm feeling sort of like a gossip talking about them **behind their backs**. Let's just be thankful they're back together now.

D **UNDERSTAND IDIOMS AND EXPRESSIONS**   Choose the word or phrase with the same meaning.

1 It's hard to patch things up after a breakup.
  a repair a relationship
  b have financial problems
  c get a divorce

2 I didn't realize they'd split up.
  a separated
  b gotten back together
  c gotten out of touch

3 Lyn and Ed had a falling out about the children.
  a argued
  b agreed not to talk
  c made strict rules

4 Our relationship started going downhill last year.
  a improving
  b getting worse
  c getting back together

5 Anne hit the nail on the head when she figured out the underlying problem.
  a realized what the real reason was
  b became violent
  c made a lot of money

6 A husband and wife should discuss their problems before things start to fall apart.
  a get bad
  b get interesting
  c get better

7 When you talk about people behind their backs, you are a gossip.
  a so they know what you think about them
  b so they don't know what you say about them
  c so they're thankful

E **THINK AND EXPLAIN**   Answer the questions with a partner. Then discuss with the class.

1 What is your opinion of the decision to have Max stay home to care for the kids?

2 Why do you think some couples get back together after breaking up?

SPEAKING   **GROUP WORK**   Tell your classmates about a time you or someone you know…

• had a difference of opinion with a parent or child
• had a falling out with a friend, relative, or colleague

Provide specific examples and use language from Spotlight and Preview if possible.   87

A ▶4:12 **GRAMMAR SPOTLIGHT**   Read the information in the article. Notice the spotlighted grammar.

FALLING BIRTHRATES

Current trends show the size of families is changing, impacting societies worldwide. Women are marrying later, and couples are waiting longer to have children. And **the longer** couples wait to have children, **the fewer** children they have.

Two key factors that impact family size are the education and the employment of women. Studies show that **the more** education women get, **the smaller** families they have. Moreover, **the longer** women stay in school, **the better** their opportunities for employment. Working women are less likely to marry young and have large families.

In addition to the falling birthrate, there is a rising life expectancy. With people living **longer and longer**, families are going to have to face the challenges posed by an aging population. **The longer** people live, **the more** care they require. Traditionally, children have cared for their elderly parents at home. However, **the more** the birthrate falls, **the harder** the future may be for the elderly. With fewer children, families may find it **more and more** difficult to care for their older members.

B   **PAIR WORK**   Discuss the questions.

1 According to the article, what factors explain why more couples are having fewer children?

2 Why do you think populations are living longer? What problems can be caused by a larger elderly population?

C   **GRAMMAR**   REPEATED COMPARATIVES AND DOUBLE COMPARATIVES

Repeated comparatives

Use repeated comparatives to describe continuing increases and decreases.

> The birthrate is getting **lower and lower**.
> By the end of the twentieth century, couples were waiting **longer and longer** to marry.
> Changes are occurring **faster and faster**.

Use repeated comparatives with <u>more</u> or <u>less</u> to modify adjectives or adverbs that don't use an -er comparative form. When the adjective or adverb is understood, it may be omitted.

> It's becoming **more and more difficult** to predict life expectancy.
> It's **less and less possible** to raise birthrates in modern societies.
> That's happening **more and more** (often) these days.

Use repeated comparatives with <u>more</u>, <u>less</u>, and <u>fewer</u> to compare nouns. When the noun is understood, it may be omitted.

> **More and more** people are marrying later.
> **Fewer and fewer** (people) are having children before they are thirty.

Double comparatives

Use double comparatives to describe a cause-and-effect process.

> **The more** education women get, **the later** they marry. [Women are getting more education, so they're marrying later.]
> **The less** children studied, **the more** slowly they learned. [Children studied less, so they learned more slowly.]
> **The older** one gets, **the harder** it can be to find a husband or wife.

Note: When <u>be</u> is used in double comparatives, it is sometimes omitted.

> **The better** the quality of health care (is), **the higher** the life expectancy (is).

GRAMMAR BOOSTER   p. 137

· Making comparisons: review and expansion
· Other uses of comparatives, superlatives, and comparisons with <u>as</u> ... <u>as</u>

Be careful!
Don't use the present or past continuous in either clause of a double comparative statement. Use the simple present or the simple past tense instead.

The longer couples **wait** to have children, the fewer children they **have**.

NOT The longer couples ~~are waiting~~ to have children, the fewer they~~'re having~~.

D **NOTICE THE GRAMMAR**   Find a sentence using a double comparative in Spotlight on page 87.

E ▶ 4:13 **LISTEN TO ACTIVATE GRAMMAR**   Listen to three people talking about trends in marriage and family life. Then listen again and complete each statement, according to what the speaker implies, using double comparatives.

1 .... education mothers get, ... medical care they receive.

2 .... couples date, ... they marry.

3 .... children stay in school, ... their life expectancy.

F **GRAMMAR PAIR WORK**   First complete the statements logically, using the cues and double comparatives. Then, with a partner, discuss whether you agree or disagree with each statement. Support your opinion.

1 .... people are when they marry, ... children they have.
old ... few

2 .... the life expectancy, ... the elderly population is.
high ... large

3 .... people work, ... they are.
hard ... successful

4 .... the quality of health care is, ... the death rate.
good ... low

5 .... the country is, ... the life expectancy.
developed ... low

6 .... women are when they have children, ... they are to get
young ... likely
a higher education.

G **GRAMMAR PRACTICE**   On a separate sheet of paper, rewrite the sentences, using repeated comparative forms.

1 (An increasing number of) couples are having (a decreasing number of) children.

2 Divorces are taking place (with decreasing frequency).

3 People say that children are growing up (with increasing speed).

H **GRAMMAR PRACTICE**   Correct the errors in the sentences.

1 The more I'm eating, the later I'm sleeping.

2 The fewer grammar mistakes I'm making when I speak English, the better I am communicating.

NOW YOU CAN   Describe family trends

A **PAIR WORK**   With a partner, take turns making statements with repeated and double comparatives about the way families are changing in your country.

> ❝Families have been getting smaller and smaller.❞

B **SUMMARIZE**   On a separate sheet of paper, write a paragraph developing one of the statements you made in Exercise A. Add details.

> In the last few decades, family size has declined. Fewer and fewer people are having big families, so their standard of living is higher. The higher the standard of living is, the healthier the population will be.

C **DISCUSSION ACTIVATOR**   In small groups, discuss family trends in your country. Talk about how changing trends will impact the families of the future. Include the ideas below in your discussion. Say as much as you can.

Ideas
- birthrate
- life expectancy
- age at marriage
- health
- education
- income
- employment opportunities
- generational differences

> ❝It seems like more and more people are having fewer and fewer children. This could be a problem later because ...❞

DIGITAL STRATEGIES   **A** ▶ 4:14 **VOCABULARY** **DESCRIBING PARENT AND TEEN BEHAVIOR**
Read and listen. Then listen again and repeat.

Parents can sometimes be …

(too) strict	(too) lenient	overprotective

They set a lot of restrictions and expect kids to obey rules.	They let their kids have or do anything they want.	They worry too much about their kids.

Teenagers can sometimes be …

rebellious	spoiled	disrespectful

They refuse to obey family rules and just do whatever they want.	They expect to have or get whatever they want.	They are rude and often talk back to adults.

B **VOCABULARY PRACTICE**   Complete each statement with one of the adjectives. Use <u>too</u>
with the adjective if that represents your opinion.

1 Parents who always allow their teenage children to stay out late are ....

2 Teenagers who demand that their parents buy everything they ask for are ....

3 When parents never let their children do things because they are afraid they'll get sick or hurt,
they are being ....

4 If a father tells his teenage son not to get a tattoo and he disobeys and gets one anyway, we say
he is ....

5 Parents who make their teenage children clean their rooms every day are ....

6 Teens who act uninterested in class are ....

parent and teen behavior. Then listen again and determine which adjective from the
Vocabulary best completes each statement.

1 She thinks he's ....

2 She thinks he's acting ....

3 He thinks she's ....

4 He's angry because she's being ....

5 He thinks she's ....

6 She criticizes him for being ....

D **MAKE PERSONAL COMPARISONS**   Are you or anyone you know like any of the speakers in the
conversations in Exercise C? Explain.

E **PROVIDE EXAMPLES**   With a partner, describe people you know who exhibit the following kinds of
behavior. Explain, providing real details.

1 a parent who is too strict

2 a parent who is too lenient

3 a parent who is overprotective

4 a teenager who is rebellious

5 a teenager who is spoiled

6 a teenager who is disrespectful

NOW YOU CAN   Discuss parent-teen issues

A ▶ 4:16 **CONVERSATION SPOTLIGHT**
Read and listen. Notice the spotlighted
conversation strategies.

A: What do you think
parents should do if
their teenage kids
start smoking?

B: Well, I'm sorry to say
there's not much they
can do.

A: Why's that?

B: Well, teenagers are out of the house
most of the day, so parents can't
control everything they do.

A: I suppose. But they can ground
them if they don't shape up.

▶ 4:18
I'm sorry to say
I hate to say it, but
To tell you the truth,
Unfortunately,
The sad fact is

B ▶ 4:17 **RHYTHM AND INTONATION**
Listen again and repeat. Then practice
the conversation with a partner.

C **CONVERSATION ACTIVATOR**
Create a similar conversation. Use the
Vocabulary, examples of bad behavior
from the list, and language from Preview
on page 86. Start like this: *What do you
think parents [or teenagers] should do
if...?* Be sure to change roles and then
partners.

DON'T STOP!
• Give examples of your
own experiences.
• Discuss other
parent-teen issues.
• Say as much as you can.

Examples of bad behavior
• acting up at school
• staying out late without permission
• being rude or disrespectful
• becoming a troublemaker
• another example: ....

D **DISCUSSION**   If you could give parents
one piece of advice, what would it be?
If you could give teenagers one piece
of advice, what would it be? Provide
reasons.

GOAL Compare generations

A ▶ 4:19 **LISTENING WARM-UP** **WORD STUDY** **TRANSFORMING VERBS AND ADJECTIVES INTO NOUNS**
Listen and repeat.

Noun Suffixes	Nouns	Noun Suffixes	Nouns
-ation -tion -ssion	expect → expectation explain → explanation frustrate → frustration permit → permission	-ness	fair → fairness rebellious → rebelliousness selfish → selfishness strict → strictness
-ment	develop → development involve → involvement	-ity	generous → generosity mature → maturity mobile → mobility secure → security productive → productivity
-y	courteous → courtesy difficult → difficulty		
-ility	responsible → responsibility reliable → reliability capable → capability dependable → dependability disabled → disability	-ance -ence	important → importance significant → significance independent → independence lenient → lenience obedient → obedience

B **WORD STUDY PRACTICE** Circle all the words that are nouns.
Check a dictionary if you are not sure about the meaning of a word.

PRONUNCIATION BOOSTER	p. 147
Stress placement: prefixes and suffixes	

1 dependency   depend   dependence   dependent

2 confidence   confident   confide   confidently

3 consider   consideration considerate   considerately

4 different   difference   differentiate differentiation

5 attraction   attract   attractive   attractiveness

6 impatient   impatience   impatiently

7 unfair   unfairness   unfairly

8 closeness   close   closely

9 happily   happy   happiness

C ▶ 4:20 **LISTEN FOR SUPPORTING INFORMATION**
Listen to Part 1 of a man's description of the
generation gap in his family. Then answer the questions.

1 How did Rimas grow up differently from his parents?

2 Why does Rimas's father think teenagers nowadays
have more problems than when he was growing up?

D ▶ 4:21 **LISTEN FOR DETAILS** Listen to Part 1
again. Then complete each statement.

1 Rimas grew up in .... , but his
parents grew up in ....

2 Rimas's extended family includes ....
aunts and uncles on his mother's side.

3 When Rimas's mother was growing
up, every evening she ate dinner
....

However, when Rimas and his sister
were kids, they sometimes had to eat
....

Rimas Vilkas
Vilnius, Lithuania

	How are they different?	
	Rimas's parents' generation	**Rimas's generation**
career choices		
mobility		
influences from other cultures		
age at marriage and childbearing		
work experience		
closeness of family		

F RELATE TO PERSONAL EXPERIENCE Discuss the questions.

1 Rimas's parents worry about him and their own future. From your experience, why do you think parents worry about their children and the future?

2 In what ways is the Vilkas family's story story similar to or different from yours?

NOW YOU CAN Compare generations

A NOTEPADDING Compare your parents' generation with your generation. Write your ideas. Discuss them with a partner.

	My parents' generation	**My generation**
music		
style of clothes		
hairstyles / facial hair		
attitude toward elders		
family responsibility		
language (idioms, slang)		
marriage and childbearing		
values and beliefs		
use of technology		
other:		

B DISCUSSION Discuss these questions with your classmates. Use information from your notepads for examples.

1 In what ways is your generation the most different from your parents' generation? What do you like best or respect the most about your parents' generation?

2 What contributions do you think your generation will make to the next generation? How do you think the next generation will differ from yours?

OPTIONAL WRITING Summarize your discussion in writing.

A **READING WARM-UP** In your country, how are older family members traditionally cared for?

DIGITAL STRATEGIES **B** ▶ 4:23 **READING** Read the report on the increase in the global population of older people. What will some consequences of this demographic shift be?

WORLDWIDE GROWTH OF AGING POPULATIONS

ELEANOR HARRIS (left) lived on her own until last year, when her daughter found her in the kitchen cooking what she thought was soup, but which was actually just a pot of boiling water. It became obvious that she could no longer take care of herself. She is now living in a group home for elderly people.

The world is facing a huge demographic shift without precedent. For the first time in history, we soon will have more elderly people than children, and more extremely old people than ever before. As the population of older people gets larger and larger, key questions arise: will aging be accompanied by a longer period of good health, social engagement, and productivity, or will it be associated with more illness, disability, and dependency?

What we do know is that the more elderly people there are in the population, the more cases of age-related diseases such as heart disease, stroke, diabetes, and cancer there will be. Societies will have to find ways to address this growing need. And the older people get, the higher the prevalence of dementia, especially Alzheimer's disease; an estimated 25–30 percent of people aged 85 or older have dementia and lose their ability to remember, have difficulty reasoning, and undergo some personality changes.

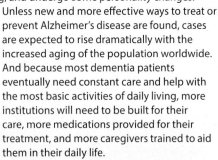

Unless new and more effective ways to treat or prevent Alzheimer's disease are found, cases are expected to rise dramatically with the increased aging of the population worldwide. And because most dementia patients eventually need constant care and help with the most basic activities of daily living, more institutions will need to be built for their care, more medications provided for their treatment, and more caregivers trained to aid them in their daily life.

What are some of the other social and economic consequences of this demographic shift? Even if they don't have dementia,

SALVADOR DUARTE is in rehabilitation to learn to walk after a stroke. In the coming decades more and more elderly patients like Mr. Duarte will require costly rehabilitation.

many of the oldest-old lose their ability to live independently, and many require some form of long-term care, which can include nursing homes, assisted living facilities, in-home care, and specialized hospitals.

The significant costs associated with providing this support may need to be borne by families and society. And as fewer and fewer adult children are able or want to stay home to care for older relatives, the shift to institutional care for elders will represent an immense social change, especially in those cultures where older generations have traditionally lived with younger ones. And the more residents of developing countries seek jobs in cities or other areas far from where they grew up, the less access to informal family care their older relatives back home will have.

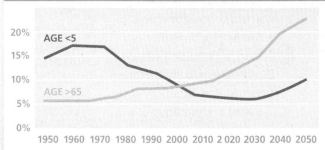

YOUNGER AND OLDER PEOPLE AS A PERCENT OF WORLDWIDE POPULATION BY DECADE

AGE <5

AGE >65

20% 15% 10% 5% 0%

1950 1960 1970 1980 1990 2000 2010 2 020 2030 2040 2050

C **SUMMARIZE** In your own words, summarize the changes described in the article.

D **UNDERSTAND MEANING FROM CONTEXT** Paraphrase the statements, based on your understanding of the underlined words and phrases.

1 The world is facing a huge demographic shift.

2 These changes are without precedent.

3 We soon will have more elderly people than children.

4 And the older people get, the higher the prevalence of dementia.

5 Many of the oldest of the elderly population lose their ability to live independently.

6 Many require some form of long-term care.

7 Institutional care for the elderly will represent an immense social change.

E CRITICAL THINKING Choose the best answer about the future, based on information in the report.

1 Who will pay for long-term care of people who can no longer live independently?
   a Stay-at-home adults.
   b Families and society.
   c Older people themselves.

2 Why will fewer old people be able to get informal home care?
   a Because their younger relatives may have moved elsewhere.
   b Because there will be more institutional care available for them.
   c Because they will seek work.

DIGITAL
EXTRA
CHALLENGE
F DRAW CONCLUSIONS Based on information in the report, what challenges do you think you will face as the people in your immediate or extended family age?

NOW YOU CAN   Discuss caring for the elderly

A FRAME YOUR IDEAS With a partner, discuss these statements and check those you think are true about care for the elderly in your country.

- ☐ Most elderly people are adequately cared for.
- ☐ The way the elderly are cared for has been changing.
- ☐ The elderly usually live with younger family members.
- ☐ The elderly usually live in their own homes or apartments.
- ☐ The elderly usually live in special nursing homes.

- ☐ The government makes sure the elderly have affordable care.
- ☐ Younger people accept care for elderly relatives as their responsibility.
- ☐ Older people generally prefer not to socialize with younger people.
- ☐ Other: ....
  ....

B PAIR WORK With a partner, discuss the challenges each person is facing and recommend solutions.

Suzanne is divorced and has three young daughters. Her mother died years ago, and her seventy-five-year-old father can no longer take care of himself. He often forgets things. She worries that he might get hurt.

Peter's parents, who live in another city, are in their nineties. They continue to have a full social life, and they still enjoy traveling with organized tours. But they are not as strong as they used to be and need help with cooking and cleaning.

David and his wife have two children and live in a small two-bedroom apartment. They both work long hours to make ends meet. David's mother just turned eighty and lives alone. David is concerned about his mother's well-being.

 C DISCUSSION How do you think the elderly will be cared for by the time you are old? How would *you* like to be cared for? Use Frame Your Ideas for support.

A **WRITING SKILL** Study the rules.

Note two common errors that writers often make when joining two sentences:

Run-on sentences (connecting sentences or independent clauses without using punctuation)

INCORRECT: My grandmother was strict with my mom however, my mom isn't at all strict with me.

Comma splices (connecting two sentences or independent clauses with a comma and no conjunction)

INCORRECT: My dad and I used to have lots of arguments, now we get along great.

To correct a run-on sentence or a comma splice, choose one of the following techniques:

• Use a period, and capitalize the following word.	My grandmother was strict with my mom. However, my mom isn't at all strict with me. My dad and I used to have lots of arguments. Now we get along great.
• Use a semicolon.	My grandmother was strict with my mom; my mom isn't at all strict with me. My dad and I used to have lots of arguments; now we get along great.
• Use a comma and a coordinating conjunction.	My grandmother was strict with my mom, but my mom isn't at all strict with me. My dad and I used to have lots of arguments, but now we get along great.

Coordinating conjunctions

and	for	or	yet
but	nor	so	

B **PRACTICE** All the sentences have errors. Label each sentence R (for run-on) or C (for comma splice). Then, on a separate sheet of paper, correct each sentence, using one of the techniques.

.... **1** Older people will use a lot of societal resources in the future, they will require caregivers and special institutions.

.... **2** In the future, there will be many more people in the oldest demographic however, we expect to have more treatments for some of their most common ailments.

.... **3** I worry a lot about my grandparents they both have had diabetes for many years.

.... **4** It's very difficult for my mother to stay home to care for my great-grandfather, he needs care because he has Alzheimer's disease.

C **PRACTICE** On a separate sheet of paper, rewrite the paragraph, correcting any run-on sentences or comma splices.

My husband and I don't know what to do with our teenage daughter, Beth. Beth has always been a bit rebellious however, lately her behavior has really been going downhill. Yesterday, Beth's teacher told us that she was disrespectful in class she hadn't done her homework. We're at our wits' end with her. At home Beth has developed a spoiled attitude, she isn't willing to help at all. She used to make her bed and clean up her room, recently she has been leaving her things everywhere. My husband and I may have been too lenient with Beth as she was growing up, now that she's a teenager we have to get her to shape up.

D **APPLY THE WRITING SKILL**

Write a blog post with advice for parents and teens who don't have a good relationship. Use the vocabulary and expressions from this unit. Write at least three paragraphs, each one with a topic sentence stating its main idea.

SELF-CHECK

☐ Did I avoid run-on sentences and comma splices?

☐ Do all the sentences support the topic sentence?

☐ Did I use the vocabulary and expressions I learned in this unit?

A ▶ 4:24 **Listen to the conversations about generational issues. Then listen to each conversation again and complete the statement with the correct comparative.**

1 Jordan has been spending ...... time on the Internet.
   a more and more
   b less and less

2 ...... , the more her mother worries.
   a The later Sandi stays out
   b The older Sandi gets

3 The stricter Jill's father gets, ... she becomes.
   a the more rebellious
   b the more spoiled

4 The older the sisters get, ...
   a the smarter they become
   b the more they appreciate their parents

B **Write the adjective that best describes the behavior in each statement.**

1 Mark's parents don't allow him to watch more than two hours of TV a day, but most of his friends can watch as much as they want. He feels that his parents are
....

2 Karen has a closet full of expensive clothes, yet she always complains about not having anything to wear. Her parents usually buy her whatever she wants. A lot of people think Karen is ....

3 Even though she has had her driver's license for a year and a half, Marissa's parents worry about her driving at night. They say that it's too dangerous, but Marissa thinks they're just being ....

4 When Clyde's grandfather asked him to turn down the volume of his music, he ignored him. Clyde's grandfather thought this was very ....

5 Rodney and Carolyn believe parents don't need to be so concerned about their children. They rarely set rules for their kids. Carolyn's sister thinks this is a bad idea. She feels they're ....

6 Deanna wears clothing that her parents find shocking. She also has friends that her parents don't approve of. Her mother wishes she weren't so
....

C **Read the sentences. If the underlined word is in the incorrect part of speech, correct it.**

1 Teenagers were given a lot more <u>responsibility</u> when I was young.

2 I think teenagers today lack the <u>mature</u> to make decisions for themselves.

3 The main reason young people are rebellious today is <u>selfishness</u>.

4 If kids today were taught about <u>courteous</u>, they would be better behaved.

5 There's no question that teenagers today demand more <u>independent</u> than they did fifty years ago.

6 It's important for parents to be involved in their children's <u>development</u>.

7 Young people have a lot more <u>mobile</u> than they did several generations ago.

8 It seems like there's a lot more <u>rebellious</u> among teenagers today.

TEST-TAKING SKILLS BOOSTER p. 158

Web Project: Elder Care
www.english.com/summit3e

Facts, Theories, and Hoaxes

COMMUNICATION GOALS

1 Speculate about everyday situations
2 Present a theory
3 Discuss how believable a story is
4 Evaluate the trustworthiness of news sources

PREVIEW

A **FRAME YOUR IDEAS** Take the quiz with a partner and discuss your answers.

THE WORLD'S EASIEST QUIZ... OR IS IT?

Be careful: The answers may seem obvious, but they might not be what you think! Will you "take a wild guess" by closing your eyes and just choosing A, B, C, or D? Or will you use "the process of elimination" by rejecting the answers that can't possibly be true?

1 How long did the Hundred Years' War in Western Europe last?
- A 100 years
- B 116 years
- C 50 years
- D 200 years

2 Where do Panama hats come from?
- A Panama
- B The Philippines
- C Ecuador
- D Italy

3 From which animals do we get catgut for violin strings?
- A cats
- B sheep
- C sharks
- D dogs

4 The former U.S.S.R. used to celebrate the October Revolution in which month?
- A October
- B November
- C December
- D June

5 What is a camel hair paintbrush made of?
- A camel hair
- B squirrel hair
- C cat hair
- D human hair

6 The Canary Islands in the Atlantic Ocean are named after which animal?
- A the canary
- B the cat
- C the dog
- D the camel

7 What was King George VI of England's first name?
- A George
- B Charles
- C Joseph
- D Albert

8 What color is a male purple finch?
- A dark purple
- B pinkish-red
- C sky blue
- D white

9 What country do Chinese gooseberries come from?
- A China
- B Japan
- C Sweden
- D New Zealand

10 How long did the Thirty Years' War in Central Europe last?
- A 30 years
- B 40 years
- C 20 years
- D 100 years

SCORING

1–2 CORRECT
We TOLD you they weren't so easy!

3–5 CORRECT
Not bad! Did you already know a few of the answers?

6–10 CORRECT
Either you're a great guesser, or you're a true scholar!

ANSWERS 1. B 116 years (from 1337 to 1453, with interruptions) **2. C** Ecuador (And Ecuadorians hate that everyone thinks the hats come from Panama!) **3. B** sheep (The word *catgut* may have come from *kitgut*—*kit* meaning violin— and someone confused it with the word for a young cat: *kitten*.) **4. B** November (Russians used to use the Julian calendar.) **5. B** squirrel hair (The brush inventor's surname was Camel.) **6. C** the dog (In Latin, *canarias* means dogs.) **7. D** Albert (British kings usually took new names when they become king.) **8. B** pinkish-red (And the female is brown.) **9. D** New Zealand (New Zealanders renamed them *kiwi fruit* to avoid confusion.) **10. A** 30 years, of course! (from 1618 to 1648)

B **DISCUSSION** Did you have a reason for each answer you chose? Did you just take wild guesses, or did you use the process of elimination? Which method do you think works better? Why?

C ▶ 5:01 **SPOTLIGHT** Read and listen to a conversation about a mystery. Notice the spotlighted language.

Boris: Have you been keeping up with all the news about that missing military jet?

Tina: Yeah. Very mysterious, don't you think? The whole thing **doesn't make sense**.

Boris: No, it doesn't. I mean, how can a military plane just **vanish without a trace** over the Mediterranean Sea? Where's the evidence of a crash?

Tina: I have no idea, but apparently there was bad weather. Most likely the pilot lost control and it crashed into the water.

Boris: They claim that's the probable explanation but, in my opinion, they**'re barking up the wrong tree**.

Tina: What do you mean?

Boris: Well, I know I**'m going out on a limb** with this, but the plane might have been taken over by someone and flown to a secret location.

Tina: Oh come on! How could anyone take over a military plane? You **don't really buy that**, do you?

Boris: Why not? Rumor has it that there were two high-level government scientists aboard. Maybe someone wanted the information they might have had.

Tina: I'm sorry, but that seems really **far-fetched to me**. It's just not believable! There's no question the plane crashed. The only question is where.

D **UNDERSTAND IDIOMS AND EXPRESSIONS** With a partner, find these expressions in Spotlight and discuss the meaning of each. Explain what it means when…

1 something "doesn't make sense"

2 something "vanishes without a trace"

3 someone "barks up the wrong tree"

4 someone "goes out on a limb"

5 someone "doesn't buy" an idea

6 something seems "far-fetched"

E **DISCUSSION** Discuss the questions with a partner.

1 Do you think Boris's theory is far-fetched? Why or why not?

2 Do you generally believe what you hear or read in the news? Why or why not?

SPEAKING

A **PAIR WORK** Read each rumor and discuss how believable you think it is. Explain your reasons, using the expressions from Exercise D.

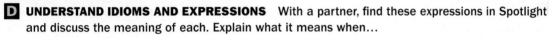

		most likely true	might be true	doesn't make sense	sounds far-fetched
1	That vaccines cause physical harm to young children	○	○	○	○
2	That the British monarchy controls the world's economy	○	○	○	○
3	That aliens from other planets have visited Earth	○	○	○	○
4	That the 1969 moon landing never actually happened	○	○	○	○

B **DISCUSSION** Which did you find more difficult to do: express an opinion on the rumors in Exercise A, or answer the questions in the quiz on page 98? Why?

GOAL Speculate about everyday situations

A ▶5:02 **VOCABULARY** **DEGREES OF CERTAINTY** Read and listen. Then listen again and repeat.

I wonder what happened to Clare.

very certain
Clearly, It's obvious (that) } she got stuck in traffic. There's no question (that)

almost certain
Most likely Probably I'll bet } she got stuck in traffic. I suppose

not certain
Maybe It's possible (that) } she got stuck in traffic. I wonder if

B ▶5:03 **LISTEN TO ACTIVATE VOCABULARY** Listen to each conversation and circle the phrase that best completes the statement. Then explain your choices.

1 She is (very certain / almost certain / not certain) about the reason Jade got grounded.
He is (very certain / almost certain / not certain) about the reason Jade got grounded.

2 She is (very certain / almost certain / not certain) about the reason Jack is in debt.
He is (very certain / almost certain / not certain) about the reason Jack is in debt.

3 She is (very certain / almost certain / not certain) why Linda got her kids a puppy.
He is (very certain / almost certain / not certain) why Linda got her kids a puppy.

C **APPLY THE VOCABULARY** Write three sentences about each situation, each with a different degree of certainty. (a = very certain, b = almost certain, c = not certain) Compare sentences with a partner.

1

You're trying to take the elevator downstairs to get some lunch. You've been waiting for the elevator for over ten minutes.

a ..... Clearly, the elevator isn't working. ....
b ....
c ....

2

It's 9:30, and your teacher hasn't arrived yet for your 9:00 class.

a ....
b ....
c ....

3

You go to your favorite restaurant. The lights are on, but the doors are locked, and there's no one inside.

a ....
b ....
c ....

4

You expected a package to arrive on Monday. It's Friday, and it still hasn't come.

a ....
b ....
c ....

NOW YOU CAN   Speculate about everyday situations

A ▶ 5:04 **CONVERSATION SPOTLIGHT**
Read and listen. Notice the spotlighted conversation strategies.

A: **I wonder** where Stacey is. She said she'd be here by ten.
B: Do you think something happened?
A: No idea. But **I'm sure it's nothing.** I'll bet she got stuck in traffic.
B: **I suppose you're right.** But I'm surprised she hasn't called.
A: I am, too.
B: **There must be a good explanation.** Maybe she left her phone at home.
A: Could be. I forget mine all the time.

▶ 5:06 **Ways to say "I don't know."**	▶ 5:07 **Responding to speculation**
No idea.	Could be.
No clue.	Maybe.
Beats me.	I suppose.

B ▶ 5:05 **RHYTHM AND INTONATION** Listen again and repeat. Then practice the conversation with a partner.

C **CONVERSATION ACTIVATOR** Create a similar conversation, using one of the situations in Exercise C on pages 100–101 (or another situation.) Start like this: *I wonder ...* Be sure to change roles and then partners.

DON'T STOP!
• Continue to speculate, using varying degrees of certainty.
• Say as much as you can.

RECYCLE THIS LANGUAGE
· It doesn't make sense.
· I don't buy that.
· That sounds far-fetched.
· There's no question...

GOAL Present a theory

A ▶5:08 **GRAMMAR SPOTLIGHT** Read about Rapa Nui. Notice the spotlighted grammar.

ISLAND OF MYSTERY

Rapa Nui (or Easter Island) is the most remote inhabited island in the world. Its huge stone figures (called *moai*) are world-famous, but their origin, as well as much of the island's history, is shrouded in mystery.

Experts believe the stone figures **may have been used** to establish religious and political authority and power, but no one knows for sure. Islanders moved a total of 540 figures across the island—some as far as 22 kilometers. Several experts believe the *moai* **could have been "walked"** upright, using ropes to rock the figures back and forth. Others theorize the islanders **must have laid** the figures down flat and **rolled** them over logs. They point out that moving each figure **could not have been accomplished** without the help of 70 or more people and probably took days to achieve.

In the early twentieth century, Norwegian explorer Thor Heyerdahl noticed cultural similarities between the people on Rapa Nui and the Incas in Peru. He argued that the island **might have been inhabited** by people who came in boats from South America. To prove it was possible, he successfully sailed a raft called the Kon-Tiki on that route. However, experts citing more recent DNA evidence confirmed that the original inhabitants **had to have sailed** from Polynesia, which lies to the west.

The first arrivals most likely found an inviting habitat lush with palm forests. However, today, the native trees are extinct. Some experts believe that, as the population of this small island increased, trees **must have been cut** down to build houses and boats and to make logs for moving the huge *moai*.

These are some of the theories about Rapa Nui, its stone figures, and the people who created them. Perhaps someday we will learn all the answers.

the Kon-Tiki

B **DRAW CONCLUSIONS** Which theory of how the *moai* were moved seems most believable to you? Explain your reasons.

DIGITAL INDUCTIVE ACTIVITY **C** **GRAMMAR** PERFECT MODALS FOR SPECULATING ABOUT THE PAST: ACTIVE AND PASSIVE VOICE

Active voice
You can form perfect modals using <u>may</u>, <u>might</u>, <u>could</u>, <u>must</u>, or <u>had to</u> to speculate with different degrees of certainty about the past. Remember: A perfect modal is formed with a modal + <u>have</u> and a past participle.

very certain:	The islanders **had to have come** from Polynesia.
	They **couldn't** (or **can't**) **have come** from Peru.
almost certain:	The figures **must have been** very important.
	They **must not have been** easy to move.
not certain:	They **might** (or **may**) **have moved** the *moai* by "walking" them.
	However, they also **could have laid** the *moai* flat on logs.

PRONUNCIATION BOOSTER p. 149
Reduction and linking in perfect modals in the passive voice

Passive voice
Use the passive voice if the performer of the action is unknown or if you want to focus on the receiver of the action. To form the passive voice with perfect modals, use a modal + <u>have been</u> and a past participle. In negative statements, place <u>not</u> before the auxiliary <u>have</u>.

The stone figures **must have been moved** using ropes and logs.
The secrets of Rapa Nui **might not have been lost** if their writing system had survived.
The island **couldn't have been inhabited** originally by people from South America.

GRAMMAR BOOSTER p. 138
Perfect modals: short responses (active and passive voice)

DIGITAL MORE EXERCISES **D** **UNDERSTAND THE GRAMMAR** Read the Grammar Spotlight again. Circle the perfect modals that are in the active voice. Underline those that are in the passive voice.

E GRAMMAR PRACTICE On a separate sheet of paper, rewrite the sentences with perfect modals in the active voice.

1 Scientists believe that <u>it's possible some form of life existed</u> on the planet Mars billions of years ago.

2 Heyerdahl thought <u>it was possible that they had come</u> on a raft like the Kon-Tiki.

3 Some historians think that <u>the Rapa Nui islanders probably didn't move</u> the *moai* using logs.

4 <u>It's possible someone forced the pilot</u> to fly the plane to a different location.

5 Experts suggest that originally <u>the Rapa Nui people most likely wrote</u> on banana leaves.

6 <u>There's no question that hunting was</u> the cause of the carrier pigeon's extinction as a species.

> *Scientists believe that some form of life could have existed on the planet Mars billions of years ago.*

F GRAMMAR PRACTICE Complete the conversations, using perfect modals in the passive voice.

> **Harvard Professor Claims Egyptian Pyramids Built by Aliens from Space**

1 A: I suppose they .... by aliens.

B: Come on! You don't really buy that, do you?

> **New Zealand Scientist Argues Dinosaurs Killed by Giant Tsunami**

2 A: That sounds far-fetched to me. I think the dinosaurs .... by something else.

B: I suppose you're right.

> **SHOCKING NEW REVELATION:**
> **Artist Vincent van Gogh was actually murdered by brother**

3 A: Do you think that's possible?

B: Of course not. He .... by his brother. Everyone knows he killed himself!

> **Woman Attacked by Lion While Shopping in London**

4 A: That just doesn't make sense!

B: Don't be so sure. Someone .... by a lion if it had escaped from the zoo.

NOW YOU CAN Present a theory

A FRAME YOUR IDEAS Read about each mystery. On a separate sheet of paper, write a theory to explain each one, using perfect modals. Your theories can be believable or far-fetched.

The Yeti For centuries, people in Asia's remote Himalayan Mountains have claimed to have seen a shy, hairy, human-like creature. However, no one has ever captured a yeti or taken its photo. These sightings continue to be reported today.

Stonehenge Stonehenge was built over 3,000 years ago in England. Experts say the huge stones came from mountains 257 kilometers away. No one knows for sure how the stones were carried or put into place. The purpose of the stones is unknown.

The Nazca Lines These huge shapes were carved into the earth in Peru more than 1,500 years ago and can only be seen from an airplane. No one knows how they were designed or made.

B DISCUSSION ACTIVATOR Speculate about each mystery, using active or passive perfect modals when possible. Use Degrees of Certainty vocabulary from page 100. Say as much as you can.

> ❝I believe the stones at Stonehenge **may have been used** for religious purposes. That's what makes the most sense to me. ❞

C PRESENTATION Choose one of the mysteries. Present the theory that you think best explains the mystery and tell the class why you believe it.

GOAL Discuss how believable a story is

A **READING WARM-UP** What kind of information would you need to determine whether or not a news story is true?

DIGITAL STRATEGIES **B** ▶ 5:09 **READING** Read the article. Which details do you think are the most questionable or the least believable?

THE ROSWELL INCIDENT

On June 25th 1947, pilot Kenneth Arnold was flying a plane in the northwest of the U.S. when he saw something strange: objects that looked like plates, or saucers, flying across the sky like a small flock of birds. His story led to numerous other news stories in which people claimed to have seen similar unidentified flying objects (UFOs)—or "flying saucers."

Shortly after, on July 8th, a secret military balloon crashed near Roswell, New Mexico, in the southwest. However, the local newspaper reported that a flying saucer had crashed, and the news media from all over demanded more information. Because the balloon was a secret, the military made an official announcement: that the object that had crashed was just an ordinary weather balloon.

A weather balloon

No one questioned that story for more than thirty years—until 1978. UFO lecturer Stanton Friedman interviewed a man who claimed to have seen something stranger than a weather balloon in the wreckage of the 1947 crash, and the story of a flying saucer was reborn. Although versions of that story differ, most people who believe there was a military conspiracy to hide the truth agree on these basic details: a flying saucer crashed near Roswell in 1947. And because it didn't want anyone to know the truth, the military kept the incident top secret and continues to do so today.

However, many details have been added to the story over the years. Eleven additional "crash sites" have been identified. While some people claim that alien beings from other planets must have been captured alive and imprisoned by the military in a secret

location, others believe that aliens might have died in the crash and were most likely being kept frozen for research. Roswell conspiracy fans meet at annual conferences to debate the various versions.

The military eventually admitted that it had been a secret military balloon. However, Roswell "experts" claim to have interviewed hundreds of witnesses who say they saw evidence of a flying saucer, proving, therefore, that the conspiracy theory must be true. B.D. Gildenberg, who has examined such claims, believes that the Roswell conspiracy stories are a hoax—"the world's most famous, most exhaustively investigated, and most thoroughly debunked UFO claim." Other skeptics of the conspiracy, who accept the military's version, point out that all the interviews occurred more than thirty years after the crash and that many of the statements made in the interviews were highly questionable. For example, one witness's name was changed after it became clear that she didn't exist. Furthermore, witnesses often seemed to confuse details with military plane crashes that had occurred in the area at about the same time.

All the same, a CNN / *Time* poll in the U.S. showed that a majority of the people who responded found the UFO story very believable. Conspiracy critic Kal Korff admits, "Let's not pull any punches here: The Roswell UFO myth has been very good business for UFO groups, publishers, Hollywood, the town of Roswell, [and] the media."

Attendees at annual "Roswell" conferences debate conflicting theories about alien visitors and UFOs.

C **CONFIRM POINT OF VIEW** Write A, B, or C to classify the people or organizations based on their point of view.

A = a skeptic of the military's version of the Roswell incident
B = a skeptic of the Roswell conspiracy theory
C = not enough information in the article to know for sure

1 .... Kenneth Arnold
2 .... Stanton Friedman
3 .... Roswell "experts"
4 .... Roswell conspiracy fans
5 .... CNN / *Time*
6 .... B.D. Gildenberg
7 .... Kal Korff

INFER INFORMATION   Based on information from the article, infer the answers to these questions.

1 What did Stanton Friedman's first witness probably tell him he saw in 1947?

2 When B.D. Gildenberg says the Roswell conspiracy is a "hoax," what does he mean?

3 When Kal Korff says the Roswell conspiracy is "very good business," what does he mean?

DIGITAL EXTRA CHALLENGE

4 When the military finally admitted years later that they hadn't told the truth about the weather balloon in 1947, how would you guess Roswell conspiracy fans responded?

DIGITAL STRATEGIES

E ▶ 5:10 **WORD STUDY**   **ADJECTIVES WITH THE SUFFIX -ABLE**   Listen and repeat.

believable	can be accepted as true because it seems possible
debatable	more than one explanation is possible
unprovable	cannot be shown to be true
questionable	likely to be untrue

F **WORD STUDY PRACTICE**   Use the adjectives from Exercise E to complete each statement.

1 His story is really .... So many of the details sound far-fetched.

2 I think she's telling the truth. Her description of the events sounds very .... to me.

3 Your claims are .... It isn't difficult to find another explanation for what happened.

4 That the military found a flying saucer is .... There is no evidence to show that they did.

NOW YOU CAN   Discuss how believable a story is

A **NOTEPADDING**   With a partner, create a story for each of two imaginary witnesses of the 1947 Roswell event: one supporting the conspiracy theory and one supporting the military's version.

Witness	What did the witness claim to have seen or heard?
1 a bus driver	He saw a flying saucer on the road. Some injured aliens were lying on the ground nearby. Some soldiers were ...

Witness	What did the witness claim to have seen or heard?
1	
2	

B **GAME**   "TO TELL THE TRUTH"   Divide the class into two opposing groups. Group A will argue that there was a Roswell conspiracy. Group B will defend the military's version. Students from each group role-play the witnesses, making their stories as believable as possible. Students in the opposing group ask questions in order to determine if the witness is telling the truth.

66 How many aliens did you see? 99

66 What did they look like? 99

C **DISCUSSION**   Vote to decide which witnesses told the most believable stories. Explain your reasons.

66 I thought the first witness's story was **questionable** because he must have ... 99

RECYCLE THIS LANGUAGE
· It doesn't make sense.
· I don't buy that.
· You're barking up the wrong tree.
· [You] really went out on a limb.
· That's just far-fetched.
· There's no question...

GOAL Evaluate the trustworthiness of news sources

A **LISTENING WARM-UP** **DISCUSSION** Look at the photo. Speculate about the purpose of the object behind the people.

Falcon Heene (front left) with his parents, Richard and Mayumi, and his brothers.

B 5:11 **LISTEN FOR MAIN IDEAS** Listen to Part 1 of this true story and discuss the questions.

1 What was the story that was being reported in the news?

2 Why did the Heene family contact the authorities?

3 What happened to the balloon?

4 What surprise did everyone discover afterward?

C ▶ 5:12 **LISTEN TO DRAW CONCLUSIONS** Listen to Part 2 of the story. Complete the statements. Explain your choices.

1 News agencies grew suspicious about the story because ....

   a Falcon's father answered interviewers' questions   **b** Falcon got sick during the interviews

2 Authorities grew suspicious when they learned about Falcon's father's ....

   a interests   **b** inventions

3 A publicity stunt is when someone tries to ....

   a hide the truth from the authorities   **b** get the attention of the media

4 Falcon's parents agreed to pay $36,000 as ....

   a a donation   **b** a punishment

D **CRITICAL THINKING** Discuss these questions. Listen to Part 2 again if necessary.

1 Do you think the authorities should have been less lenient or more lenient toward Falcon's parents? Why or why not?

2 Do you agree that the media probably made errors in judgment in the way they reported the story? Explain your opinion.

3 Do you think the media generally do a good job reporting the news? Provide examples of good or bad reporting.

A **FRAME YOUR IDEAS** Complete the survey and calculate your score. Then compare results with a partner. Which one of you is generally more skeptical?

ARE YOU A *skeptic?*

	NOT SKEPTICAL					VERY SKEPTICAL	
	100%	90%	70%	50%	30%	10%	0%
What percentage of the news you read in the newspaper do you think is true?	○	○	○	○	○	○	○
What percentage of the news you hear on TV or radio do you think is true?	○	○	○	○	○	○	○
What percentage of what you see on the Internet do you think is true?	○	○	○	○	○	○	○
What percentage of what politicians say do you think is true?	○	○	○	○	○	○	○
What percentage of what advertisers say do you think is true?	○	○	○	○	○	○	○
What percentage of what your family says do you think is true?	○	○	○	○	○	○	○
What percentage of what your friends say do you think is true?	○	○	○	○	○	○	○

HOW SKEPTICAL ARE YOU?
First add up all the percentage numbers you checked to get your total. Then calculate your average score by dividing your total by 7.

TOTAL [ ][ ][ ]   AVERAGE SCORE [ ][ ][ ]

B **NOTEPADDING** On the notepad, write news sources you trust and ones you don't. Include sources from newspapers, magazines, TV, radio, and the Internet. Explain your reasons.

The news sources I trust the most	Some news sources I don't trust
Why?	Why not?

C **DISCUSSION** Why do you trust some news sources and not others? Do you and your classmates agree on any? How can you determine if the information you read or hear is true or not?

RECYCLE THIS LANGUAGE		
· I'm sorry to say …	· There's no question …	· believable
· I hate to say it, but …	· I don't buy [that story].	· questionable
· To tell you the truth, …	· … doesn't make sense to me.	· reliable
· Unfortunately, …	· They're barking up the wrong tree.	· troubling
· The sad fact is …	· They went out on a limb.	· careful / careless
		· disappointed / disappointing

OPTIONAL WRITING Write about a news source you trust, or one you don't trust. Explain your reasons.

A WRITING SKILL Study the rules.

A sentence fragment is a group of words that does not express a complete thought. Here are two common fragments.

A dependent clause
A dependent clause is a group of words that contains both a subject and a verb but begins with a subordinating conjunction, making it an incomplete thought.

> FRAGMENT: ~~Because the military hadn't told the truth.~~
> FRAGMENT: ~~After his mother admitted to lying.~~

A phrase
A phrase is a group of words that is not a complete sentence. Common phrases are prepositional phrases, verb phrases, embedded questions, infinitive phrases, relative clauses, etc.

> FRAGMENT: ~~The people who were at the airport.~~
> FRAGMENT: ~~At the end of the year.~~
> FRAGMENT: ~~Are very reliable.~~
> FRAGMENT: ~~Where the balloon landed.~~
> FRAGMENT: ~~To solve the mystery.~~

To correct a sentence fragment, do one of the following:

- Attach a dependent clause to an independent clause to complete the thought.
    People believed the conspiracy theories because the military hadn't told the truth.
    After his mother admitted to lying, **everyone knew the story was a hoax**.

- Complete the thought by adding missing information to a phrase so it's a complete sentence.
    The people who were at the airport **couldn't board their planes**.
    They were freed from prison at the end of the year.
    Most newspapers are very reliable.
    That's where the balloon landed.
    To solve the mystery, **they interviewed all the witnesses**.

Remember:

An independent clause ...
- contains a subject and a verb.
- expresses a complete thought.

A complete sentence ...
- starts with a capital letter.
- ends with a period.
- expresses a complete thought.
- needs at least one independent clause.

Subordinating conjunctions that begin a dependent clause

after	since
as soon as	unless
because	until
before	when
even though	whenever
if	while

B PRACTICE Underline the sentence fragments in this paragraph. Then, on a separate sheet of paper, rewrite the paragraph correctly.

DIGITAL WRITING PROCESS

> When John Tyler did not appear at his wedding. His bride and the wedding guests were worried. They called the police for help. The police used helicopters. To search for John's car. An hour later, John called his bride by phone. She was shocked. Because John told her that he had been carjacked. According to his story. The carjackers had locked him in the trunk of his car. Meanwhile, the police had found John's car. In the parking lot of a hotel. Furthermore, John was found in a hotel room. Speaking with his wife on the phone. Apparently, he had been having doubts about getting married and had made up the whole story about the carjacking. John had to repay the town the $3,000 spent trying to rescue him during his carjacking hoax. He and his bride were married two weeks later.

C APPLY THE WRITING SKILL
On a separate sheet of paper, write a short news article about one of these topics:

a A real or imaginary mysterious event, such as a UFO sighting, a disappearance, or the discovery of a previously unknown place

b A real or imaginary story in which the media succeeded at telling, or failed to tell, the truth

SELF-CHECK

☐ Do all my sentences express complete thoughts?
☐ Did I avoid sentence fragments?
☐ Did I avoid run-on sentences?

A ▶ 5:13 **Listen to the conversations. Then listen to each conversation again and choose the statement that is closer in meaning to what each person said.**

1 The woman says ....
   a it's possible Bill overslept
   b Bill couldn't possibly have overslept

2 The woman says ....
   a it's possible the wallet is Gina's
   b it's almost certain that the wallet is Gina's

3 The man thinks ....
   a the president may have been involved in the scandal
   b the president had clearly been involved in the scandal

4 The man thinks ....
   a the story could possibly be a hoax
   b the story couldn't possibly be true

B **Rewrite each statement in the passive voice.**

1 The military must have moved the aliens' bodies to a secret place.

....

2 Witnesses might have seen evidence of the event.

....

3 Stanton Friedman must have written the first account of the Roswell conspiracy.

....

4 They couldn't have moved the stones without lots of help.

....

5 Richard Heene had to have asked Falcon to lie to the authorities.

....

6 The islanders might not have used the stone figures for religious purposes.

....

C **On a separate sheet of paper, write your own response to each question, using varying degrees of certainty. Explain your theories.**

1 Do you think it's possible that there could really be a human-like creature in the Himalayas called a yeti?

> *I suppose it's possible, but I really don't believe it because ...*

2 Do you think the conspiracy theory about the Roswell incident could be true?

3 Does it make sense to you that the Bermuda Triangle might cause ships and planes to disappear?

4 Do you think it's possible that the Nazca Lines were designed by aliens?

TEST-TAKING SKILLS BOOSTER p. 159

Web Project: Mysteries
www.english.com/summit3e

COMMUNICATION GOALS

1 Suggest ways to reduce stress
2 Describe how you got interested in a hobby
3 Discuss how mobile devices affect us
4 Compare attitudes about taking risks

PREVIEW

A **FRAME YOUR IDEAS** Complete the survey about your free time.

HOW DO YOU LIKE
to spend your time?

RATE THESE ACTIVITIES ON A SCALE OF 0 TO 3.

3 = extremely important
2 = fairly important
1 = somewhat important
0 = not important to me at all

1 spending time with my family — 0 1 2 3

2 hanging out with my friends — 0 1 2 3

3 spending time alone relaxing and doing nothing — 0 1 2 3

4 immersing myself in my work or studies — 0 1 2 3

5 seeking excitement — 0 1 2 3

6 engaging in quiet activities at home — 0 1 2 3

7 participating in sports — 0 1 2 3

8 working out to stay in shape — 0 1 2 3

9 rooting for my favorite teams — 0 1 2 3

10 attending cultural events — 0 1 2 3

11 enjoying my hobbies and other interests — 0 1 2 3

B **PAIR WORK** Compare your survey responses. Ask questions about your partner's free time.

C ▶5:14 **VOCABULARY** **WAYS TO DESCRIBE PEOPLE** Listen and repeat. Then use the words and the survey to describe your partner.

- **sociable:** likes being around other people
- **a loner:** prefers being alone or hanging out with close friends or family
- **active:** enjoys doing lots of activities, has lots of interests
- **sedentary:** somewhat inactive physically
- **laid back:** relaxed, easygoing
- **other** ....

> My partner is really sociable. She likes to spend time with her family and hang out with her friends.

D ▶ 5:15 **SPOTLIGHT**   Read and listen to a conversation between two friends after work. Notice the spotlighted language.

Ava: *[phone rings]* Don't you need to take that?

Erin: Nah. It's my new boss. It can wait till tomorrow.

Ava: Really? What if it's urgent?

Erin: She needs to know I'm not always **on call**. And besides, my workday ended over two hours ago … I have a life!

Ava: Well, you're a lot more laid back than I am. I've got **a lot on my plate** at work these days. I'd worry my boss might think I was **slacking off**.

Erin: But he knows that's not true! You work really hard.

Ava: I do. But I feel like I need to take my work home with me. Or I'll never be able to **keep up**.

Erin: Well, my previous boss was always calling me on the weekend. Finally, I had to put a stop to it. I just decided I wouldn't take any more calls after hours. You just have to **draw the line** somewhere, right?

Ava: I suppose so. But if I did that, I'd be **a nervous wreck** that I might lose my job.

Erin: Me, I can't live like that. When I'm at work, I **give it my all**. But my free time is mine … *[phone rings]* Is that yours?

Ava: I guess so … Oh no … I forgot I was supposed to call my boss at 7:00. Excuse me for a minute …

Erin: Come on! Don't tell me you're going to take that!

Ava: Stop that! Shhh!

E **UNDERSTAND IDIOMS AND EXPRESSIONS**   Find these expressions in Spotlight. Match each with its correct meaning.

.... **1** be on call
.... **2** have a lot on one's plate
.... **3** slack off
.... **4** keep up
.... **5** draw the line
.... **6** be a nervous wreck
.... **7** give something one's all

a not work as hard as one should
b finish everything that needs to get done
c make it clear that something is unacceptable
d be anxious or worried about something
e make oneself available for someone to contact any time
f do something with maximum effort
g have lots of things that need to get done

F **DISCUSSION**   Whose philosophy about taking work calls after hours makes the most sense to you — Ava's or Erin's? Explain your reasons.

SPEAKING   **PAIR WORK**   Complete the chart. Then tell your partner about the people. Use the Vocabulary from page 110.

> Unfortunately, Chris is a little sedentary because he's always immersed in his studies.

Someone I know who …	Name	Relationship to you
is always immersed in his or her work or studies		
has a lot on his or her plate right now		
is good at drawing the line between work and private time		
maintains a very active life		
slacks off a little too often		
gives everything his or her all		

111

GOAL Suggest ways to reduce stress

DIGITAL STRATEGIES **A** ► 5:16 **VOCABULARY** **WAYS TO REDUCE STRESS** Read and listen to the suggestions for reducing the stress of work. Then listen again and repeat.

 TAKE A BREATHER.
Stop what you're doing from time to time. Take a rest or get some exercise.

 SET ASIDE SOME DOWN TIME.
Schedule time that's just for you so you can focus on relaxing.

 SLOW DOWN.
Don't do everything so fast. Take time to think about what you're doing and do it right.

REDUCING THE STRESS OF WORK

 SET LIMITS.
Learn to draw the line and say no to others' demands on your private time.

 LEARN TO LAUGH THINGS OFF.
Stop taking things so seriously. Remember to see the humor in everything.

 TAKE UP A HOBBY.
Start doing something you'd enjoy in your free time, such as making, collecting, fixing, or taking care of things.

B ► 5:17 **LISTEN TO ACTIVATE VOCABULARY** Read the suggestions. Then listen to six people's complaints. Write the number of a speaker in the box next to the suggestion you'd give him or her.

☐ "If I were you, I'd take a breather every few hours."

☐ "You should set aside some down time each week."

☐ "Slow down a bit so you can do the job right."

☐ "If I were you, I'd try to set some limits."

☐ "Why don't you try to laugh things off at work."

☐ "I think you should take up a hobby."

> **GRAMMAR BOOSTER** p. 139
> Be supposed to: expansion

DIGITAL INDUCTIVE ACTIVITY **C** **GRAMMAR** **EXPRESSING AN EXPECTATION WITH BE SUPPOSED TO**

Use be supposed to + a base form to express expectation. Use a present form of be for a present or future expectation. Use a past form of be for an expectation in the past.

We're **supposed to arrive** on time today. (Someone expects it.)
Marcy **is supposed to bring** snacks tomorrow. (Someone will expect it.)
You **were supposed to come** yesterday. (Someone expected it.)

Note: The negative form of be supposed to can also express a prohibition.
We're not supposed to text during class.

Negative statements

They **aren't supposed to know** about the party.
She **wasn't supposed to stay** past 5:00.

Yes / no questions

Is Paul **supposed to give** his presentation tomorrow?
Was the school **supposed to pay** you a refund?

Information questions

When **were** we **supposed to buy** the tickets?
Who's **supposed to call** us today?

Be careful!
Don't use auxiliary verbs or modals with be supposed to.
Don't say: Marcy ~~will be~~ supposed to bring the snacks.

Don't confuse be supposed to with the verb suppose.
I suppose I should call her. (= I assume I should.)
What do you suppose is wrong? (= What do you guess is wrong?)

DIGITAL MORE EXERCISES **D** **UNDERSTAND THE GRAMMAR** Speculate about who might have an expectation.

1 Jeff is supposed to call home before he leaves the office. ❝His wife might expect it.❞

2 Our teacher is supposed to tell us our final grades today.

3 Customers are supposed to leave a 15% tip after their meal.

E **ERROR CORRECTION** On a separate sheet of paper, rewrite these sentences correctly.

1 You don't suppose to smoke cigarettes inside the office.

2 Wasn't everyone suppose to turn off their phones during the talk?

3 Lena and Gil didn't supposed to finish their report before the meeting yesterday.

4 When will he be supposed to let his boss know he's taking time off?

5 What we suppose to do for tomorrow's class?

F **GRAMMAR PRACTICE** Rewrite each instruction to express an expectation, using <u>be supposed to</u>. Make any other necessary changes.

PRONUNCIATION BOOSTER p. 150
Vowel sounds /eɪ/, /ɛ/, /æ/, and /ʌ/

1 "Please bring your homework with you tomorrow."
(we / bring) ....

2 "Please tell Sara to call her mother after class."
(Sara / call) ....

3 "Please inform Walter that he needs to pay his bill by Friday."
(Walter / pay) ....

4 "Don't tell anyone about Tom's surprise birthday party on Sunday."
(I / tell) ....

5 "Don't tip people for their service when you're traveling in Japan."
(you / tip) ....

6 "All of our store clerks should be friendly, helpful, and courteous."
(Our store clerks / be) ....

NOW YOU CAN Suggest ways to reduce stress

A ▶5:18 **CONVERSATION SPOTLIGHT** Read and listen. Notice the spotlighted conversation strategies.

A: **Uh-oh.** I really messed up.

B: Why? What did you do?

A: **I just realized** we were supposed to turn in our reports this morning. It completely slipped my mind.

B: **Well, frankly,** I'm not surprised.

A: What do you mean?

B: **It's just that** you've been working so hard lately. **Let's face it** … you need a break.

A: You're probably right. I've got way too much on my plate.

B: **You know what?** It's time to slow down a little.

B ▶5:19 **RHYTHM AND INTONATION** Listen again and repeat. Then practice the conversation with a partner.

C **CONVERSATION ACTIVATOR** Create a similar conversation in which one of you is stressed out about forgetting to do something. Start like this: *Uh-oh. I really messed up…* Be sure to change roles and then partners.

DON'T STOP!

- Suggest and discuss other ways to reduce stress.
- Say as much as you can.

RECYCLE THIS LANGUAGE	
· be on call	· give it one's all
· be a nervous wreck	· draw the line
· can't keep up	

Some ideas
You were supposed to …
- get someone a birthday gift.
- pick someone up at the airport.
- finish your homework.
- be at a meeting at work or school.
- prepare a presentation for an event.

113

GOAL Describe how you got interested in a hobby

A ▶5:20 **GRAMMAR SPOTLIGHT** Read about how these people got interested in their hobbies. Notice the spotlighted grammar.

ASSEMBLING MODELS

When I was a kid, I was crazy about airplanes. My dad did a lot of traveling for his job, so he **would bring** me back model kits from different airlines. I**'d assemble** them and paint them, and it was fun. My dad **was always showing** off my work to his friends, so I decided to get serious and make it a real hobby. Now I build my own models with engines that can really fly.

QUILTING

When I was young, my mom **was always collecting** old pieces of colorful cloth. At some point, she **would sew** them together into shapes, and then she **would combine** the shapes together to make a huge bed cover. I used to think it was embarrassing to have my friends come over and see all those pieces of cloth lying around. But today I'm really proud of the quilts my mom made.

PRACTICING A MARTIAL ART

When I was about eight, my friends were all learning martial arts. They**'d walk** past my house in their uniforms on their way to karate class, and I really wanted to join them. So I told my mom, and she agreed to let me. I've been practicing now for more than ten years. It's helped me to feel really confident physically.

B **PAIR WORK** With a partner, discuss which hobby in Exercise A is the most appealing to you. Explain your reasons.

> GRAMMAR BOOSTER p. 139
> · Would: review
> · Placement of adverbs of manner

C **GRAMMAR** DESCRIBING PAST REPEATED OR HABITUAL ACTIONS

You can use <u>would</u> + a base form to describe past repeated or habitual actions.

When I was a kid, my mom **would sew** pieces of cloth together to make quilts.
Every weekend, I **would walk** around the neighborhood and take photos.

You can also use the past continuous with the frequency adverb <u>always</u> to describe a past habitual action.

Our grandfather **was always fixing** things in his garage.
We **were always taking care of** other people's pets.

Remember: You can also use <u>used to</u> + a base form to describe past habitual actions that are no longer true.

My mom **used to make** quilts. [But she doesn't anymore.]
I **used to love** assembling model cars. [But I don't have the time now.]

Be careful!
With non-action verbs that don't describe repeated actions, use <u>used to</u>, not <u>would</u>.
We **used to be** interested in martial arts.
NOT We ~~would be~~ interested in martial arts.
She **used to dislike** sewing.
NOT She ~~would dislike~~ sewing.

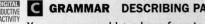

D **NOTICE THE GRAMMAR**   Find an example of the past continuous with _always_ in Spotlight on page 111. Restate the sentence, using _used to_.

E **GRAMMAR PRACTICE**   Write an X next to the statements that cannot be rewritten using _would_ for past repeated or habitual actions. Explain your decision for each item.

☐ **1** Nick used to like everything about going to school.

☐ **2** My brother used to collect soda cans when we were kids.

☐ **3** We used to visit antique stores to look for beautiful old things.

☐ **4** The prices of the model cars I liked the best used to be astronomical.

☐ **5** My family used to live next door to a karate school.

☐ **6** When Jan first started her new job, she used to immerse herself in her work.

☐ **7** When I was a teenager, I used to seek excitement by taking risks.

> ❝ In item 1, _like_ is a non-action verb. You can't use _would_ for repeated actions with non-action verbs. ❞

F **GRAMMAR PRACTICE**   On a separate sheet of paper, rewrite each statement from Exercise E that can be rewritten with _would_.

> _My brother would collect soda cans when we were kids._

G **GRAMMAR PRACTICE**   With a partner, take turns restating each statement from Exercise F, using the past continuous with _always_.

> ❝ My brother was always collecting soda cans when we were kids. ❞

NOW YOU CAN   Describe how you got interested in a hobby

A **NOTEPADDING**   Using the Grammar Spotlight as a guide, write statements about one of your hobbies. Use _would_ or the past continuous for past repeated or habitual actions when possible.

B **DISCUSSION ACTIVATOR**   Using your notepad, discuss your hobby with a partner. Find out about your partner's hobby. Say as much as you can.

C **PRESENTATION**   With your partner, tell your class about how you each got interested in your hobbies.

OPTIONAL WRITING   Write about how your partner got interested in his or her hobby.

| What is your hobby? |
| How did you first get interested in it? |
| |
| |
| |
| |
| How did your interest change over time? |
| |
| |
| |
| |
| |

A   **READING WARM-UP**   Do you think technology increases or reduces stress in your life? Provide examples.

B   ▶ 5:21   **READING**   Read the article. How would you summarize the author's main points about technology today?

ALWAYS CONNECTED?

The Consequences of Never Switching Off

Alison Murphy

Advances in technology come with the promise of increased efficiency, making us more productive and providing more time to relax and enjoy our leisure time. However, some experts claim that the opposite is true— that we're actually working more and have less time to relax. And, as a result, we are becoming more stressed out.

Next time you're in a public place, look around. Odds are you'll see a large percentage of people on their phones or tablets texting, chatting, checking messages, or surfing the net. We're more connected to our mobile devices than ever before, which provides us 24/7 contact with our work, social media, and the Internet. The devices even follow us into our bedrooms, where we use technology as a means to unwind at the end of a long day.

According to a recent poll, a majority of respondents said they use their devices right before going to bed. Most also reported that using their devices keeps them up at night and that they don't get enough sleep. Zack Panatera, a student at Stanford University, complained, "I'll take a quick look at something interesting, and the next thing I know, I've spent a few hours online." According to psychiatrist Kyla Greenham, "The light from our devices throws off our normal sleep cycle and actually reduces production of the sleep hormone melatonin." She advises, "Switch off any kind of technology at least an hour before going to bed." Lack of sleep may not seem so important, but it can have a huge effect on one's performance the next day, making it harder to pay attention or remember things.

At work, technology is in fact a contributing factor in a growing trend toward longer hours and less time off. When we leave the office, we continue to stay connected. We are inviting our work world into our private lives in ways that never would have been imaginable in the past. We're constantly "on call," and our time is never entirely our own. We just don't know how to "switch off" our work when we get home.

In our leisure time, technology appears to be reducing the face-to-face human interaction that we've traditionally enjoyed. For example, the trend has been away from the shared experiences of going out to the movies or shopping at the mall, toward the more private acts of watching movies at home or shopping online. Common leisure activities of the past, such as participating in clubs, took place in the community and provided extended time to communicate with others and develop relationships. In contrast, today's online posts and tweets with family, friends, and colleagues are shorter, more superficial, and less satisfying. Recent research has in fact suggested that face-to-face family time is decreasing in homes with Internet connections.

No one wishes to turn back the clock on what technology can do. However, switching off our devices from time to time may be one of the most important decisions we can make to ensure that we are living full, satisfying lives.

C   **UNDERSTAND MEANING FROM CONTEXT**   With a partner, find these words and phrases in the article. Match each one with its correct meaning.

.... **1** switch off

.... **2** 24/7

.... **3** a means to unwind

.... **4** keeps [someone] up at night

.... **5** lack of

.... **6** throws off

.... **7** face-to-face

a a way to relax

b all day and night

c insufficient amount or quantity

d prevents from sleeping

e by talking to someone directly, in person

f turn off

g makes something not work right

D IDENTIFY SUPPORTING DETAILS Answer the questions, according to the article.
Find examples or information in the article to support your answers.

1 What is wrong with always being "on call" for an employer?

2 What are the consequences of checking one's devices before going to sleep?

3 Why is it a problem to rely on technology for social interaction?

E INFER POINT OF VIEW Answer the following questions. Explain your reasons.

1 What kinds of leisure activities do you think the author would recommend?

2 Do you think the author's opinion of electronic devices is more positive or negative? Explain.

DIGITAL
EXTRA
CHALLENGE

NOW YOU CAN Discuss how mobile devices affect us

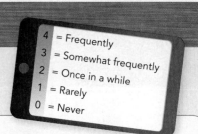

4 = Frequently
3 = Somewhat frequently
2 = Once in a while
1 = Rarely
0 = Never

A FRAME YOUR IDEAS Complete the survey. Then compare answers with a partner. Describe your habits and explain why you do what you do.

HOW CONNECTED ARE YOU?

	0	1	2	3	4	not sure
I text to connect with other people.	○	○	○	○	○	○
I make calls to other people.	○	○	○	○	○	○
I stop whatever I'm doing to respond to calls or texts.	○	○	○	○	○	○
I check my messages as soon as I wake up.	○	○	○	○	○	○
I check my messages as soon as I get home.	○	○	○	○	○	○
I check my messages before going to sleep.	○	○	○	○	○	○
I wake up during the night and check my messages.	○	○	○	○	○	○
I switch off my devices during the day.	○	○	○	○	○	○
I switch off my devices at night.	○	○	○	○	○	○

BASED ON YOUR SURVEY RESPONSES, WHICH STATEMENT BELOW BEST DESCRIBES YOU?

○ I'm almost always connected, and I think that's great.

○ I'm almost always connected, but I wish I weren't.

○ I think it's important to be connected, but I know when to switch off my devices.

○ I'm hardly ever connected, but I wish I were more often.

○ I'm hardly ever connected, and I'm glad.

B DISCUSSION Discuss the following questions in small groups. Then share your ideas with the class.

1 In your opinion, do technological advances save us time or waste more of our time? How?

2 What are your recommendations for the best ways to use our devices at work or school? In public places? At home?

3 Do you think technology adds to or interferes with your leisure time? Explain how.

❝ Texting keeps me in touch with more of my friends and makes it easier to get together. I don't think it interferes with my leisure time at all. ❞

GOAL Compare attitudes about taking risks

A **LISTENING WARM-UP** **DISCUSSION** Which of the following risks would you find the easiest to take? Which would you find the most difficult? Explain your reasons.

Jumping out of an airplane

Changing your career after the age of 40

Driving way over the speed limit

Climbing a live volcano

DIGITAL STRATEGIES

B ▶ 5:22 **LISTEN FOR MAIN IDEAS** Listen to the interview with a psychologist. Then listen again and write a description for each of the two personality types the psychologist describes.

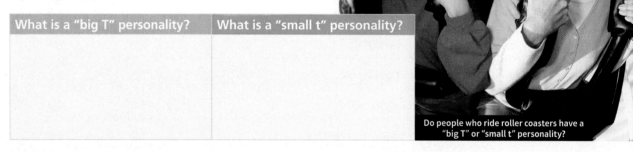
Do people who ride roller coasters have a "big T" or "small t" personality?

What is a "big T" personality?	What is a "small t" personality?

C ▶ 5:23 **LISTEN FOR SUPPORTING DETAILS** Read each summary of some of Franklin's main points. Listen again, and complete each explanation by providing details from the interview.

		Explanation
1	Franklin notes that one cannot simply classify people's personalities as either 100% "big T" or "small t."	
2	She clarifies that having a "big T" personality isn't always a positive trait.	
3	She argues that even if you are willing to ride on a roller coaster, you don't necessarily have a "big T" personality.	

D ▶ 5:24 **LISTEN TO UNDERSTAND MEANING FROM CONTEXT** Listen to each of the following comments from the interview and complete the statements.

1 If you are "faint of heart" and "wouldn't dare" to do certain things, you have more of a (big T / small t) personality.

2 A person who "takes chances" and chooses to "live on the edge" has more of a (big T / small t) personality.

3 If you feel an "adrenaline rush" when you go "right up to the edge," you have more of a (big T / small t) personality.

RELATE TO PERSONAL EXPERIENCE   Where do you fit on the risk-taking continuum?
Do you have more of a "big T" or "small t" personality? Explain your reasons.

◄ Risk-Avoider   Risk-Taker ►

DIGITAL
STRATEGIES
F ▶ 5:25 **WORD STUDY**   **ADVERBS OF MANNER**
Most adverbs of manner are formed by adding -ly
to an adjective. Listen and repeat.

Adjective		Adverb
confident	→	confident**ly**
mysterious	→	mysterious**ly**
quick	→	quick**ly**
quiet	→	quiet**ly**
safe	→	safe**ly**

Exceptions: If an adjective ends in ...

- -y, change to -ily. (noisy → nois**ily**)
- -l, add -ly. (careful → careful**ly**)
- -ble, change to -bly. (comforta**ble** → comforta**bly**)

Usage note
Use an adverb of manner to modify a verb or adjective.

Risk-taking affects you **physically**.
[modifies the verb: describes how it affects you]

I'm afraid of activities that are **physically** dangerous.
[modifies the adjective: describes how they are dangerous]

Some adverbs such as luckily, fortunately, unfortunately, and sadly express the speaker's attitude. They are generally used at the beginning or end of a sentence.
Luckily, no one was hurt. I was really frightened, **unfortunately**.

G **WORD STUDY PRACTICE**   Complete each statement, using an adverb of manner.

1 (dangerous) Many people who seek excitement like to live ....

2 (fortunate) My niece climbed a live volcano. Nothing terrible happened, ...

3 (easy) I don't like taking risks when I drive. Someone could .... get hurt.

4 (nervous) He .... checked his parachute before he jumped out of the plane.

5 (sad) .... , he was badly injured when he jumped off the cliff.

6 (extreme) The hike through the desert is .... challenging.

7 (beautiful) The stories about her adventures are .... written.

8 (accidental) She .... walked into a high-crime neighborhood.

9 (mysterious) Our teacher was .... absent over the last week.

NOW YOU CAN   Compare attitudes about taking risks

A **NOTEPADDING**   Interview a partner about the riskiest thing he or she has ever done. Take notes on your notepad. Use adverbs of manner if you can.

DIGITAL
SPEAKING
BOOSTER
B **DISCUSSION**   In small groups, compare your partners' experiences. Then decide who is the biggest risk-taker.

OPTIONAL WRITING   Write a paragraph about why you think a person becomes a risk-taker or a risk-avoider.

	Description of what happened:
Name	
Time and place	
Where?	

WRITING   Presenting and supporting opinions clearly

A WRITING SKILL   Study the rules.

When you write to critique or comment on another person's ideas, it is important to present and support your own opinions clearly. Use connecting words and phrases to present your ideas logically, and support your ideas with reasons.

Present your ideas logically

First of all, I agree with Alison Murphy's main point.

In addition, she makes a good point about modern technology.

Furthermore, she's right about its effect on sleep.

Finally, I believe we need to decide what we want technology to do for us.

Support your ideas with reasons

Since they are able to work from home, people have more free time.

Because of the Internet, people are working more efficiently.

Actually, new technology increases leisure time. **That is why** I think the author is wrong.

Due to new technological advances, people are more connected than ever.

> **Citing the writer's words**
> Use direct speech to quote short statements. For example:
>
> *Murphy says, "It may be one of the most important decisions we can make."*
>
> For longer statements, use indirect speech to paraphrase what Murphy says. For example:
>
> *Murphy argues that technology is interfering with our sleep.*

B PRACTICE   Write statements using the connecting words.

1 Smart phones are so convenient. It seems like everyone needs to have one. (since)

....

2 Online shopping is the reason fewer people shop at the mall these days. (because of)

....

3 Murphy's arguments are very strong. I agree with her opinions. (that is why)

....

4 The light from their devices is the reason people aren't getting enough sleep. (due to)

....

C PRACTICE   On a separate sheet of paper, rewrite this paragraph by adding connecting words and phrases. Use a comma where necessary.

> **1** .... I completely agree with Murphy when she suggests we switch off our devices more often. It's just common sense. **2** .... I agree with her argument that our devices are keeping us up at night. **3** .... I always check my messages before going to bed, I know exactly what she means. **4** .... she makes a good point when she says that people are interacting face-to-face less and less. My family is trying to change that by setting aside family time. **5** .... I think she's right when she says, "Switching off our devices may be one of the most important decisions we can make." **6** .... I've decided to switch off my phone every evening at 7:00 P.M.

DIGITAL WRITING PROCESS

D APPLY THE WRITING SKILL   Write a critique of the article "Always Connected?" on page 116. Begin by stating your opinion. To comment on the article's point of view, and to support yours, use quotes or paraphrase what the writer says. Write at least two paragraphs.
Idea: first, underline sentences in the article you want to comment on.

> **SELF-CHECK**
>
> ☐ Did I use connecting words and phrases to present and support my opinions?
>
> ☐ Did I use quotation marks when citing the writer's own words?
>
> ☐ Did I paraphrase the writer's words when I didn't use direct speech?

A ▶ 5:26 **Listen to the conversations. Complete each statement with the correct idiom or expression.**

1 He has decided to ....
 a slack off   **b** draw the line   **c** be on call

2 She's ....
 a slacking off   **b** got a lot on her plate   **c** giving it her all

3 He's managing to ....
 a keep up   **b** be on call   **c** slack off

4 Her boss might think she was ....
 a keeping up   **b** giving it her all   **c** slacking off

B **Use the prompts to write questions using be supposed to.**

1 (we / read / the article before class tomorrow)

....

2 (why / I / contact / the authorities tomorrow morning)

....

3 (what / they / bring / to the party later tonight)

....

4 (what time / we / call / the office next Friday)

....

5 (how long / Daniel / stay at the library this afternoon)

....

6 (where / Lisa / go / tomorrow)

....

C **Respond to each statement in your own words, using expressions from Preview or Lesson 1.**

1 	❝Uh-oh. I really messed up. ❞

You: ....
....

2 	❝I'm so sorry I forgot to call you! It completely slipped my mind. ❞

You: ....
....

3 	❝Let's face it. You're working too hard. ❞

You: ....
....

D **Write an adverb form for each adjective.**

1 angry   ....
2 busy   ....
3 responsible   ....
4 appropriate   ....
5 happy   ....

6 preferable   ....
7 respectful   ....
8 honest   ....
9 polite   ....

TEST-TAKING SKILLS BOOSTER p. 160

Web Project: Extreme Sports
www.english.com/summit3e

Reference Charts

PRONUNCIATION TABLE

These are the pronunciation symbols used in *Summit 1*.

Vowels

Symbol	Key Word	Symbol	Key Word
i	beat, feed	ə	banana, among
ɪ	bit, did	ɚ	shirt, murder
eɪ	date, paid	aɪ	bite, cry, buy, eye
ɛ	bet, bed	aʊ	about, how
æ	bat, bad	ɔɪ	voice, boy
ɑ	box, odd, father	ɪr	beer
ɔ	bought, dog	ɛr	bare
oʊ	boat, road	ɑr	bar
ʊ	book, good	ɔr	door
u	boot, food, student	ʊr	tour
ʌ	but, mud, mother		

Consonants

Symbol	Key Word	Symbol	Key Word
p	pack, happy	z	zip, please, goes
b	back, rubber	ʃ	ship, machine,
t	tie		station, special,
d	die		discussion
k	came, key, quick	ʒ	measure, vision
g	game, guest	h	hot, who
tʃ	church, nature,	m	men, some
	watch	n	sun, know,
dʒ	judge, general,		pneumonia
	major	ŋ	sung, ringing
f	fan, photograph	w	wet, white
v	van	l	light, long
θ	thing, breath	r	right, wrong
ð	then, breathe	y	yes, use, music
s	sip, city,	t̬	butter, bottle
	psychology	t̚	button

IRREGULAR VERBS

base form	simple past	past participle	base form	simple past	past participle
be	was / were	been	forget	forgot	forgotten
beat	beat	beaten	forgive	forgave	forgiven
become	became	become	freeze	froze	frozen
begin	began	begun	get	got	gotten
bend	bent	bent	give	gave	given
bet	bet	bet	go	went	gone
bite	bit	bitten	grow	grew	grown
bleed	bled	bled	hang	hung	hung
blow	blew	blown	have	had	had
break	broke	broken	hear	heard	heard
breed	bred	bred	hide	hid	hidden
bring	brought	brought	hit	hit	hit
build	built	built	hold	held	held
burn	burned / burnt	burned / burnt	hurt	hurt	hurt
burst	burst	burst	keep	kept	kept
buy	bought	bought	know	knew	known
catch	caught	caught	lay	laid	laid
choose	chose	chosen	lead	led	led
come	came	come	leap	leaped / leapt	leaped / leapt
cost	cost	cost	learn	learned / learnt	learned / learnt
creep	crept	crept	leave	left	left
cut	cut	cut	lend	lent	lent
deal	dealt	dealt	let	let	let
dig	dug	dug	lie	lay	lain
do	did	done	light	lit	lit
draw	drew	drawn	lose	lost	lost
dream	dreamed / dreamt	dreamed / dreamt	make	made	made
drink	drank	drunk	mean	meant	meant
drive	drove	driven	meet	met	met
eat	ate	eaten	mistake	mistook	mistaken
fall	fell	fallen	pay	paid	paid
feed	fed	fed	put	put	put
feel	felt	felt	quit	quit	quit
fight	fought	fought	read /rid/	read /rɛd/	read /rɛd/
find	found	found	ride	rode	ridden
fit	fit	fit	ring	rang	rung
fly	flew	flown	rise	rose	risen
forbid	forbade	forbidden	run	ran	run

base form	simple past	past participle	base form	simple past	past participle
say	said	said	spring	sprang / sprung	sprung
see	saw	seen	stand	stood	stood
sell	sold	sold	steal	stole	stolen
send	sent	sent	stick	stuck	stuck
set	set	set	sting	stung	stung
shake	shook	shaken	stink	stank / stunk	stunk
shed	shed	shed	strike	struck	struck / stricken
shine	shone	shone	string	strung	strung
shoot	shot	shot	swear	swore	sworn
show	showed	shown	sweep	swept	swept
shrink	shrank	shrunk	swim	swam	swum
shut	shut	shut	swing	swung	swung
sing	sang	sung	take	took	taken
sink	sank	sunk	teach	taught	taught
sit	sat	sat	tear	tore	torn
sleep	slept	slept	tell	told	told
slide	slid	slid	think	thought	thought
smell	smelled / smelt	smelled / smelt	throw	threw	thrown
speak	spoke	spoken	understand	understood	understood
speed	sped / speeded	sped / speeded	upset	upset	upset
spell	spelled / spelt	spelled / spelt	wake	woke / waked	woken / waked
spend	spent	spent	wear	wore	worn
spill	spilled / spilt	spilled / spilt	weave	wove	woven
spin	spun	spun	weep	wept	wept
spit	spit / spat	spit / spat	win	won	won
spoil	spoiled / spoilt	spoiled / spoilt	wind	wound	wound
spread	spread	spread	write	wrote	written

STATIVE VERBS

amaze	desire	hear	need	seem
appear*	dislike	imagine	owe	smell*
appreciate	doubt	include*	own	sound
astonish	envy	know	please	suppose
be*	equal	like	possess	surprise
believe	exist	look like	prefer	taste*
belong	fear	look*	realize	think*
care	feel*	love	recognize	understand
consist of	forget	matter	remember*	want*
contain	hate	mean	resemble	weigh*
cost	have*	mind	see*	

*These verbs also have action meanings. Example: *I see a tree.* (non-action) *I'm seeing her tomorrow.* (action)

VERBS FOLLOWED BY A GERUND

acknowledge	consider	endure	imagine	prevent	resent
admit	delay	enjoy	justify	prohibit	resist
advise	deny	escape	keep	propose	risk
appreciate	detest	explain	mention	quit	suggest
avoid	discontinue	feel like	mind	recall	support
can't help	discuss	finish	miss	recommend	tolerate
celebrate	dislike	forgive	postpone	report	understand
complete	don't mind	give up	practice		

EXPRESSIONS THAT CAN BE FOLLOWED BY A GERUND

be excited about	be opposed to	believe in	blame [someone or something] for
be worried about	be used to	participate in	forgive [someone or something] for
be responsible for	complain about	succeed in	thank [someone or something] for
be interested in	dream about / of	take advantage of	keep [someone or something] from
be accused of	talk about / of	take care of	prevent [someone or something] from
be capable of	think about / of	insist on	stop [someone or something] from
be tired of	apologize for	look forward to	
be accustomed to	make an excuse for		
be committed to	have a reason for		

VERBS FOLLOWED DIRECTLY BY AN INFINITIVE

afford	choose	grow	mean	pretend	threaten
agree	claim	hesitate	need	promise	volunteer
appear	consent	hope	neglect	refuse	wait
arrange	decide	hurry	offer	request	want
ask	demand	intend	pay	seem	wish
attempt	deserve	learn	plan	struggle	would like
can't wait	expect	manage	prepare	swear	yearn
care	fail				

VERBS FOLLOWED BY AN OBJECT BEFORE AN INFINITIVE*

advise	choose*	force	need*	remind	urge
allow	convince	get*	order	request	want*
ask*	enable	help*	pay	require	warn
beg	encourage	hire	permit	teach	wish*
cause	expect*	instruct	persuade	tell	would like*
challenge	forbid	invite	promise*		

*In the active voice, these verbs can be followed by the infinitive without an object (example: *want to speak* or *want someone to speak*).

ADJECTIVES FOLLOWED BY AN INFINITIVE*

afraid	content	disturbed	glad	proud	sorry
alarmed	curious	eager	happy	ready	surprised
amazed	delighted	easy	hesitant	relieved	touched
angry	depressed	embarrassed	likely	reluctant	upset
anxious	determined	encouraged	lucky	sad	willing
ashamed	disappointed	excited	pleased	shocked	
certain	distressed	fortunate	prepared		

*Example: *I'm willing **to accept** that.*

VERBS THAT CAN BE FOLLOWED BY A GERUND OR AN INFINITIVE

with a change in meaning			without a change in meaning	
forget (+ gerund)	=	forget something that happened	begin	love
(+ infinitive)	=	forget something that needs to be done	can't stand	prefer
regret (+ gerund)	=	regret a past action	continue	start
(+ infinitive)	=	regret having to inform someone about an action	hate	try
remember (+ gerund)	=	remember something that happened	like	
(+ infinitive)	=	remember something that needs to be done		
stop (+ gerund)	=	stop a continuous action		
(+ infinitive)	=	stop in order to do something		

PARTICIPIAL ADJECTIVES

alarming	–	alarmed	disturbing	–	disturbed	paralyzing	–	paralyzed
amazing	–	amazed	embarrassing	–	embarrassed	pleasing	–	pleased
amusing	–	amused	entertaining	–	entertained	relaxing	–	relaxed
annoying	–	annoyed	exciting	–	excited	satisfying	–	satisfied
astonishing	–	astonished	exhausting	–	exhausted	shocking	–	shocked
boring	–	bored	fascinating	–	fascinated	soothing	–	soothed
comforting	–	comforted	frightening	–	frightened	startling	–	startled
confusing	–	confused	horrifying	–	horrified	stimulating	–	stimulated
depressing	–	depressed	inspiring	–	inspired	surprising	–	surprised
disappointing	–	disappointed	interesting	–	interested	terrifying	–	terrified
disgusting	–	disgusted	irritating	–	irritated	tiring	–	tired
distressing	–	distressed	moving	–	moved	touching	–	touched

Grammar Booster

The Grammar Booster is optional. It offers more information and extra practice, as well as Grammar for Writing. Sometimes it further explains or expands the unit grammar and points out common errors. In other cases, it reviews and practices previously learned grammar that would be helpful when learning new grammar concepts. If you use the Grammar Booster, you will find extra exercises in the Workbook in a separate section labeled Grammar Booster. The Grammar Booster content is not tested on any *Summit* tests.

UNIT 1

Infinitives: review, expansion, and common errors

Statements

Using an infinitive as the subject of a sentence sounds extremely formal in speaking. There are two ways to express the same idea: (1) Make the infinitive a subject complement, or (2) use an impersonal <u>it</u>.

To be a mother is my greatest wish. $\rightarrow$

1 My greatest wish is **to be** a mother.

2 **It's** my greatest wish **to be** a mother.

When making a statement with an impersonal <u>It</u> and an infinitive about a specific person or people, use a phrase with **for** + a noun or a pronoun to name that person or people.

It isn't hard **for me** to learn new languages.

It usually takes time **for new students** to get to know each other.

It's too late **for Ella and Paul** to go out for dinner now.

With causative <u>get</u>

Use an infinitive, not a base form, with causative <u>get</u>.

We **got** everyone **to fill out** the survey.

The teacher **got** me **to compare** my personality with my mother's personality.

In indirect speech

Use an infinitive to replace an imperative in indirect speech.

The manager said, "Be at the meeting at 2:15 sharp." $\rightarrow$ The manager said **to be** at the meeting at 2:15 sharp.

She told us, "Don't call before dinner." $\rightarrow$ She told us **not to call** before dinner.

> **Be careful!** You can't use an adjective of feeling or emotion in statements with <u>It's</u> + adjective and infinitive. You have to use an actual subject.
> **My sister** is happy to graduate.
> NOT <s>It's</s> happy to graduate.

> **Some adjectives of feeling or emotion:**
> | | | | |
> |---|---|---|---|
> | afraid | ashamed | excited | sad |
> | amazed | depressed | glad | shocked |
> | angry | disappointed | happy | sorry |
> | anxious | embarrassed | pleased | upset |

A On a separate sheet of paper, rewrite each sentence, changing the subject infinitive to a subject complement.

1 To be successful is every new graduate's wish.

2 To cook dinner is my chore for the evening.

3 To win the game is every player's dream.

4 To rescue hikers lost in the woods is the responsibility of the park police.

5 To win the election is every candidate's task.

B Rewrite each sentence, beginning with an impersonal <u>it</u>.

1 To be disciplined about an exercise program is difficult for an easygoing person.

2 To get to work on time is a good idea.

3 To be outgoing in new situations is helpful.

4 To act friendly is always worthwhile.

5 To be too talkative can sometimes be a problem.

6 To pass the examination is not the easiest thing in the world.

7 To live in an English-speaking country might be an exciting experience.

8 To know when to use an infinitive and when to use a gerund is pretty confusing.

C Insert a phrase with <u>for</u> in each of the following sentences.

 for new drivers
1 It's hard⌃to drive in a lot of traffic.

2 It's important to remember that some difficult things are just a part of life.

3 It's smart to realize that it's better to be safe than sorry.

4 It's too late to make the early show.

5 It's essential to use insect repellent when you camp in the woods.

6 It's good to avoid being too outgoing when you're starting a new job.

D On a separate sheet of paper, rewrite each statement in indirect speech.

1 Celine said, "Don't be late for the meeting."

2 Last night they told me, "Always take care when you go out in the evening."

3 My sister said, "Don't call me before 7:00 A.M."

4 The tour guide told them, "Just roll with the punches."

✏ Grammar for Writing: parallelism with gerunds and infinitives

A common error in formal written English is mixing gerunds and infinitives when listing items in a series. A list of items should be either all gerunds or all infinitives.

> When I take time off from work, I prefer **relaxing** at home, **spending** time with my family, and **getting** things done around the house. NOT I prefer relaxing at home, spending time with my family, and ~~to get~~ things done around the house.
>
> I can't stand **getting up** late and **missing** the bus. NOT I can't stand getting up late and ~~to miss~~ the bus.

In a series, either use <u>to</u> with all the infinitives or use it only with the first one.

> When I take time off from work, I prefer **to relax** at home, **spend** time with my family, and **get** things done around the house. NOT When I take time off from work, I prefer to relax at home, spend time with my family, and ~~to~~ get things done around the house.

E On a separate sheet of paper, correct the errors in parallelism in the following sentences.

1 After she arrived in London, she began to write long letters home and calling her parents at all hours of the night.

2 There are two things I really can't stand doing: speaking in front of large audiences and chat with people I don't know at parties.

3 Right before midnight, everyone began to sing, dance, and to welcome in the new year.

4 There's no question I prefer using all my vacation time and take a long vacation.

F Complete the following sentences, using appropriate gerund or infinitive forms. Refer to pages 122–124 in the Reference Charts if necessary.

1 I would suggest .... out the form immediately and .... a copy for your records.
                                       fill   *make*

2 Did you remember .... off the stove, ... the windows, and .... the door before you left?
                                      turn   *close*   *lock*

3 It's obvious from her e-mails that she really loves .... the culture, ... new people, and just .... there.
                              experience   *meet*   *be*

4 They prohibit .... photographs or .... a recorder.
                        take   *use*

5 I really wouldn't mind .... them out to dinner or .... them around if you'd like me to.
                        take   *show*

6 He promised .... the report home, ... it carefully, and .... to any questions by the next day.
                    take   *read*   *respond*

UNIT 2

Finished and unfinished actions: summary

Finished actions

Use the simple past tense or the past of <u>be</u> for an action finished at a specified time in the past.

> They **watched** some movies yesterday.

Use the present perfect for an action finished at an unspecified time in the past.

> They**'ve watched** that movie three times.

Use the past perfect for an action that was finished before another action in the past.

When I arrived, they **had** already **watched** the movie.

Note: Although the continuous aspect is used for actions in progress, the present perfect continuous is sometimes used for very recently completed actions, especially to emphasize duration.

They**'ve been watching** movies all afternoon, but they're done now.

Unfinished actions

Use the past continuous for unfinished actions that continued for a period of time or during a specific time in the past.

I **was relaxing** at home all morning.

At noon, I **was watching** a movie.

Use the present perfect OR the present perfect continuous for unfinished actions that began in the past and may continue into the future. Use the present perfect continuous to further emphasize that the action is continuous.

She**'s listened** to R&B for years. [And she may continue.]

OR She**'s been listening** to R&B for years. [And she may continue.]

A Complete the article, using the simple past tense, the past of <u>be</u>, or the present perfect.

World Music is not really a true genre of music—it is a combination of musical genres from around the world. More recently recording companies .... the term to describe the music of artists who

1 use
they felt could appeal to new audiences across cultures. The concept of World Music .... first

2 be
created after U.S. singer / songwriter Paul Simon .... his hugely successful *Graceland* album

3 record
in 1986. At that time, he .... South Africa's male choir Ladysmith Black Mambazo and rock

4 invite
group Savuka to accompany him on the recording. Both groups later .... with him around

5 tour
the world. This exciting collaboration immediately .... to European and North American

6 appeal
audiences, who were attracted to this different sound.

Since that time, as more artists .... to reach new audiences, there .... an

7 try   8 be
increased amount of "crossover"—that is, musicians influencing each other across cultures. Enthusiasm for music from other cultures .... steadily. Artists such as Angélique Kidjo and Carlos Vives, who

9 rise
were well-known within specific regions such as Africa or Latin America, ... international

10 become
stars, and mainstream music .... many of the features of these artists.

11 incorporate

B Read each statement. Then decide which description is closer in meaning.

1 By the time I heard about it, the concert had sold out.

  a First I heard about the concert. Then it sold out.

  b First the concert sold out. Then I heard about it.

2 After he'd won the award, he got a big recording contract.

  a First he got the recording contract. Then he won the award.

  b First he won the award. Then he got the recording contract.

3 We wanted to go to his performance because we'd heard his new album.

  a First we heard his album. Then we wanted to go to his performance.

  b First we wanted to go to his performance. Then we heard his album.

4 He'd played at a lot of different halls before he performed at Carnegie Hall.

  a First he performed at Carnegie Hall. Then he played at a lot of different halls.

  b First he played at a lot of different halls. Then he performed at Carnegie Hall.

Noun clauses: review and expansion

Remember: A noun clause functions as a noun and is often introduced with <u>that</u>. When a noun clause is a direct object, use of <u>that</u> is optional.

> I didn't realize **(that) art therapy could be so helpful**.

Introduce a noun clause with <u>if</u> or <u>whether</u> when it is an embedded <u>yes</u> / <u>no</u> question. Use a question word when it is an embedded information question.

> (Does she come from the U.S.?) Do you know **if she comes from the U.S.**?
>
> (When does the concert begin?) I'm not sure **when the concert begins**.

A noun clause can also function as the subject of a sentence. A noun clause introduced with a question word can also function as a subject complement.

> **What he said** was very interesting. (subject)
>
> **That she's a therapist** surprises me. (subject)
>
> Teaching children is **what I love**. (subject complement)

> **Be careful!** Don't use question word order in noun clauses that are embedded questions.
>
> I don't know **where the band is performing**.
> NOT I don't know where is the band performing.
>
> Does he understand **what the lyrics mean**?
> NOT Does he understand what do the lyrics mean?
>
> Use a period with an embedded question within a statement. Use a question mark with an embedded question within a question.
>
> **I don't know** who is singing**.**
>
> **Do you know** who is singing**?**

C Complete each noun clause with <u>that</u>, <u>if</u> (or <u>whether</u>), or a question word. (Some have more than one possible answer.)

1 She thinks .... classical music is boring.

2 Catching up with friends on social media is .... I spend Saturday mornings.

3 I don't remember .... bands we saw in concert last year.

4 .... I like most is electronic pop.

5 Did anyone tell you .... I'm showing my paintings at the Henderson gallery?

6 Robert asked me .... I had bought tickets for the ballet yet.

7 I can't imagine .... life would be like without the arts.

8 I don't really know .... to cook very well.

9 New York is .... the Empire State Building is located.

10 I wonder .... the concert begins.

D Complete each statement, using a noun clause based on the question in parentheses.

1 (Where did Mozart live?) I don't know ....

2 (What type of music does our teacher like?) I have no idea ....

3 (When did the Black Eyed Peas recently perform in Chicago?) She asked me ....

4 (Are ballet tickets really expensive?) I don't know ....

5 (How long is the musical Annie?) I'm not sure ....

6 (Will the movie end before 6:00?) He's asking ....

✏ Grammar for Writing: noun clauses as adjective and noun complements

As adjective complements

To more formally make a point, use <u>It</u> + <u>be</u> or another linking verb + an adjective with a noun clause beginning with <u>that</u>. <u>That</u> is optional.

> **It is clear (that)** Hensley has done a lot of research.
>
> **It seems obvious (that)** the band needs a new lead singer.
>
> **It was surprising (that)** they never performed together again.

As noun complements

To more formally focus on an issue or topic, complete the meaning of a noun phrase with a noun clause. <u>That</u> is necessary.

> The fact **that her songs were extremely popular** made her very wealthy.
>
> The belief **that vaccines might be harmful** led some people to refuse them.

Some adjectives used in expressions with <u>It</u> + <u>be</u> or another linking verb:

It	is was will be could be seems	obvious important essential unacceptable surprising interesting	(that)

Some noun phrases used to introduce noun clauses:

The announcement that	The idea that
The argument that	The news that
The belief that	The possibility that
The chance that	The proposal that
The claim that	The recommendation that
The demand that	The report that
The fact that	The suggestion that

E On a separate sheet of paper, rewrite each sentence, using <u>It</u> + <u>be</u> (or a linking verb) + an adjective and a noun clause as an adjective complement.

1 That developing countries address the problems caused by global warming is extremely important.

2 That the president plans on resigning appears obvious to everyone.

3 That not providing disaster relief will only worsen the situation seems quite clear.

4 That a cure for cancer will be discovered in the next twenty years is certainly possible.

5 That the governments of Argentina and Chile will reach an agreement looks very likely.

6 That Max Bianchi won't be participating in the Olympics next year is not important.

F Read each quote from a radio news program. Then, on a separate sheet of paper, complete each statement, using the noun clause as a noun complement.

Example: "Volkswagen announced **that they would unveil a new car design early next year**. This is causing a lot of excitement in the auto industry." [The announcement …]

> *The announcement that Volkswagen would unveil a new car design*
> *early next year is causing a lot of excitement in the auto industry.*

1 "The Health Ministry announced **that they will begin vaccinating all infants for measles**. This was greeted with criticism from the opposition party." [The announcement …]

2 "The president said it was possible **that he would resign by the end of this year**. This has taken everyone by surprise, including the news media." [The possibility …]

3 "The London Sun reports **that Dr. Regina Blair of the Glasgow Medical Center has discovered a new protein**. This is attracting much interest in the world of science." [The report …]

4 "The Auckland Times claimed **that a ninety-five-year-old New Zealand man had broken the world record for growing the longest beard**. This has triggered similar claims across three continents." [The claim …]

UNIT 3

The past unreal conditional: inverted form

The conditional clause of past unreal conditional sentences can be stated without <u>if</u> by simply inverting <u>had</u> and the subject of the clause. Clauses using inverted word order are more formal than those using usual (non-inverted) word order.

> **Be careful!** Don't contract <u>not</u> with <u>had</u> in inverted negative clauses.
> Had they not been there, they wouldn't have known the truth.
> NOT ~~Hadn't~~ they been there, they wouldn't have known the truth.

Usual word order		Inverted word order
If I had known it would take up so much room, I wouldn't have bought it.	→	**Had I known** it would take up so much room, I wouldn't have bought it.
I might have gotten another brand **if I had realized** it would be so hard to operate.	→	I might have gotten another brand **had I realized** it would be so hard to operate.
If we hadn't been so busy, we could have shopped around.	→	**Had we not been** so busy, we could have shopped around.
If she had told me this thing wouldn't operate without batteries, I would never have considered getting it.	→	**Had she told** me this thing wouldn't operate without batteries, I would never have considered getting it.

A On a separate sheet of paper, rewrite the following past unreal conditional sentences, using the inverted form.

1 They would have lent her their car if she had asked.

2 If I hadn't spent so much money on my vacation, I would have considered buying a stationary bicycle.

3 If the Carsons hadn't moved into such a small apartment, they would have bought a treadmill.

4 Could you have gotten the car if they hadn't raised the price?

B On a separate sheet of paper, complete the statements of buyer's remorse, using the inverted form and the Vocabulary from page 28.

1 … I would never have gotten that espresso maker.

2 … we never would have bought such a large sofa.

3 … I could have gotten an entertainment center with fewer pieces.

4 … we probably would have bought a more economical car.

5 … I would have gotten a DVR with simpler directions.

The future continuous

Use the future continuous for actions that will be in progress at a specific time or over a period of time in the future. To form the future continuous, use <u>will</u> + <u>be</u> + a present participle OR <u>be going to</u> + <u>be</u> + a present participle.

At this time next week, I { **'ll be lying** / **'m going to be lying** } on a beach in Hawaii. [specific time]

I { **'ll be studying** / **'m going to be studying** } English in the United States for about two years. [period of time]

Sometimes sentences in the simple future and the future continuous have almost the same meaning. Choose the future continuous to emphasize a continuous or uninterrupted activity.

Next year, I**'ll study** English in the United States.

Next year, I**'ll be studying** English in the United States.

Questions and short answers

Will you **be working** at home? Yes, I **will**. / No, I **won't**.

Are you **going to be working** at home? Yes, I **am**. / No, I**'m not**.

Use the future continuous and a time clause with <u>while</u> or <u>when</u> to describe a continuous activity that will occur at the same time as another activity. Do not use a future form in the time clause.

I**'ll be looking** for a job while my wife **continues** her studies.

NOT I'll be looking for a job while my wife ~~will be continuing~~ her studies.

When the teacher **is speaking**, we**'ll be listening** carefully.

NOT When the teacher ~~will be speaking~~, we'll be listening carefully.

> **Remember:** Don't use a continuous form with a stative verb. Stative verbs are "non-action" verbs such as <u>be</u>, <u>have</u>, <u>know</u>, <u>remember</u>, <u>like</u>, <u>seem</u>, <u>appreciate</u>, etc.
>
> Do not use the continuous with stative verbs.
> DON'T SAY By next month, ~~I'll be having~~ a new car.
>
> For a complete list of stative verbs, see page 123 in the Reference Charts.

C On a separate sheet of paper, correct the errors in the following sentences.

1 She'll be staying at the Newton Hotel when she's going to be attending the meeting.

2 We won't be spending much time sightseeing while we'll be visiting London.

3 When he's going to stay in town, he's going to be meeting with some friends.

4 She'll be correcting homework while the students will take the test.

5 While Michelle will be serving dessert, Randy will already be washing the dishes.

6 Won't they be going to sleep in New York when you'll be getting up in Taipei?

D Complete the following sentences, using the future continuous with <u>will</u> when possible. If the future continuous is not possible, use the simple future with <u>will</u>.

1 After I've completed my studies, I .... for a job.

　　　　　　　　　　　　　　　　　　look

2 She .... historic sites while she's in Turkey.

　　photograph

3 In a few years, they .... all the problems they had.

　　　　　　　　not / remember

4 .... he .... very long between flights?

　　　　　　　　　　　wait

5 I'm sure she .... when you call tonight.

　　　　not / sleep

The future perfect continuous

Use the future perfect continuous to emphasize the continuous quality of an action that began before a specific time in the future. To form the future perfect continuous, use <u>will</u> (or <u>won't</u>) + <u>have been</u> and a present participle.

> By next year, I'**ll have been studying** English for five years. [Describes an action that began before "next year" and may still continue.]

Combine a statement using the future perfect continuous with a time clause to show the relationship between two future actions. Use the simple present tense in the time clause.

> **By the time I arrive** in New York, I'**ll have been sitting** in a plane for over ten hours.
> NOT By the time ~~I'll arrive~~ in New York, I'll have been sitting in a plane for over ten hours.

E Complete the postcard, using the future continuous or the future perfect continuous.

> Dear Ida,
>
> Venice was great, but finally on to Paris! By tomorrow afternoon, I .... down
> the Champs Elysées and .... in the beautiful sights of that great city.
> _{1 stroll}   _{2 take}
> In the evening, I .... an opera by Bizet in the city where he was born.
> _{3 enjoy}
> Just think, by Saturday, I .... delicious French food for a whole week!
> _{4 eat}
> Plus, I .... my French with real native speakers. Then, after Paris, it's off to
> _{5 practice}
> the Riviera, where I .... around on the beaches of Nice and Saint-Tropez
> _{6 lounge}
> for a week. By that time, I .... for three weeks, and it will almost be time
> _{7 travel}
> to come home—a long trip for a homebody like me!
>
> See you soon!
>
> Pavel

UNIT 4

Quantifiers: <u>a few</u> and <u>few</u>, <u>a little</u> and <u>little</u>

Use <u>a few</u> with plural count nouns and <u>a little</u> with non-count nouns to mean "some."
Use <u>few</u> with plural count nouns and <u>little</u> with non-count nouns to mean "not many" or "not much."

<u>A few</u> / <u>few</u>

> **A few companies** are allowing their employees to dress casually on Fridays. [= some companies]
> **Few companies** are allowing their employees to dress casually on Fridays. [= not many companies]

<u>A little</u> / <u>little</u>

> Employees are showing **a little interest** in this new dress code. [= some interest]
> Employees are showing **little interest** in this new dress code. [= not much interest]

Quantifiers used without referents

Quantifiers can be used without the noun they describe, as long as the context has been made clear earlier.

> Most people don't think we'll find life on other planets in our lifetime, but **a few** do.
> Several workers in our office think people should dress down every day, but **most** don't.

A Change the underlined quantifiers to <u>a few</u>, <u>few</u>, <u>a little</u>, or <u>little</u>.

1 Would you like to listen to <u>some</u> music? ^{a little}

2 We actually eat <u>almost no</u> meat.

3 There were <u>several</u> new students in my class today.

4 I've seen <u>hardly any</u> movies in the last month.

5 I enjoy visiting Ames, but there's <u>not much</u> to do there.

6 If you look in the fridge, there should be <u>some</u> eggs.

Quantifiers: using _of_ for specific reference

Use _of_ when a noun is preceded by a possessive adjective, a possessive noun, a demonstrative adjective, or the article _the_.

More general	More specific
any friends	**any of** her friends
some students	**some of** his students
one cat	**one of** my cats
all employees	**all of** our employees
most co-workers	**most of** Jack's co-workers
several companies	**several of** these companies
many books	**many of** those books
a few choices	**a few of** the choices
a little cake	**a little of** the cake

> **possessive adjectives** = my, her, their, etc.
> **possessive nouns** = John's, the doctor's
> **demonstrative adjectives** = this, that, these, those

Using _of_ after _all_ or _both_ is optional, with no change in meaning.

all of our employees	OR	**all** our employees	NOT	**all** ~~of~~ employees
both of those choices	OR	**both** those choices	NOT	**both** ~~of~~ choices

> **Be careful!** In the superlative, do not use _of_ after _most_.
> DON'T SAY Tokyo is the city with the most ~~of~~ people in Japan.
>
> _Of_ must be included when using an object pronoun.
> **both of** them NOT ~~both them~~

One and _each_ are used with singular nouns only. But _one of_ and _each of_ are used with plural nouns only. However, the meaning of both expressions is still singular.

One student	—	**One of** the students
Each class	—	**Each of** the classes

Some quantifiers must include _of_ when they modify a noun or noun phrase.

a lot of	a majority of	a couple of	a bit of
lots of	plenty of	a number of	a great deal of

B Only one of each pair of sentences is correct. Check the correct sentence and correct the mistake in the other one.

1. a ☑ She went with several of her classmates.
   b ☐ Several ~~of~~ classmates went out for coffee.
2. a ☐ Most of companies in the world are fairly formal.
   b ☐ Most of the companies in the United States have dress-down days.
3. a ☐ All of hot appetizers were delicious.
   b ☐ Everyone tried all of the cold appetizers.
4. a ☐ A lot of my friends have traveled to exotic places.
   b ☐ There are a lot places I'd like to see.
5. a ☐ I read a few of Steinbeck's novels last year.
   b ☐ A few of novels by Steinbeck take place in Mexico.
6. a ☐ Several managers were interviewed, and many them liked the new policy.
   b ☐ Many of the employees we spoke with liked the new policy.

✎ Grammar for Writing: subject-verb agreement of quantifiers followed by _of_

In quantifiers with _of_, the verb must agree with the noun that comes after _of_.

Some of **the movie is** in English.	—	Some of **the movies are** in English.
A lot of **the music was** jazz.	—	A lot of **the musicians were** young.

In formal written English, _none of_ is traditionally followed by a singular verb. However, in spoken English it is almost always used with a plural verb. The plural verb is acceptable and correct.

Formal: **None of** the students **was** late for class.
Informal: **None of** the students **were** late for class.

> **Be careful!** The quantifiers _one of_, _each of_, and _every one of_ are always followed by a plural noun, but they always take a singular verb.
> **One of** the students **likes** rap music.

C Choose the verb that agrees with each subject.

1 Every one of these choices (sound / sounds) terrific!

2 One of the teachers (was / were) going to stay after class.

3 A lot of the problem (is / are) that no one wants to work so hard.

4 Each of the employees (want / wants) to work overtime.

5 Half of the city (was / were) flooded in the storm.

6 None of the players (is coming / are coming) to the game.

7 Only 8 percent of their workers prefer shorter work weeks, while at least 90 percent (don't / doesn't).

UNIT 5

Conjunctions with <u>so</u>, <u>too</u>, <u>neither</u>, or <u>not either</u>

Use <u>and so</u> or <u>and ... too</u> to join affirmative statements that are similar.

Spitting on the street is offensive, **and so** is littering. OR ... , **and** littering is, **too**.

Playing loud music bothers me, **and so** does smoking. OR ... , **and** smoking does, **too**.

Use <u>and neither</u> or <u>and ... not either</u> to join negative statements that are similar.

Playing loud music isn't polite, **and neither** is smoking. OR ... **and** smoking isn**'t either**.

Spitting on the street doesn't bother me, **and neither** does littering. OR ... **and** littering doesn**'t either**.

If the first clause uses the verb <u>be</u>, an auxiliary verb, or a modal, use the same structure in the second clause.

Tokyo **is** a huge city, and so **is** São Paulo.

New York **doesn't** have a lot of industry, and neither **does** London.

Mexico City **has** grown a lot, and so **has** Los Angeles.

Nancy **can't** tolerate loud music, and neither **can** Tom.

I **haven't** been to Tokyo, and neither **have** you.

If the first clause is an affirmative statement in the simple present or simple past tense, use <u>do</u>, <u>does</u>, or <u>did</u> in the second clause.

John **thinks** graffiti is a big problem, and so **does** Helen.

My wife **enjoyed** visiting Paris, and so **did** I.

> **Notice the subject-verb order.**
> ... and so **is littering**.
> ... and **littering is**, too.
>
> ... and neither **does littering**.
> ... and **littering doesn't** either.

> **Be careful!**
> Use a negative verb, auxiliary verb, or modal with <u>either</u> and an affirmative with <u>neither</u>.
> ... and littering **doesn't either**.
> NOT ... and littering ~~does either~~.
> ... and **neither does** littering.
> NOT ... and ~~neither doesn't~~ littering.
>
> With <u>so</u> and <u>neither</u>, the verb (or auxiliary verb or modal) goes before the subject.
> Tokyo is a huge city, and so **is São Paulo**.
> NOT ... and so ~~São Paulo is~~.
> Nancy can't stand loud music, and neither **can Tom**.
> NOT ... neither ~~Tom can~~.

A Find and underline the nine errors. On a separate sheet of paper, write each sentence correctly.

New York is one of the most famous cities in the world, and so does London. While these two cities differ in many ways, they also share a number of characteristics. Here's a quick comparison:

- If you're looking for peace and quiet, New York is not the place to be, and neither London is. They are both exciting and noisy places. If you're not used to it, New York's traffic can be deafening at times, and so does London's.

- The best way to get around in both cities is the subway (or the Tube in London). New York's subway system is quite old and elaborate, and is London's, too.

- If you're looking for first-rate entertainment, New York is filled with theaters, and so London does.

- Hungry? London's restaurants feature exciting dishes from around the world, and New York's are, too.

- Both cities offer a huge choice of museums to visit. The museums in New York can't possibly be seen in a day, and either London's can't.

- New York offers some of the world's most famous tourist sites—for example, the Statue of Liberty and the Empire State Building—and so is London, with Buckingham Palace and the Millennium Wheel.

It's clear that New York shouldn't be missed, and neither London shouldn't!

B On a separate sheet of paper, rewrite each statement, using the word in parentheses. Make any necessary changes in verbs or possessive adjectives.

Example: Both Quito and Cuenca have large historic sections. (so)

> Quito has a large historic section, and so does Cuenca.

1 Both Bangkok and São Paulo face many problems caused by too much traffic. (so)
2 Both Beijing and London have hosted the Olympic Games in the past. (too)
3 Vancouver and Taipei don't ever get very cold. (neither)
4 Seoul and Jakarta won't experience a decrease in their populations any time soon. (not either)
5 Both Hong Kong and Rio de Janeiro are famous for their physical beauty. (so)
6 Prague and Krakow attract people who like old historic architecture. (too)
7 The Prado Museum in Madrid and the Louvre in Paris shouldn't be missed. (neither)
8 Tokyo and Mexico City haven't lost their places among the world's largest cities yet. (not either)

So, too, neither, or not either: short responses

Use <u>so</u>, <u>too</u>, <u>neither</u>, or <u>not either</u> in short responses to express agreement.

A: I hate littering.
B: So do I. OR I do, **too**.
   NOT So do I ~~hate~~. / I do ~~hate~~, too.

A: I can't stand smoking.
B: I can't **either**. OR **Neither** can I.
   NOT I can't ~~stand~~ either. / Neither can I ~~stand~~.

It is common to express agreement with <u>Me, too</u> or <u>Me neither</u>.

A: I hate littering.
B: Me, too.

A: I can't stand smoking.
B: Me neither.

C Agree with each statement three ways, using short responses with so, too, neither, or (not) either.

1 "I've never been to Ulan Bator."
   You: ....

2 "I can't figure this out."
   You: ....

3 "I loved going there!"
   You: ....

4 "I have to get some cash."
   You: ....

5 "I'm getting really tired."
   You: ....

6 "I used to travel more."
   You: ....

7 "I'll call her tomorrow."
   You: ....

8 "I'm not going to tell her she's late."
   You: ....

UNIT 6

Modals and modal-like expressions: summary

Make polite requests
Could I get your phone number?
Can my son have just one more cookie?
Would you please hold this for a second? (with <u>you</u> only)
May I have a cup of coffee? (formal, with <u>I</u> or <u>we</u> only)

Express preferences
I **would like to** see that movie.
Would you **like to** go running?
I**'d rather not** see a movie.
I **would rather** have left earlier.

Give or ask for permission
You **can** open the window if you want.
Can I leave this here?
You **may** leave early if you need to. (formal)
May I leave my coat here? (formal, with <u>I</u> or we only)

Express ability or lack of ability
He **can** complete the job for you in an hour.
Can you write well in English?
We **couldn't** finish the report yesterday.
Couldn't you find the restaurant?
My grandmother **isn't able to** walk any more.
Is she **able to** take care of herself?
She **was able to** do a lot more when she was younger.

Give a warning
Your mother **had better** see a doctor right away.
You **had better not** forget about your appointment.
He **had better have** called this morning.
They **had better not have** hurt any animals when they made that movie.

> **Note:** <u>Had better</u> is generally not used in questions. In spoken English, the contraction <u>'d better</u> is almost always used.

Modals and modal-like expressions: summary (continued)

Express possibility

It **may** rain this afternoon.

He **may not** be able to come this morning.

She **may have** forgotten to lock the door.

She **may not have** remembered.

It **might** be noisy at that restaurant.

She **might not** want to eat anything.

He **might have** gone home already.

He **might not have** paid yet.

It **could** rain tomorrow.

We **could have** paid less.

Draw conclusions

Your father **must** be very smart.

She **must not** think it's important.

They **must have** been exhausted when they got home.

He **must not have** sent it.

Suggest alternatives

You **could** take the next train.

Give suggestions

They really **should** think about staying longer.

He **shouldn't have** waited to make a reservation.

They **should have** called first.

You **shouldn't** stay at that hotel.

They really **ought to** think about staying longer.

They **ought to have** called first.

Should we have called first?

> **Note:** Ought to is not usually used in negative statements or questions. Use shouldn't or should instead.

Express necessity

We **have to** take the test tomorrow.

We**'ve got to** arrive on time. [informal, spoken]

All students **must** take the test. [formal]

Express lack of necessity

You **don't have to** have a passport.

She **didn't have to** pay a late fee.

Express prohibition or deny permission

New employees **cannot** (OR **shouldn't**) park their cars in the garage.

New employees **must not** park their cars in the garage. [formal]

New employees **may not** park their cars in the garage. [formal]

> **Note:** In questions, have to is generally used. Questions with must are very formal and not very common. Past necessity is expressed with had to.
> **Does** everyone **have to** take the test?
> **Must** everyone take the test?
> All students **had to** take the test.

A Cross out the one modal that *cannot* be used in each sentence or question.

1 (May / Can / Could) your mother please call me tonight?

2 I (wasn't able to / couldn't / shouldn't) get there on time because the traffic was so bad.

3 She (may / had better / can) be able to complete the job by tomorrow.

4 (Can / Should / Ought to) my students listen in while you practice?

5 Shoppers (may / have to / must) not park their cars in front of the main entrance.

6 Thank goodness she (doesn't have to / must not / was able to) renew her passport for another five years.

7 You (could / had better / should) let them know you won't be able to make it on time, or you may not get the job.

8 This restaurant is so good we (ought to / might / would rather) come here more often.

B Circle the one modal that best completes each conversation.

1 **A:** Why didn't you come to the party last night?

   B: I (had to / have to / must / have got to) study for a test.

2 **A:** You really (can't / should / mustn't / are able to) call more often.

   B: You're right. I'm sorry.

3 **A:** She ('d better not have / should have / had to have / must have) forgotten the tickets!

   B: Uh-oh. I hate to tell you this, but I think she did.

4 **A:** Do you think I ('m able to / must / would / could) get your phone number?

   B: Sure.

5 **A:** Did you get to go to the movies?

   B: Yeah. But I (must have / 'd rather have / should not have / would have) stayed at home.

6 **A:** Unfortunately, the doctor (shouldn't / has to / won't be able to / had better) see you until tomorrow.

   B: That's OK. No problem.

7 **A:** What do you think happened to Judy?

   B: She (must not have / shouldn't have / isn't able to / didn't have to) known we were starting so early.

The passive voice: review and expansion

Verbs can be transitive or intransitive. A transitive verb can have a direct object. An intransitive verb cannot have a direct object. With an intransitive verb, there can't be a "receiver" of an action.

> Transitive: We **bought** a car. (a car = a direct object)

> Intransitive: We **slept** well. (The verb <u>sleep</u> can't have an object.)

Remember: In the active voice, the subject of a sentence performs the action of the verb. In the passive voice, the subject of the sentence is the receiver of the action of a verb. Form the passive voice with a form of <u>be</u> and a past participle, or with a modal + a form of <u>be</u> and a past participle.

Common intransitive verbs	
arrive	rain
come	seem
die	sit
fall	sleep
go	stand
happen	stay
laugh	walk
live	

Statements

The simple present tense
The ad **is seen** by at least a million people a day.

The simple past tense
At the meeting, people **were called** by their first names.

The present continuous
Every house **is being painted** white.

The future with <u>be going to</u>
Maurizio's new fashions **are going to be shown** on TV tonight.

The future perfect
If I wear this dress before the event, it **will have been seen** by everyone and it won't seem new.

The past continuous
Before we had regulations, dangerous products **were being tested** on small animals.

The present perfect
We've **been helped** a lot by our friends.

The past perfect
The aloha shirt **had been worn** only on Fridays for a couple of years before people started wearing them every day.

Modals
Sometimes the truth **can't be** easily **seen**.

My teacher said my essay **should be rewritten** to make it clearer.

Note: The passive voice of the future continuous and the present perfect continuous are rarely used, so they aren't included in this list.

Questions

Invert the subject and the auxiliary verb (the form of <u>be</u> or <u>have</u>) or the modal.

Is Russian **spoken** by many people in Chicago?

Has your uncle **been hired** by an advertising company?

When **will** she **be given** a new office?

Who **have** you **been called** by?

Where **should** we **be married**?

How **can** this house **be painted** in only two days?

A Write a check mark next to the three sentences that have an intransitive verb.

☐ **1** Valentino's new line of women's purses arrives in stores next week.

☐ **2** Models are wearing very short dresses this season.

☐ **3** My parents are opening a new restaurant downtown.

☐ **4** The owner of the boutique lived in an apartment above the shop.

☐ **5** People speak French in Quebec.

☐ **6** It rained really hard last night.

☐ **7** Advertisers never tell the complete story about defective products.

B On a separate sheet of paper, rewrite in the passive voice the four sentences from Exercise A that have transitive verbs.

C On a separate sheet of paper, rewrite each statement in the passive voice.

1 Joan Saslow and Allen Ascher wrote this book.

2 Students practice English online in most language schools today.

3 Ads can persuade people to buy products.

4 Some ads have manipulated people's emotions.

5 My friend was driving the car when the accident occurred.

D On a separate sheet of paper, rewrite the sentences you wrote for Exercise C as <u>yes</u> / <u>no</u> questions.

E On a separate sheet of paper, write information questions, using the question words and phrases in parentheses.

1 That new shampoo was endorsed by Larissa La Rue. (when)

2 Those beauty products are being manufactured. (where)

3 The car can be bought at the sale price. (for how long)

4 The winner of the election will be known. (what time)

5 The new school was being built. (in what year)

Making comparisons: review and expansion

Comparative forms of adjectives and adverbs show how two things are different.

John is **taller than** Rob (is).

This movie was **less interesting than** the last one (was).

My sister types **a lot faster than** I (do).

Superlative forms of adjectives and adverbs show how one thing is different from everything else.

She was **the nicest** person I ever met!

That was **the least entertaining** movie I ever saw.

Of all the actors, she sang **the most beautifully**.

Among my friends, Ned and Stacey definitely have **the most** money.

Of all the cars we looked at, the Linkus costs **the most**.

Use the determiners <u>more</u>, <u>the most</u>, <u>less</u>, <u>least</u>, <u>little</u>, <u>the least</u>, <u>fewer</u>, and <u>the fewest</u> with nouns to compare quantities and amounts.

There is **less** corruption in the government than there used to be.

I want to be healthy, so I eat **fewer** sweets than **most** people.

Few people went to see *Horror City*, but last night had **the fewest** people in the audience.

Comparisons with <u>as</u> ... <u>as</u> show how two things are alike.

Tom is just **as tall as** George (is).

She still sings **as beautifully as** she did when she was young.

My nephew now weighs **as much as** I do.

I have **as much money** in the bank **as** I did last year.

Use <u>as</u> ... <u>as</u> with <u>almost</u>, <u>about</u>, and <u>not quite</u> to show how two things are similar, but not equal.

My nephew weighs **almost as much as** I do. [I weigh a bit more.]

The movie is **about as long as** his last one. [But it's a bit shorter.]

This coat is**n't quite as** expensive **as** it looks. [It's actually cheaper.]

Use <u>as</u> ... <u>as</u> with <u>twice</u>, <u>three times</u>, etc., to show that things are not equal at all.

A Linkus sedan is about **twice as** expensive **as** a Matsu.

My new computer is **ten times as** fast **as** my old one.

Note: In informal spoken English, it is more common to say "... as tall as me" instead of the more formal "... as tall as I (am)."

Be careful! Use <u>the</u> with a superlative form. However, you can omit <u>the</u> if the superlative is not followed by a noun.

Which student is **the tallest** OR **tallest**?

NOT ~~Which is tallest student?~~

Irregular forms

adjective	adverb	comparative	superlative
good	well	better (than)	the best
bad	badly	worse (than)	the worst
far	far	farther / further (than)	the farthest / furthest

A Read each quoted statement. Then complete each sentence using a comparative, superlative, or comparison with <u>as</u> ... <u>as</u>.

1 "The textbook we are using now is very good. The textbook we were using last year was also very good."

The textbook we're using now is .... the one we were using last year.

2 "Star shampoo costs about $6.00. Ravel shampoo costs about $7.00. Sanabel shampoo costs about $5.00."

Among the three shampoos, Sanabel is ....

3 "We paid four hundred euros each for our tickets. They paid three hundred euros."

We paid .... they did.

4 "Matt has only a little experience working with children. Nancy has a lot of experience."

Matt has .... Nancy.

5 "John's laptop weighs 2 kilos. Gerry's laptop weighs 2.1 kilos."

John's laptop isn't .... Gerry's is.

6 "Mark knows only a little Japanese. Jonah knows a lot."

Mark knows .... Jonah does.

7 "Bart ate a lot for lunch. Susan ate a lot for lunch, too."

Susan ate .... Bart did for lunch.

Other uses of comparatives, superlatives, and comparisons with <u>as</u> ... <u>as</u>

For emphasis

The Nile River is **more than** 5,500 kilometers long. [emphasizes that the river is very long]

The Dickens School now has **fewer than** 900 students. [emphasizes that this is a relatively small number]

That was **the worst** movie **ever**. [emphasizes that this was a bad movie]

This meal was **the best of all time**! [emphasizes that this was a great meal]

A newborn Asian elephant can weigh **as much as** 150 kilos. [emphasizes that this is fairly heavy]

As many as 200 of these animals are killed every year. [emphasizes that this is a high number]

Milton Academy is **one of the best** schools in the city.

Preet Gupta is **among the most intelligent** commentators on any TV news program today.

The lions in the Central Zoo are **some of the finest** examples of African wildlife you can see without going to Africa.

To show progression

My son is getting **taller** every day. [He's growing.]

The economy is **stronger** now. [It's improving.]

To show tendencies or preferences

We eat out **more than** in. [We tend to eat out.]

Sara likes being alone **more than** socializing. [She prefers to spend time alone.]

To clarify

He's a lot **friendlier than** you would think. [You may think he's not friendly, but in fact he is.]

She's **more of a singer than** a dancer. [People may think she's mainly a dancer, but in fact she's mainly a singer.]

The movie's **more annoying than** scary. [You may think this movie will be scary, but in fact it's just annoying.]

It looks **more like** snow **than** rain. [You may think it's going to rain, but in fact it looks like it's going to snow.]

B Use a comparative, a superlative, or a comparison with <u>as</u> ... <u>as</u> to complete each statement so it has a similar meaning to the information in quotes.

1 "Our meal last night was really inexpensive. It only cost 48 euros for the two of us."

Our meal last night cost .... 50 euros.

2 "Our reading club meetings are getting pretty big. On some nights there are thirty students."

Our reading club meetings sometimes have .... students.

3 "I think our teacher is really great!"

Our teacher is .... ever!

4 "The garden you planted last month has become so beautiful!"

Your garden is getting .... every day!

5 "You might think snails would taste strange, but they actually taste quite good."

Snails taste .... you may think.

6 "You may think Kate is shy, but she's actually very talkative."

Kate is .... than you might think.

7 "There were a lot of great new movies this year. *Cool Water* was one of them."

Cool Water was .... new movies this year.

UNIT 9

Perfect modals: short responses

Compare short responses with perfect modals in the active voice and passive voice.

Active voice

Do you think the first inhabitants of the island came from Sweden?

"They **might have**."
"They **must have**."
"They **had to have**."
"They **couldn't have**."

Passive voice

I wonder if the stone was moved by someone.

"It **might have been**."
"It **must have been**."
"It **had to have been**."
"It **couldn't have been**."

Be careful! In a short response to a question (or statement) with a past form of the verb <u>be</u>, always include <u>been</u>.

A: Was the story of the yeti just a joke?
B: It **must have been**. NOT It ~~must have~~.

Respond to each statement or question with a short response, using a perfect modal.

1 A: Is it most likely the Nazca Lines were created by humans?

   B: .... (must)

2 A: I wonder if the dinosaurs were killed by a meteor, too.

   B: .... (may)

3 A: Did Europeans eat potatoes before the discovery of America?

   B: .... (couldn't)

4 A: I guess people didn't realize that the carrier pigeon would become extinct.

   B: .... (must not)

5 A: The settlers in the western part of the U.S. must have known the buffalo were in danger.

   B: .... (had to)

6 A: It must not have been easy to move those huge stones.

   B: .... (can't)

UNIT 10

Be supposed to: expansion

You can also use <u>be supposed to</u> to express a broadly held opinion. It is similar to "Everyone says ... "

Green tea ice cream **is supposed to taste** really good.

Their new album **wasn't supposed to be** very good, but I loved it.

John **was supposed to have been** rude during the dinner, but I just don't believe it.

A On a separate sheet of paper, rewrite each statement, using <u>be supposed to</u>.

Example: They say the new Fernando Meirelles movie is very violent.

1 Everyone thinks our new manager is really nice.

2 Many people believe acupuncture is an effective treatment for pain.

The new Fernando Meirelles movie is supposed to be very violent.

3 I haven't heard Ashley Morgan sing, but they say she has a beautiful

4 I've never had Ethiopian food, but everyone says it's delicious.

5 They say Paulo Coelho's latest novel is his best yet.

6 Everyone says Myanmar is a fascinating place to visit.

7 It's said that corruption is one of the biggest problems in our city right now.

Would: review

Remember: The modal <u>would</u> can be used to talk about the present or future.

For polite requests in the present or future

Would you please **close** the door?

Would you **pick up** some milk on your way home?

To express a present or future result of an unreal condition

She **wouldn't be** so tired if she took a nap.

I **would go** see them in concert if the ticket prices weren't so astronomical.

The modal <u>would</u> can also be used in the following ways to talk about the past.

To express past repeated or habitual actions

As children, we **would play** in the park every Saturday.

As the past form of the future with <u>will</u>

He said he **would get** here before noon. (He said, "I'll get there before noon.")

She promised she **wouldn't forget**. (She said, "I promise I won't forget.")

To express past intentions or plans that changed

I thought I **would marry** Harry, but I changed my mind.

We didn't think we **would enjoy** eating alligator, but it was delicious.

B Write a check mark next to each sentence that expresses a past repeated or habitual action.

□ **1** I thought we would go skiing in Chile, but we didn't.

□ **2** In the summer, they would sit outside and read books or just take naps.

□ **3** I had agreed that I would make breakfast that morning.

□ **4** Every night, he would lie awake for hours thinking about her.

□ **5** She warned them that Jake would forget to bring the keys, and she was right.

□ **6** When Kyle was still living with his parents, he would work on weekdays and study on weekends.

□ **7** Leila didn't think English would be useful on her trip to Moscow, but she was wrong.

□ **8** As a student, I would stay up late every night studying for exams.

□ **9** She asked me if I would help her with her homework that afternoon.

□ **10** She wouldn't have such a hard time doing her homework if she studied harder.

□ **11** When I was younger, my dad would always help me with my homework.

□ **12** I wouldn't go see that new Tom Cruise movie if I were you.

□ **13** Would you buy an electric car if it were affordable?

□ **14** My brother thought he would be late.

🖉 **Grammar for Writing: placement of adverbs of manner**

Adverbs of manner modify adjectives or verbs. When they modify adjectives, they go before the adjective.

The path can be **dangerously** slippery.

The architecture is **incredibly** beautiful.

When they modify transitive verbs, adverbs of manner ending in -ly often go before the main verb. They can also go after a verb and its direct object.

She **slowly** opened the door. OR She opened the door **slowly**.

She should **slowly** open the door. OR She should open the door **slowly**.

When they modify intransitive verbs, adverbs of manner ending in -ly often go after the main verb. They can also go after a verb and an indirect object.

He spoke **angrily** about corruption. OR He spoke about corruption **angrily**.

Be careful! Don't place adverbs of manner without -ly before a main verb.

He drives **fast**. NOT He fast drives.

She can sing really **well**. NOT She can really well sing.

Don't place an adverb of manner between a transitive verb and its direct object.

He drank his tea **quickly**. OR He **quickly** drank his tea. NOT He drank quickly his tea.

Other adverbs of manner

angrily	poorly
badly	quietly
fast	sadly
happily	slowly
hard	softly
nicely	suddenly
noisily	well

C Write a check mark if the adverb is correctly placed. Then, on a separate sheet of paper, rewrite the sentences that you didn't check.

□ **1** When the game was over, he left quickly the court.

□ **2** As she drove into town, she sang to herself softly.

□ **3** The meeting was suddenly postponed after the CEO arrived.

□ **4** They washed noisily the dishes after dinner.

□ **5** Tom replied angrily to the text message.

□ **6** They entered quietly the room and sat in the corner.

D On a separate sheet of paper, rewrite each sentence with one or more adverbs of manner. Choose from the list above and on page 119.

1 I watched the snake until it moved.

2 We chatted until the sun came up the next morning.

3 She speaks Italian, but she doesn't really understand it.

4 He wrote about his experiences living in Cambodia.

5 A cow walked onto the road, and the bus stopped.

Pronunciation Booster

The Pronunciation Booster is optional. It provides a pronunciation lesson and practice to support speaking in each unit, making students' speech more comprehensible.

Content words and function words

In English, content words are generally stressed.
Function words are generally unstressed.

My **BOSS** is a **PAIN** in the **NECK**!

He's **REALLY** a **TERRIFIC BOSS**.

MARK is **SUCH** a **SMART GUY**.

I'm **SURE** she'll be a **GREAT MANAGER**.

Stress in compound nouns

Many compound nouns are made up of two nouns, with the first one modifying the second one. In these compounds, stress usually falls on the first noun. However when a noun is modified by an adjective, stress is equal on both words.

noun + noun		adjective + noun
I drink **APPLE** juice.	BUT	I like **RED APPLES**.
She's a **PEOPLE** person.	BUT	She's a **NICE PERSON**.
It's an **APARTMENT** building.	BUT	It's a **TALL BUILDING**.
They're **EXERCISE** machines.	BUT	They're **NEW MACHINES**.

Content words

nouns	boss, Julie, happiness
verbs	find, meet, call
adjectives	talkative, small, green
adverbs	quietly, again, very
possessive pronouns	mine, yours, his
demonstrative pronouns	this, those, that
reflexive pronouns	ourselves, herself
interrogative pronouns	what, who, where

Function words

prepositions	of, from, at
conjunctions	and, but, or
determiners	a, the, some
personal pronouns	he, she, they
possessive adjectives	my, her, their
auxiliary verbs	have + [past participle]
	be + [present participle]

Be careful! When an auxiliary verb is negative or used in short answers, it is generally stressed.

I **CAN'T GO**.	He **WON'T LIKE** it.
No, they **DON'T**.	Yes, I **HAVE**.

A ▶6:01 Listen and practice.

1 My **BOSS** is a **PAIN** in the **NECK**.

2 He's **REALLY** a **TERRIFIC BOSS**.

3 **MARK** is **SUCH** a **SMART GUY**.

4 I'm **SURE** she'll be a **GREAT MANAGER**.

B Circle the content words.

1 Learn to live in the present.

2 He reminded me to call my mother.

3 He asked me to work faster.

4 I prefer to stick closer to home.

▶6:02 Now practice reading each sentence aloud and listen to compare.* (Note that your choices may differ from what you hear on the audio.)

C ▶6:03 Listen and practice.

1 I drink **APPLE** juice. I like **RED APPLES**.

2 She's a **PEOPLE** person. She's a **NICE PERSON**.

3 It's an **APARTMENT** building. It's a **TALL BUILDING**.

4 They're **EXERCISE** machines. They're **NEW MACHINES**.

D ▶6:04 Practice reading each compound noun aloud and then listen to check.*

1 global warming

2 tennis courts

3 a reliable person

4 a telephone directory

5 office managers

6 the bullet train

*Note: Whenever you see a listening activity with an asterisk (*), say each word, phrase, or sentence in the pause after you hear each number. Then listen for confirmation.

Intonation patterns

In statements, commands, and information questions, lower pitch after the stressed syllable in the last stressed word. If the last syllable in the sentence is stressed, lower pitch on the vowel by lengthening it.

I haven't been going to many concerts lately.

Don't forget to watch them on YouTube tonight.

How long have you been listening to that song?

She's been practicing for several months.

Raise pitch after the stressed syllable in the last stressed word in <u>yes</u> / <u>no</u> questions and requests. If the last syllable in the sentence is stressed, raise pitch on the vowel by lengthening it.

Have you been listening to Christina Perri lately?

Could you pick up the tickets for me?

Do you think she has a nice voice?

Has he been checking online?

A ▶ 6:05 **Listen and practice.**

1 I haven't been going to many concerts lately.

2 Don't forget to watch them on YouTube tonight.

3 How long have you been listening to that song?

4 She's been practicing for several months.

5 Have you been listening to Christina Perri lately?

6 Could you pick up the tickets for me?

7 Do you think she has a nice voice?

8 Has he been checking online?

B Circle the last stressed content word in each of the following sentences. If that word has more than one syllable, underline the stressed syllable.

1 That song has a great beat you can dance to.

2 Her catchy lyrics make you want to sing along.

3 Didn't you like that song's melody?

4 What time do you think the concert will be finished?

5 How long has she been dancing to that song?

 ▶ 6:06 **Now practice reading each sentence aloud, using the intonation patterns you have learned. Listen to check.***

DIGITAL
PAIR
WORK

UNIT 3

Sentence rhythm: thought groups

Longer sentences are usually divided by rhythm into smaller "thought groups"—groups of words that naturally or logically go together. Exactly how statements may be divided into thought groups will vary among speakers.

My short-term goal / is to start living / within my means.

NOT ~~My short-term / goal is to / start living within my / means.~~

I don't plan / to be financially dependent / for the rest of my life.

By next year / I hope to have gotten / a good job / as a financial consultant.

Examples of thought groups	
subject + verb	I don't know
noun phrases	my short-term goal
prepositional phrases	by the end of the month
predicates	is drowning in debt
noun clauses	where the money goes
adjective clauses	that I paid off last year
adverbial clauses	when I've finished my report

Pitch in longer sentences

In longer sentences, pitch may fall—or rise—after the last stressed syllable in each thought group, with no change in meaning.

Once he tries keeping / a realistic budget / he'll find it easy / to save money. **OR**

Once he tries keeping / a realistic budget / he'll find it easy / to save money.

A ▶6:07 **Listen and practice.**

1 My short-term goal is to start living within my means.

2 I don't plan to be financially dependent for the rest of my life.

3 By next year, I hope to have gotten a good job as a financial consultant.

4 a Once he tries keeping a realistic budget, he'll find it easy to save money.

4 b Once he tries keeping a realistic budget, he'll find it easy to save money.

B **Read the following sentences. Decide how you might break each sentence into thought groups.**

1 By the end of this month, I hope to have finished paying off my student loans.

2 In two months, when we've finally paid off our house, we're going to have a big party to celebrate.

3 To be perfectly honest, I couldn't tell you where the money goes.

4 By next year, I will have completed my studies, but I don't think I will have gotten married.

▶6:08 **Now practice reading each sentence aloud, paying attention to pitch. Listen to compare.*** (Note that your choices may differ from what you hear on the audio.)

UNIT 4

Linking sounds

Linking with vowels

When the final consonant sound of a word is followed by a vowel sound, link the sounds together.

It's in style now.

She bought him an elegant tie.

I've already bought a new suit.

Linking identical consonants

When the final consonant sound of a word is followed by the same sound, link the sounds together as one sound.

The blouse is striped.

They preferred dark suits.

What an attractive vest!

A ▶6:09 **Listen and practice.**

1 It's in style now.

2 She bought him an elegant tie.

3 I've already bought a new suit.

4 The blouse is striped.

5 They preferred dark suits.

6 What an attractive vest!

B **Underline all the places where you think the sounds should be linked.**

1 She wants Susan to dress up next time.

2 It's fashionable and elegant.

3 It's out of style.

4 I wish she preferred dressing down.

5 That blouse isn't trendy enough for my taste.

6 I think Kyle has stylish taste.

DIGITAL
PAIR
WORK
▶6:10 **Now practice reading each sentence aloud and listen to check.** *

UNIT 5

Unstressed syllables: vowel reduction to /ə/

In conversation, the vowels in unstressed syllables are often reduced to the sound /ə/. The vowel sound /ə/ occurs
more often in English than any other vowel sound and contributes to maintaining the rhythm of English.

. — . .			. . — . .		
ac cept a ble	→	/ək'septəbəl/	ir re spon si ble	→	/ˌɪrə'spɑnsəbəl/
. — . .			. —		
con sid er ate	→	/kən'sɪdərət/	po lite	→	/pə'laɪt/
. . — . .			. — .		
dis o be di ent	→	/ˌdɪsə'bidiənt/	re spect ful	→	/rə'spektfəl/
. . — . .			. — . .		
in ex cus a ble	→	/ˌɪnək'skyuzəbəl/	ri dic u lous	→	/rɪ'dɪkyələs/

A ▶6:11 **Listen and practice.**

1 acceptable

2 considerate

3 disobedient

4 inexcusable

5 irresponsible

6 polite

7 respectful

8 ridiculous

B ▶6:12 **Listen to each word and circle the unstressed syllables that have the sound /ə/.**

1 un ac cept a ble

2 in con si de rate

3 im po lite

4 un pleas ant

5 ir ra tion al

6 im ma ture

7 un i mag i na ble

8 dis re spect ful

9 in ap pro pri ate

DIGITAL
PAIR
WORK
▶6:13 **Now practice reading each word aloud and listen again to check.** *

Sound reduction

In everyday speech, sounds in unstressed words are often "reduced"; that is, vowels change to /ə/ or /ɚ/ or consonants are dropped.

Vowel reduction

The /u/ sound in the function word <u>to</u> is often reduced to /ə/.

I'll be going **to** the airport after dinner. /tə/

It's ten **to** two. /tə/

The /æ/ sound in many one-syllable function words is often reduced to /ə/.

Look **at** that. /ət/

I saw **an** eagle. /ən/

That's more **than** I need. /ðən/

> **Be careful!** Function words that occur at the end of a sentence are never reduced.
>
> What a beautiful bird you **are**! /ɑr/
>
> What are you looking **at**? /æt/
>
> What are you waiting **for**? /fɔr/
>
> Who's she talking **to**? /tu/

The /ɑr/ and /ɔr/ sounds in function words are often reduced to /ɚ/.

Pets **are** no trouble. /ɚ/

Is it black **or** white? /ɚ/

Where's **your** parrot? /yɚ/

He's been gone **for** days. /fɚ/

The function word <u>and</u> is often reduced to /ən/ when it occurs between two subjects, objects, modifiers, verbs, or phrases.

They have long arms **and** legs. /ən/

She laughed **and** cried when she heard the news. /ən/

We stayed out late **and** went dancing. /ən/

> **Be careful!** The vowel sound /æ/ in <u>and</u> is generally not reduced when it occurs at the beginning of a clause, but the consonant sound /d/ may still be dropped.
>
> He wore a black suit, **and** she wore a green dress. /æn/

The initial /h/ sound is usually dropped in function words.

What does ~~h~~e mean? /dʌzi/

It's in ~~h~~is bag. /ɪnɪz/

A ▶ 6:14 **Listen and practice.**

1 I'll be going to the airport after dinner.

2 It's ten to two.

3 Look at that.

4 I saw an eagle.

5 That's more than I need.

6 Pets are no trouble.

7 Is it black or white?

8 Where's your parrot?

9 He's been gone for days.

10 They have long arms and legs.

11 She laughed and cried when she heard the news.

12 We stayed out late and went dancing.

13 He wore a black suit, and she wore a green dress.

14 What does he mean?

15 It's in his bag.

B **In the following sentences, circle the words you think will be reduced.**

1 Alternatives can be found for medical research on animals.

2 A lot can be done to make conditions better on factory farms.

3 Some animals are raised to be used for medical research.

4 Do we have to ban hunting and bullfighting?

▶ 6:15 **Now practice reading each sentence aloud and listen to check.***

Vowel sounds /i/ and /ɪ/

The sound /i/ is longer and is formed by tensing the tongue.
The sound /ɪ/ is shorter and formed with the tongue relaxed.

/i/	/ɪ/
leave	live
team	Tim
feel	fill
steal	still
feet	fit

The vowel sound /ɪ/ also appears frequently in unstressed syllables.

pla ces   mar ket   mi nute   wo men

> The vowel sounds /i/ and /ɪ/ are represented in spelling in a number of ways.
>
> | /i/ | /ɪ/ |
> |-----|-----|
> | steal | blimp |
> | steep | syllable |
> | people | busy |
> | handy | building |
> | believe | women |
> | receive | pretty |
> | boutique | been |
> | key | give |

A ▶ 6:16 **Listen and practice.**

1 leave   live   4 steal   still
2 team   Tim   5 feet   fit
3 feel   fill

B ▶ 6:17 **Listen and practice.**

1 places   2 market   3 minute   4 women

C ▶ 6:18 **Listen to each pair of words. Circle if they are the <u>same</u> or <u>different</u>.**

1 same   different   5 same   different
2 same   different   6 same   different
3 same   different   7 same   different
4 same   different   8 same   different

D ▶ 6:19 **Listen and check which sound you hear in the stressed syllable.**

	/i/ /ɪ/		/i/ /ɪ/
1	☐ ☐	8	☐ ☐
2	☐ ☐	9	☐ ☐
3	☐ ☐	10	☐ ☐
4	☐ ☐	11	☐ ☐
5	☐ ☐	12	☐ ☐
6	☐ ☐	13	☐ ☐
7	☐ ☐	14	☐ ☐

DIGITAL PAIR WORK   ▶ 6:20 **Now listen again and practice.**

Stress placement: prefixes and suffixes

Stress placement does not change when most prefixes and suffixes are added to a word.

· — ·	· · — ·	· — ·	· — · ·
im**por**tant	unim**por**tant	im**por**tance	im**por**tantly

· — · ·	· — · ·	· · — · ·	· — · · ·
o**be**dient	o**be**dience	diso**be**dience	o**be**diently

— ·	· — ·	— · ·	— · ·
happy	un**hap**py	**hap**piness	**hap**pily

However, adding the suffixes -ion, -ic, -ity, -ical, and -ian generally shifts stress to the syllable before the suffix.

— · ·		· — ·
educate	→	edu**ca**tion

— · ·		· · — ·
photograph	→	photo**graph**ic

· — · ·		· · — · ·
de**pend**able	→	dependa**bil**ity

— · ·		· — · ·
politics	→	po**lit**ical

— ·		· — ·
music	→	mu**si**cian

Some nouns and verbs have the same spelling. When the word is a noun, the stress is on the first syllable. When the word is a verb, the stress is on the second syllable.

nouns   **verbs**

— ·	· —
rebel	re**bel**

— ·	· —
protest	pro**test**

— ·	· —
present	pre**sent**

— ·	· —
object	ob**ject**

— ·	· —
progress	pro**gress**

> **Other words in this category**
> conduct
> conflict
> contrast
> convert
> permit
> record
> survey
> suspect

A ▶6:21 **Listen and practice.**

1 important   unimportant   importance   importantly
2 obedient   obedience   disobedience obediently
3 happy   unhappy   happiness   happily

B ▶6:22 **Listen and practice.**

1 educate   education
2 photograph   photographic
3 dependable   dependability
4 politics   political
5 music   musician

C Look at the stressed syllable of each word in Column A. According to the rules given in the chart on page 147, mark the stressed syllable of each word in Column B.

	A	B
1	fa <u>mil</u> iar	fa mil iar i ty
2	e <u>mo</u> tion al	e mo tion al ly
3	<u>reg</u> u late	reg u la tion
4	ap <u>pre</u> cia tive	ap pre cia tive ly
5	<u>sym</u> pa thy	sym pa thet ic
6	hy <u>poth</u> e size	hy po thet i cal
7	<u>beau</u> ty	beau ti fy
8	<u>his</u> to ry	his tor i cal
9	ma <u>te</u> ri al ist	ma te ri al is tic
10	<u>pol</u> i tics	pol i ti cian

▶ 6:23 Now practice reading each word aloud and listen to check.*

D ▶ 6:24 Listen and practice.

Nouns	Verbs	Nouns	Verbs
1 rebel	rebel	8 contrast	contrast
2 protest	protest	9 convert	convert
3 present	present	10 permit	permit
4 object	object	11 record	record
5 progress	progress	12 survey	survey
6 conduct	conduct	13 suspect	suspect
7 conflict	conflict		

E Circle the syllable you think will be stressed in each blue word.

1 A summer fishing **permit permits** you to fish all you want.

2 The **protest** was organized to **protest** government spending.

3 All the employees were **surveyed** so the results of the **survey** would be useful.

4 The **contrast** between them now is not great compared to how much they **contrast** at other times of the year.

5 We strongly **object** to the decision to sell art **objects** outside the museum.

▶ 6:25 Now practice reading each sentence aloud, paying attention to words that are both nouns and verbs. Listen to check.*

Reduction and linking in perfect modals in the passive voice

In perfect modals in the passive voice, the modal and the auxiliary verbs <u>have been</u> are said together as one unit. Note that stress falls on the modal and the main verb. In everyday speech, the /h/ sound in the auxilliary <u>have</u> is dropped and /æ/ is reduced to /ə/.

/ˈkʊdəvbɪn/
They **COULD have been KILLED**.

/ˈmaitəvbɪn/
They **MIGHT have been LOST**.

/ˈmʌstəvbɪn/
They **MUST have been MOVED**.

/ˈmeiyəvbɪn/
They **MAY have been DISCOVERED**.

With <u>had to</u>, stress <u>had</u> and the main verb. Say <u>had to</u> and <u>have been</u> as one unit.

/ˈhætuəvbɪn/
They **HAD to have been STOLEN**.

In negative perfect modals, stress falls on the modal, the word <u>not</u>, and the main verb. In everyday speech, <u>not</u> and the auxiliary verbs <u>have been</u> are generally said as one unit.

/ˈnatəvbɪn/
They **MIGHT NOT have been LOST**.
They **MUST NOT have been MOVED**.

A ▶6:26 **Listen and practice.**

1 They could have been killed.
2 They might have been lost.
3 They must have been moved.
4 They may have been discovered.
5 They had to have been stolen.
6 They might not have been lost.
7 They must not have been moved.

B Underline where you think the words should be linked and which sounds should be reduced.

1 The damage may have been caused by a storm.
2 The building could have been destroyed by a fire.
3 The gold figures couldn't have been stolen.
4 The stone statues must have been moved using animals.
5 The drawings must not have been discovered until later.
6 The islands had to have been inhabited by Polynesians.
7 The secrets of Rapa Nui might not have been lost.

DIGITAL PAIR WORK

▶6:27 **Now practice reading each sentence aloud, paying attention to reductions. Listen to check.***

Vowel sounds /eɪ/, /ɛ/, /æ/, and /ʌ/

The sound /eɪ/ is longer and is formed by tensing the tongue with the lips spread.
The sounds /ɛ/, /æ/, and /ʌ/ are shorter and are formed with the tongue relaxed.
Say /eɪ/ and /ɛ/ with the lips spread wide. Say /æ/ with the lips spread slightly and
the mouth slightly open. Say /ʌ/ with the tongue and jaw completely relaxed.

Mouth positions for vowels	
tongue tensed (long)	/eɪ/
tongue relaxed (short)	/ɛ/, /æ/, /ʌ/
lips spread	/eɪ/, /ɛ/, /æ/
jaw relaxed	/ʌ/

/eɪ/	/ɛ/	/æ/	/ʌ/
pain	pen	pan	pun
Dane	den	Dan	done
mate	met	mat	mutt
bait	bet	bat	but

The vowel sounds /eɪ/, /ɛ/, /æ/, and /ʌ/ may
be represented by these spellings.

/eɪ/	/ɛ/	/æ/	/ʌ/
pay	rest	snacks	up
weigh	sweat	have	some
shape	says	laugh	touch
wait	said	half	does
taking	friend	guarantee	blood
great	guess	relax	what

A ▶6:28 **Listen and practice.**

1 pain	pen	pan	pun
2 Dane	den	Dan	done
3 mate	met	mat	mutt
4 bait	bet	bat	but

B ▶6:29 **Listen to each word and place it in the correct column.**

age any just banned debt love edge face flashy great health
jump can't some faint enough chance text nothing trait way

/eɪ/	/ɛ/	/æ/	/ʌ/

▶6:30 **Now practice reading each word aloud and listen again to check.***

C ▶6:31 **Listen to each sentence and circle the word you hear.**

1 Give the money to the (men / man).

2 I think it's (Dan / done).

3 What is that (rag / rug) made of?

4 Do you need this (pen / pan)?

5 He's a perfect (mutt / mate).

6 My (date / debt) is causing me trouble.

7 Could you take that (bug / bag) off the counter?

8 Please put a bandage on the (cut / cat).

DIGITAL
PAIR
WORK

Now practice reading the sentences both ways.

Test-Taking Skills Booster

The Test-Taking Skills Booster is optional. It provides practice in applying some key logical thinking and comprehension skills typically included in reading and listening tasks on standardized proficiency tests. Each unit contains one Reading Completion activity and one or more Listening Completion activities.

The reading selections in the Booster are either adaptations of those from the *Summit 1* units or new reading selections about a related topic. Listening Completion exercises are based on the listening passages that can be found on the audio from the *Summit* units. None of the Reading Completion or Listening Completion tasks duplicate what students have already done in the unit.

*Note that the practice activities in the Booster are not intended to test student achievement after each unit. Complete Achievement Tests for *Summit* can be found in the *Summit* ActiveTeach.

READING COMPLETION

Read the selection. Choose the word or phrase that best completes each statement.

The Lost Ring

Last weekend, ... she was shopping for a new car, Laura Mills found a ring on the floor of one of
1
the cars she was test-driving. She picked it up and put it in her purse, intending to ask the car salesman if a

customer had .... a lost ring. However, by the time she arrived back at the car dealership, she had
2
forgotten about the ring and headed toward home, thinking about .... she should buy one of the cars
3
she had test-driven. Once home, she opened her purse to put in her keys and discovered the ring. "I felt sort

of like a thief, but I certainly hadn't .... to steal the ring. I wondered what I should do."
4

.... driving back to the car dealership immediately, she took the time to examine the ring for any
5
identifying information and found this inscription engraved inside: *To my love on our marriage. BT to LS 2005.*

In a burst of creative thinking, Mills thought one of her friends might .... the ring, so she posted the
6
photo of it on Facebook but was .... not to show the inscription. She urged her friends to share it, with
7
this message: "Have you lost this ring? I found it at Spotless Car Dealership on the floor of a car. .... it
8
is yours, identify it with the information on the inscription inside." To her surprise, she got a message from the

owner just two hours later.

1	**A** except	**B** while	**C** during	**D** because
2	**A** reported	**B** said	**C** wanted	**D** stolen
3	**A** since	**B** no matter	**C** whether	**D** after
4	**A** meant	**B** decided	**C** believed	**D** included
5	**A** Because of	**B** In spite of	**C** Rather than	**D** Due to
6	**A** relate	**B** recognize	**C** resemble	**D** resurrect
7	**A** afraid	**B** satisfied	**C** needless	**D** careful
8	**A** Whether	**B** No matter	**C** Suppose	**D** If

LISTENING COMPLETION

▶ 6:32 **You will hear a conversation. Read the paragraph below. Then listen and complete each statement with the word or short phrase you hear in the conversation. Listen a second time to check your work.**

The woman thinks that crime is out of (1) .... She says that the (2) .... is full of crime stories. The man agrees, and he thinks crime represents the whole breakdown in (3) .... The woman feels hopeless about the situation, but the man thinks there's something we can (4) .... about crime. First, he says the local (5) .... need more money to fight crime. His second suggestion is not to (6) .... a lot of jewelry on the street.

READING COMPLETION

Read the selection. Choose the word or phrase that best completes each statement.

Ludwig van Beethoven

The gifted young Ludwig van Beethoven had already composed his first piece of music by the time he was twelve. .... , at the age of sixteen, he went to study in Vienna, Austria, the .... of European
1   2
cultural life at the time and home to the most brilliant musicians and composers of the period. Beethoven proved to be an imaginative composer.

.... Beethoven remembered for his great genius, but also for his strong and difficult personality.
3
In one infamous incident, Beethoven became so annoyed with a waiter that he behaved rudely, emptying a plate of food over the man's head. .... , he could be quite egotistical, saying once, "There are and will
4
be thousands of princes. There is only one Beethoven." .... anyone in the audience talked during a
5
concert, he would stop immediately and walk out. Many in musical and aristocratic circles admired Beethoven
.... his difficult behavior, and they knew he might lose his .... at any time. They always forgave
6   7
his insults and moody temperament. Beethoven was also well-known for his .... and eccentric
8
behavior. He often walked through the streets of Vienna muttering to himself, and he completely neglected his personal appearance. Because he would always let his clothes get dirty, his friends would .... during
9
the night and replace them with new ones.

1	**A** Likewise	**B** Then	**C** Since	**D** Now that
2	**A** heart	**B** importance	**C** well-known	**D** beginning
3	**A** Neither is	**B** Even if	**C** Not only is	**D** However
4	**A** In contrast	**B** In addition	**C** While	**D** As a result
5	**A** For instance	**B** While	**C** If	**D** Because
6	**A** despite	**B** during	**C** even so	**D** even if
7	**A** music	**B** mind	**C** temper	**D** personality
8	**A** charming	**B** strange	**C** amusing	**D** likeable
9	**A** visit	**B** relax	**C** worry	**D** leave

LISTENING COMPLETION

A ▶6:33 You will hear a conversation. Read the paragraph below. Then listen and complete each statement with the word or short phrase you hear in the conversation. Listen a second time to check your work.

The man mentions that the actor Anthony Hopkins also (1) .... The woman is surprised and wants to know if the man has actually (2) .... the actor's music before. He says that he watched a video on (3) .... in which an (4) .... played one of his pieces. However, he found the music a little (5) .... for his taste.

B ▶6:34 You will hear a conversation. Read the paragraph below. Then listen and complete each statement with the word or short phrase you hear in the conversation. Listen a second time to check your work.

The woman wonders if the man likes (6) .... music and he says he's (7) .... it because it always makes him (8) .... However, she finds it (9) .... listen to because she thinks it always has the same (10) .... and every song (11) .... Whenever she hears it, she wants to (12) .... and listen to something else.

READING COMPLETION

Read the selection. Choose the word or phrase that best completes each statement.

Charitable Giving

Before deciding to .... money to a charity, it's important to look into the charity to be sure it's not a
fraud. .... we don't like to think that charitable organizations might be dishonest or take advantage of
our generosity, some charities—even ones with honest-sounding names—are not on the level.

Charities use the phone, face-to-face contact, e-mail, social networking sites, and mobile devices both
to solicit and .... donations. Scammers use the same methods to take advantage of your goodwill.
.... of how they reach you, you should .... any charity that refuses to .... detailed
information about its identity or how your money will be used. Be especially careful of a charity that uses a
name that closely resembles that of a better-known, ... organization. Another red flag is using high-
pressure tactics like trying to get you to donate immediately without giving you time to think about it or do
research. Be .... of charities that spring up too suddenly in response to current events and natural
disasters. .... they are legitimate, they probably don't have the infrastructure to get the donations
to the affected area or people. .... all the potential pitfalls, don't .... to donate to legitimate
charities. Charitable donations are one way of expressing your care for others and the environment.

1	**A** accept	**B** receive	**C** donate	**D** pay
2	**A** Because	**B** Although	**C** Nevertheless	**D** Since
3	**A** ask for	**B** return	**C** spend	**D** accept
4	**A** Because	**B** Regardless	**C** Since	**D** Otherwise
5	**A** avoid	**B** donate to	**C** select	**D** choose
6	**A** hide	**B** provide	**C** donate	**D** invest
7	**A** dishonest	**B** not on the level	**C** reputable	**D** illegal
8	**A** trusting	**B** wary	**C** shameful	**D** satisfied
9	**A** Even if	**B** Especially if	**C** Whether	**D** Because
10	**A** Although	**B** In spite of	**C** In case	**D** Similar to
11	**A** stop	**B** think	**C** hesitate	**D** remember

LISTENING COMPLETION

A ▶ 6:35 You will hear a conversation. Read the paragraph below. Then listen and complete each statement
with the word or short phrase you hear in the conversation. Listen a second time to check your work.

The man is asking the woman if she wants (1) .... for dinner. At first, she declines because she's
trying (2) .... But he insists, saying that he just got a big raise, and he suggests that they (3) ....
Again, she says no because she doesn't (4) .... right now, but the man offers to (5) ....

B ▶ 6:36 You will hear a conversation. Read the paragraph below. Then listen and complete each statement
with the word or short phrase you hear in the conversation. Listen a second time to check your work.

A man is visiting a woman and admiring her (6) .... furniture. He thinks the sofa is
(7) .... He imagines that it must have been (8) .... and asks her how she managed to pay
for it. She says that she (9) .... , putting away (10) ....very month. The man is envious and
wishes he could do the same thing. He feels bad because all his money is gone by (11) .... In spite of
the fact that he makes (12) .... , he just doesn't know where all (13) .... goes.

READING COMPLETION

Read the selection. Choose the word or phrase that best completes each statement.

> ### The Media and Women's Self-esteem
>
> It has been reported that 75 percent of women in the United States think they are "too fat." What is the cause of this? .... **1** some people, media such as television, movies, and magazines actually define a woman's "beauty" for us by providing images that represent the ideal. .... **2** the ideal today is tall and thin, women want to be tall and thin, too, ... **3** for the majority, this goal is unattainable. .... **4** hair color or weight, which are somewhat under our control, height and body type are largely determined by genetics and .... **5** are not controllable. .... **6** , since the average fashion model is 5 feet, 11 inches (1.83 meters) tall and weighs 117 pounds (53 kilograms), ... **7** the average woman is only 5 feet, 4 inches (1.65 meters) tall and weighs approximately 140 pounds (63.5 kilograms), very few women could fall into the "ideal" range. .... **8** , many women are left feeling either fat or unattractive.
>
> Perhaps more important is the fact that constantly viewing images of models and actresses causes even very young girls to grow up with a negative self-image and .... **9** self-esteem. .... **10** it would be impractical to try to change the images being presented in the media, we can make an effort to help young people understand that they are being targeted as a consumer group so advertisers can convince them to buy products.

1	**A** Because	**B** As a consequence of	**C** According to	**D** Therefore
2	**A** Due to the fact that	**B** As a result	**C** Although	**D** Consequently
3	**A** because	**B** even though	**C** as a consequence	**D** likewise
4	**A** Unlike	**B** Like	**C** In similar fashion	**D** Whereas
5	**A** not either	**B** therefore	**C** however	**D** as well
6	**A** Because	**B** In contrast	**C** Furthermore	**D** Although
7	**A** whereas	**B** even though	**C** similarly	**D** unlike
8	**A** However	**B** In contrast	**C** For instance	**D** As a result
9	**A** excellent	**B** high	**C** happy	**D** low
10	**A** Although	**B** Following that	**C** Before	**D** After that

LISTENING COMPLETION

A ▶6:37 You will hear a conversation. Read the paragraph below. Then listen and complete each statement with the word or short phrase you hear in the conversation. Listen a second time to check your work.

The first woman is looking at a (1) .... and would like the other woman's opinion of it. She is thinking of wearing it for her presentation at the (2) .... She asks the other woman if it might be (3) .... The second woman thinks the dress might be better on a younger woman. She thinks clothes for women their age should be more (4) ....

B ▶6:38 You will hear a conversation. Read the paragraph below. Then listen and complete each statement with the word or short phrase you hear in the conversation. Listen a second time to check your work.

The customer is shopping for a shirt for (5) .... He's thinking he'd like something in a (6) .... color, perhaps in a (7) .... or green. The salesman asks whether the customer is looking for a (8) .... or a (9) .... shirt. The customer says that he'd like a long-sleeve one, and the clerk offers to show him some (10) .... ones for him (11) .... from.

READING COMPLETION

Read the selection. Choose the word or phrase that best completes each statement.

Avoiding Urban Crime

.... the 21st century, there has been a steady increase in the number of foreign visitors to the great
1
cities of the world. Unfortunately, ... tourists to those places are particularly vulnerable to criminal
2
activities. Yet, there are precautions you can take to .... that you don't become a crime victim.
3

To begin with, avoid going out alone if .... There's usually safety in numbers, but don't
4
.... that tourist attractions also attract thieves. Stay aware of what's happening around you—as if you
5
had eyes in the back of your head. On the street, ... using a smartphone or tablet nor fumbling with a
6
map or guidebook is a good idea—unless of course you need to. Be particularly careful in crowds at festivals
or on buses and trains. And a warning to women: be careful if you carry a cross-body purse. Although wearing
one may .... it harder for a criminal to grab it from you, you could be injured if the purse-snatcher is on
7
a motorcycle.

At the hotel, ... leaving valuables unprotected in your room, where a burglar might break in and
8
take them. Ask the front desk to keep them for you. Better safe than sorry! Keep in mind that, all in all, crime
rates are going down worldwide, and the chances you will become a crime victim are low. So don't let
worrying about crime .... you from having a great time!
9

1	A Since	B In	C Now that	D As a result of
2	A part-time	B resident	C foreign	D friendly
3	A ensure	B avoid	C know	D attract
4	A unfamiliar	B expensive	C possible	D afraid
5	A remember	B forget	C realize	D worry
6	A not only	B neither	C either	D both
7	A make	B ensure	C take	D require
8	A remember	B forget	C avoid	D never
9	A confuse	B interfere	C encourage	D keep

LISTENING COMPLETION

▶6:39 You will hear part of a report. Read the paragraph below. Then listen and complete each statement
with the word or short phrase you hear in the report. Listen a second time to check your work.

Pete Frates was diagnosed with a rare disease called ALS that (1) .... the nervous system. He
came up with a big idea in order to (2) .... awareness of this terrible disease and to encourage people to
(3) .... to finding a cure. All people had to do was (4) .... in which they dump a bucket of icy
water over their heads and challenge (5) .... to either do the same or donate a hundred dollars. In social
media, people all over the world posted videos of (6) .... On Facebook, these videos were viewed
(7) .... times. Everyone (8) .... about the Ice Bucket Challenge. Even famous
(9) .... and (10) .... were taking the challenge and posting videos.

UNIT 6

READING COMPLETION

Read the selection. Choose the word or phrase that best completes each statement.

Saving the American Buffalo

One remarkable conservation story is the sustained effort to save the American buffalo, ... was successfully brought back from near extinction. .... the arrival of European settlers in North America, there were more than 50 million buffalo roaming in huge herds across the continent's central flatlands, which are today known as the Great Plains. For Native Americans living on the plains, these magnificent creatures .... food as well as clothing and shelter. The buffalo played an enormously important .... in the plains ecosystem, sustaining other animals and plants on the plains. For example, weaker buffalo provided food for predators such as bears and wolves. Buffalo attracted birds that picked at their fur for insects. And thousands of hooves walking over the landscape kept aggressive plants .... control.

.... , as new settlers moved from the East to settle the West, whole herds were slaughtered, often just for sport. Buffalo were considered an obstacle to the settlers' desire to grow crops and raise cattle. .... , the resource that had sustained Native Americans for centuries began to disappear. By the end of the 1800s, there were as few as 750 buffalo remaining. Many people were shocked that the buffalo, long considered a symbol of the West, had been allowed to come so close to extinction. Fortunately, ... efforts to save them were begun in 1905. The remaining herds were gathered together and protected. As a result, steady .... was made, increasing their numbers to today's population of about 350,000. What conclusion can we draw from this story? It illustrates that conservation efforts can make a difference if they are begun early enough.

1	**A** which	**B** even though	**C** now that	**D** so that
2	**A** While	**B** Because	**C** Before	**D** In fact
3	**A** provided	**B** took	**C** made	**D** sold
4	**A** species	**B** character	**C** role	**D** place
5	**A** as	**B** over	**C** out of	**D** under
6	**A** To sum up	**B** Secondly	**C** In summary	**D** Unfortunately
7	**A** In contrast	**B** Consequently	**C** Similarly	**D** Still
8	**A** environment	**B** ecology	**C** habitat	**D** conservation
9	**A** progress	**B** reduction	**C** conservation	**D** distance

LISTENING COMPLETION

▶6:40 You will hear part of a lecture. Read the paragraph below. Then listen and complete each statement with the word or short phrase you hear in the lecture. Listen a second time to check your work.

The lecturer says that most species can be placed into one of two (1) .... : predator or prey. However, she points out that many animals play (2) .... in nature, as predator and prey. She further explains that animals that are prey rely on (3) .... in order to protect themselves from predators. As an example, she points out that fish swim in huge (4) .... in which they move as if the group were one (5) .... This behavior (6) .... predators, causing them to only eat the fish that are outside the group. The lecturer further points out that predators also often travel in groups called (7) .... in order to make it easier to hunt their prey and ensure their own (8) .... She notes that (9) .... in a group makes it possible to kill (10) .... animals.

READING COMPLETION

Read the selection. Choose the word or phrase that best completes each statement.

Compulsive Shopping: the Problem and the Solution

In the last hundred years, the way in which we consume material goods has changed radically. .... ,
for our grandparents, shopping was for buying things that were necessary to satisfy physical needs. Today,
1
.... , although we continue to buy necessities, we now .... additionally to indulge ourselves in
2 **3**
luxuries, such as expensive gym shoes or the latest electronic and digital technology. .... , shopping
4
itself has for many of us become entertainment. While there is no harm in being entertained, some people
have unfortunately gone entirely overboard. .... for most people an occasional indulgence may
5
cause them to come up a bit short at the end of the month, for others spending becomes a catastrophe
with extremely troubling consequences. Such people cannot resist temptation, and they often buy merely
to acquire. Then .... do they find themselves in considerable debt, but they sink into psychological
6
distress .... Recent studies suggest that extreme impulse buying is on the increase, affecting an
7
estimated 5 to 10 percent of the adult population in many countries. .... , what can or should be done
8
about this growing worldwide problem? Some say that .... compulsive shoppers shop to avoid or hide
9
their feelings of anxiety or loneliness, the only way to combat the problem is with psychological counseling
and self-awareness. .... experts, problem shoppers need to learn that "you can't buy happiness."
10

1	**A** Likewise	**B** To begin with	**C** Secondly	**D** Similarly
2	**A** whereas	**B** furthermore	**C** in contrast	**D** following that
3	**A** entertain	**B** travel	**C** work	**D** shop
4	**A** Third	**B** Least importantly	**C** Secondly	**D** Even though
5	**A** Because	**B** When	**C** Finally	**D** Whereas
6	**A** while	**B** furthermore	**C** not only	**D** in addition
7	**A** since	**B** as well	**C** didn't either	**D** however
8	**A** Finally	**B** For instance	**C** Therefore	**D** For one thing
9	**A** yet	**B** because	**C** like	**D** however
10	**A** According to	**B** Whereas	**C** In contrast to	**D** Not only

LISTENING COMPLETION

▶ 6:41 **You will hear two conversations. Read each paragraph. Then listen and complete each statement
with the word or short phrase you hear. Listen a second time to check your work.**

Nina greets Ross in the store and he asks her what she's (1) .... She tells him that she needs
(2) .... for her (3) .... because her old one is (4) .... She has been told that
the store has some really (5) .... ones. If she can find one with a good price she might buy one for her
(6) .... too because their air conditioner is really old.

The woman sees a (7) .... that she really likes. Her husband agrees that it's (8) .... , but he
wonders if it's (9) .... since it has no price tag on it. The wife guesses that the store purposely doesn't put
the price on items in the window so customers have to (10) .... and ask. The husband says stores like it
when customers do that because then if you don't buy the item, they might be able to talk you into (11) ....
They're happy they (12) .... one.

READING COMPLETION

Read the selection. Choose the word or phrase that best completes each statement.

The Consequences of an Aging Population

For the first time in history, we soon will have more .... people than children. However, even more
important than the ratio of old to young people is the increase in their actual numbers .... an increase
in life expectancy. .... the population of older people gets larger, there will be more cases of age-
related conditions and diseases .... , there will be increased needs for medications and
equipment. .... , some of the most elderly patients will eventually need constant care and assistance
with their most basic activities of daily living, ... more nursing homes will need to be built and more
caregivers will have to be trained. .... governmental resources may not be able to cover costs, much
of the expense will need to be borne by families and .... institutions.

.... the economic consequences of the growth in the elderly population, there will be significant
cultural and social consequences as well. .... in the past it was common for adult children to stay
home to care for older relatives, fewer adults are able or willing to take on that role today. .... , the shift
to institutional rather than home care will represent an immense social change, especially in cultures where
older and younger generations have traditionally lived together.

1	**A** elderly	**B** young	**C** married	**D** unhappy
2	**A** because	**B** due to	**C** until	**D** nevertheless
3	**A** In conclusion	**B** Whereas	**C** As	**D** For example
4	**A** as well	**B** either	**C** yet	**D** not either
5	**A** Because	**B** Since	**C** While	**D** Consequently
6	**A** Even though	**B** Nevertheless	**C** First of all	**D** Furthermore
7	**A** for instance	**B** so	**C** whereas	**D** yet
8	**A** Nevertheless	**B** Because	**C** All the same,	**D** Therefore
9	**A** educational	**B** sporting	**C** technical	**D** charitable
10	**A** Furthermore	**B** While	**C** In addition to	**D** Unlike
11	**A** Whenever	**B** So	**C** Yet	**D** While
12	**A** As a result	**B** Even though	**C** First of all	**D** It's possible

LISTENING COMPLETION

▶ 6:42 **You will hear a conversation. Read the paragraph below. Then listen and complete each statement
with the word or short phrase you hear in the conversation. Listen a second time to check your work.**

A father and his daughter are discussing her (1) .... The father doesn't like the boy because he
thinks he's (2) .... He explains by saying that the boyfriend is always (3) .... The daughter
complains that her father doesn't have any (4) .... for her (5) .... She tells him that just
because he's (6) .... doesn't mean he knows everything. The father gets angry at her tone of voice and tells
her (7) .... Now she won't be able to see any movies or make any (8) .... for two weeks!

UNIT 9

READING COMPLETION

Read the selection. Choose the word or phrase that best completes each statement.

The Roswell Incident

.... pilot Kenneth Arnold was flying a plane in the northwest of the U.S. on June 25th, 1947, he saw
1
something strange: objects that looked like plates, or saucers, flying across the sky like a small flock of birds.

His story led to numerous other news stories in which people claimed to have seen similar unidentified flying

objects (UFOs)—or "flying saucers." Shortly after, on July 8th, a secret military balloon crashed near Roswell,

New Mexico, in the southwest. Nevertheless, the local newspaper reported .... that a flying saucer
2
had crashed, and the news media from all over demanded more information. However, because the balloon

was a secret, the military .... an official story: that the object that had crashed was just an ordinary
3
weather balloon.

No one questioned that story for more than thirty years. Then, in 1978, UFO lecturer Stanton Friedman

interviewed a man who .... he had seen something stranger than a weather balloon in the wreckage
4
of the 1947 crash. .... the story of a flying saucer was reborn. Even though versions of that story
5
.... , most people who believe there was a military conspiracy to hide the truth agree on this basic
6
detail: a flying saucer crashed near Roswell in 1947. .... the military didn't want anyone to know the
7
truth, it kept the incident top secret and continues to do so today. Because many details have been added

to the story over the years, many still .... there was a military cover-up. .... , the story has
8   **9**
become a part of popular culture, and Roswell conspiracy fans meet at annual conferences to debate the

various versions.

1	**A** If	**B** Because	**C** While	**D** Whenever
2	**A** instead	**B** likewise	**C** also	**D** besides
3	**A** turned on	**B** began	**C** opened	**D** invented
4	**A** insisted	**B** forgot	**C** questioned	**D** told
5	**A** Yet	**B** But	**C** So	**D** Likewise
6	**A** different	**B** vary	**C** agree	**D** interest
7	**A** Since	**B** While	**C** If	**D** Despite that
8	**A** forget	**B** remember	**C** believe	**D** wonder
9	**A** Despite that	**B** Similarly	**C** As a result	**D** Even if

LISTENING COMPLETION

▶ 6:43 **You will hear a description. Read the paragraph below. Then listen and complete each statement
with the word or short phrase you heard. Listen a second time to check your work.**

It is believed that the people of Easter Island may have used the stone figures to (1) .... religious and
political (2) .... and (3) .... In total, 540 figures were moved (4) .... the island.
They may have (5) " .... " the figures to their final destination by using (6) .... to rock the
figures back and forth. It's also possible that they were laid down flat and rolled on logs. However, moving the figures
either way couldn't have been (7) .... with fewer than 70 people. Explorer Thor Heyerdahl believed the
island might have been (8) .... by South Americans. He sailed a raft called the Kon-Tiki in order to
(9) .... that his theory was possible. Ultimately, DNA evidence (10) .... that the original
inhabitants must have come from Polynesia.

UNIT 10

READING COMPLETION

Read the selection. Choose the word or phrase that best completes each statement.

When You Never Switch Off

In the next few days, ... you find yourself in a public place, look around. Odds are you'll see a large
¹
percentage of people on their phones or tablets texting, chatting, checking messages, or surfing the net.

We're more connected to our mobile devices .... we have ever been before.
²

Our devices even follow us into our bedrooms, ... we use all this technology as a means to unwind
³
at the end of a long day. According to a recent poll, a majority of respondents said they use their devices

right before going to sleep. Most also reported that using their devices .... keeps them up at night
⁴
but prevents them from getting enough sleep. Zack Panatera, a student at Stanford University, complained,

"I'll take a quick look at something interesting and, the next thing I know, I've spent a few hours online."

.... some experts, the light from an electronic device can throw off our normal sleep cycle. Therefore,
⁵
they .... people to switch off any kind of technology at least an hour before going to bed.
⁶

While lack of sleep may not seem so important, the .... can be huge: one's performance the next
⁷
day may be affected and it may be harder to pay attention or remember things. .... , technology is a
⁸
contributing factor in a growing trend toward longer hours at work and less time off. Even though we have left

the office, we continue to stay connected. We are .... our work world to enter our private lives in ways
⁹
that never would have been imaginable in the past.

1	**A** whereas	**B** if	**C** even if	**D** if only
2	**A** where	**B** and	**C** than	**D** since
3	**A** where	**B** which	**C** that	**D** even if
4	**A** not only	**B** neither	**C** either	**D** but
5	**A** Due to	**B** Accordingly	**C** To illustrate	**D** According to
6	**A** advise	**B** suggest	**C** recommend	**D** report
7	**A** technology	**B** concern	**C** consequences	**D** symptoms
8	**A** Moreover	**B** Still	**C** Otherwise	**D** In contrast
9	**A** stopping	**B** allowing	**C** telling	**D** preventing

LISTENING COMPLETION

▶6:44 **You will hear a speaker. Read the paragraph below. Then listen and complete each statement
with the word or short phrase you hear. Listen a second time to check your work.**

The speaker points out a (1) .... toward longer hours at work and less time off. People seem to be
(2) .... their work world into their (3) .... in ways that weren't (4) .... in the past.
Even in people's (5) .... time, technology has reduced face-to-face human (6) .... Instead of
going out with others, people are (7) .... at home and (8) .... online. And communication with
family, friends, and colleagues—now mainly online—is shorter and more (9) .... than it was in the past. At
the end, the lecturer also claims that face-to-face family time is (10) ....